Learning Perl

Learning Perl

Second Edition

Randal L. Schwartz
and Tom Christiansen

O'REILLY®

Beijing · Cambridge · Farnham · Köln · Paris · Sebastopol · Taipei · Tokyo

Learning Perl, Second Edition
by Randal L. Schwartz and Tom Christiansen

Copyright © 1997, 1993 O'Reilly & Associates, Inc. All rights reserved.
Printed in the United States of America.

Published by O'Reilly & Associates, Inc., 101 Morris Street, Sebastopol, CA 95472.

Editor: Steve Talbott

Production Editor: Mary Anne Weeks Mayo

Printing History:

November 1993:	First Edition.
April 1994:	Minor corrections.
August 1994:	Minor corrections.
July 1997:	Second Edition.

ISBN: 1-56592-284-0   [2/01]

[M]

Table of Contents

List of Tables

Foreword

Attention, class! Attention! Thank you.

Greetings, aspiring magicians. I hope your summer vacations were enjoyable, if too short. Allow me to be the first to welcome you to the College of Wizardry and, more particularly, to this introductory class in the Magic of Perl. I am not your regular instructor, but Professor Schwartz was unavoidably delayed, and has asked me, as the creator of Perl, to step in today and give a few introductory remarks.

Let's see now. Where to begin? How many of you are taking this course as freshmen? I see. Hmmm, I've seen worse in my days. Occasionally. *Very* occasionally.

Eh? That was a joke. Really! Ah well. No sense of humor, these freshmen.

Well now, what shall I talk about? There are, of course, any number of things I *could* talk about. I could take the egotistical approach and talk about myself, elucidating all those quirks of genetics and upbringing that brought me to the place of creating Perl, as well as making a fool of myself in general. That might be entertaining, at least to me.

Or I could talk instead about Professor Schwartz, without whose ongoing efforts the world of Perl would be much impoverished, up to and including the fact that this course of instruction wouldn't exist.

That might be enlightening, though I have the feeling you'll know more of Professor Schwartz by the end of this course than I do.

Or, putting aside all this personal puffery, I could simply talk about Perl itself, which is, after all, the subject of this course.

Or is it? Hmmm... .

When the curriculum committee discussed this course, it reached the conclusion that this class isn't so much about Perl as it is about you! This shouldn't be too surprising, because Perl is itself also about you—at least in the abstract. Perl was created for someone like you, by someone like you, with the collaboration of many other someones like you. The Magic of Perl was sewn together, stitch by stitch and swatch by swatch, around the rather peculiar shape of your psyche. If you think Perl is a bit odd, perhaps that's why.

Some computer scientists (the reductionists, in particular) would like to deny it, but people have funny-shaped minds. Mental geography is not linear, and cannot be mapped onto a flat surface without severe distortion. But for the last score years or so, computer reductionists have been first bowing down at the Temple of Orthogonality, then rising up to preach their ideas of ascetic rectitude to any who would listen.

Their fervent but misguided desire was simply to squash your mind to fit their mindset, to smush your patterns of thought into some sort of hyperdimensional flatland. It's a joyless existence, being smushed.

Nevertheless, your native common sense has shown through in spots. You and your conceptual ancestors have transcended the dreary landscape to compose many lovely computer incantations. (Some of which, at times, actually did what you wanted them to.) The most blessed of these incantations were canonized as Standards, because they managed to tap into something mystical and magical, performing the miracle of Doing What You Expect.

What nobody noticed in all the excitement was that the computer reductionists were still busily trying to smush your minds flat, albeit on a slightly higher plane of existence. The decree, therefore, went out (I'm sure you've heard of it) that computer incantations were only allowed to perform one miracle apiece. "Do one thing and do it well" was the rallying cry, and with one stroke, shell programmers were condemned to a life of muttering and counting beads on strings (which in these latter days have come to be known as pipelines).

This was when I made my small contribution to saving the world. I was rolling some of those very beads around in my fingers one day and pondering the hopelessness (and haplessness) of my existence, when it occurred to me that it might be interesting to melt down some of those mystical beads and see what would happen to their Magic if I made a single, slightly larger bead out of them. So I fired up the old Bunsen burner, picked out some of my favorite beads, and let them melt together however they would. And lo! the new Magic was more powerful than the sum of its parts and parcels.

That's odd, thought I. Why should it be that the Sedulous Bead of Regular Expressions, when bonded together with the Shellacious Bead of Gnostic Interpolation, and the Awkward Bead of Simple Data Typology, should produce more Magic, pound for pound, than they do when strung out on strings? I said to myself, could it be that the beads can exchange power with each other because they no longer have to commune with each other through that skinny little string? Could the pipeline be holding back the flow of information, much as wine doth resist flowing through the neck of Doctor von Neumann's famous bottle?

This demanded (of me) more scrutiny (of it).

So I melted that larger bead together with a few more of my favorite beads, and the same thing happened, only more so. It was practically a combinatorial explosion of potential incantations: the Basic Bead of Output Formats and the Lispery Bead of Dynamic Scoping bonded themselves with the C-rationalized Bead of Operators Galore, and together they put forth a brilliant pulse of power that spread to thousands of machines throughout the entire civilized world. That message cost the Net hundreds if not thousands of dollars to send everywhere. Obviously I was either onto something, or on something.

I then gathered my courage about me and showed my new magical bead to some of you, and you then began to give me your favorite beads to add in as well. The Magic grew yet more powerful, as yet more synergy was imbued in the silly thing. It was as if the Computational Elementals summoned by each bead were cooperating on your behalf to solve your problems for you. Why the sudden peace on earth and good will toward mentality? Perhaps it was because the beads were your favorite beads? Perhaps it was because I'm just a good bead picker?

Perhaps I just got lucky.

Whatever, the magical bead eventually grew into this rather odd-looking Amulet you see before you today. See it glitter, almost like a pearl.

That was another joke. Really! I assure you! Ah well. I was a freshman once too... The Amulet isn't exactly beautiful though; in fact, up close it still looks like a bunch of beads melted together. Well, all right, I admit it. It's downright ugly. But never mind that. It's the Magic that counts. Speaking of Magic, look who just walked in the door! My good buddy Merlyn, er, I should say, Professor Schwartz, is here just in the nick of time to begin telling you how to perform miracles with this little Amulet, if you're willing to learn the proper mysterious incantations. And you're in good hands; I must admit that there's no one better at muttering mysterious incantations than Professor Schwartz. Eh, Merlyn?

Anyway, to sum up. What you'll need most is courage. It is not an easy path that you've set your foot upon. You're learning a new language: a language full of

xiv   *Foreword*

strange runes and ancient chants, some easy and some difficult, many of which
sound familiar, and some of which don't. You may be tempted to become discour-
aged and quit. But think you upon this: consider how long it took you to learn
your own native tongue. Was it worth it? I think so. And have you finished
learning it? I think not. Then do not expect to learn all the mysteries of Perl in a
moment, as though you were consuming a mere peanut, or an olive. Rather, think
of it as though you were consuming, say, a banana. Consider how this works.
You do not wait to enjoy the banana until after you have eaten the whole thing.
No, of course not. You enjoy each bite as you take it. And each bite motivates
you to take the next bite, and the next.

So then, speaking now of the fruit of Merlyn's labors, I would urge you to enjoy
this, um, course. The fruit course, of course. Ahem, that was a joke too. Ah well.

Here then, Professor, I present to you your new class. They seem to have no
sense of humor whatsoever, but I expect you'll manage somehow.

Class, I present to you Professor Randal L. Schwartz, Doctor of Syntax, Wizard at
Large, and of course, Just Another Perl Hacker. He has my blessings, just as you
have my blessings. May you Learn Perl. May you do Good Magic with Perl. And
above all, may you have Lots of Fun with Perl. So be it!

So do it!

Larry Wall
September, 1993

Second Edition Update

You too, Tom.

Larry Wall
May, 1997

Preface

What This Book Is About

Among other things, this book is about 260 pages long. It is also a gentle introduction to Perl. By the time you've gone through this book, you'll have touched on the majority of the simpler operations and common language idioms found in most Perl programs.

This book is not intended as a comprehensive guide to Perl; on the contrary, in order to keep the book from growing unmanageably large, we've been selective about covering only those constructs and issues that you're most likely to use early in your Perl programming career.

As a prelude to your more advanced study, however, we've included a heavier chapter at the end of the book. It's about CGI programming, but along the way, it touches upon library modules, references, and object-oriented programming in Perl. We hope it whets your appetite for these more advanced topics.

Each chapter ends with a series of exercises designed to help you practice what you have just read. If you read at a typical pace and do all the exercises, you should be able to get through each chapter in about two to three hours, or about 30 to 40 hours for the entire book.

This book is meant to be a companion volume to the classic *Programming Perl, Second Edition*, by Larry Wall, Randal L. Schwartz, and Tom Christiansen, published by O'Reilly & Associates, the complete reference book on the language.

Initially designed as a glue language under the UNIX operating system, Perl now runs virtually everywhere, including MS-DOS, VMS, OS/2, Plan 9, Macintosh, and any variety of Windows you care to mention. It is one of the most portable programming languages available today. With the exception of those few sections related to UNIX systems administration, the vast majority of this book is applicable to any platform Perl runs on.

Retrieving Exercises

The exercises in this book are available electronically in a number of ways: by FTP, FTPMAIL, BITFTP, and UUCP. The cheapest, fastest, and easiest ways are listed first. If you read from the top down, the first one that works is probably the best. Use FTP if you are directly on the Internet. Use FTPMAIL if you are not on the Internet but can send and receive electronic mail to Internet sites. Use BITFTP if you send electronic mail via BITNET. Use UUCP if none of the above works.

Note: The exercises were prepared using a UNIX system. If you are running UNIX, you can use them without modification. If you are running on another platform, you may need to modify these exercises slightly. For example, whereas under UNIX every line ends with a line-feed character (the carriage return is implicit), under DOS every line must end with explicit line-feed and carriage-return characters. Depending upon your own configuration and transfer method, you may need to append carriage returns. See the *README* file accompanying the exercises for additional information.

FTP

To use FTP, you need a machine with direct access to the Internet. A sample session is shown below.

```
% ftp ftp.oreilly.com
Connected to ftp.uu.net.
220 ftp.oreilly.com FTP server (Version 6.34 Thu Oct 22 14:32:01 EDT 1992)
ready.
Name (ftp.oreilly.com:username): anonymous
331 Guest login ok, send e-mail address as password.
Password: username@hostname          Use your username and host here
230 Guest login ok, access restrictions apply.
ftp> cd /published/oreilly/nutshell/learning_perl2
250 CWD command successful.
ftp> get README
200 PORT command successful.
150 Opening ASCII mode data connection for README (xxxx bytes).
226 Transfer complete.
local: README remote: README
xxxx bytes received in xxx seconds (xxx Kbytes/s)
ftp> binary
200 Type set to I.
ftp> get examples.tar.gz
200 PORT command successful.
150 Opening BINARY mode data connection for examples.tar.gz (xxxx bytes).
226 Transfer complete. local: exercises remote: exercises
```

```
xxxx bytes received in xxx seconds (xxx Kbytes/s)
ftp> quit
221 Goodbye.
%
```

FTPMAIL

FTPMAIL is a mail server available to anyone who can send electronic mail to and receive it from Internet sites. This includes any company or service provider that allows email connections to the Internet. Here's how you do it.

You send mail to *ftpmail@online.oreilly.com*. In the message body, give the FTP commands you want to run. The server will run anonymous FTP for you and mail the files back to you. To get a complete help file, send a message with no subject and the single word "help" in the body. The following is an example of a UNIX mail session that gets the examples. This command sends you a listing of the files in the selected directory and the requested example files. The listing is useful if there's a later version of the examples you're interested in.

```
% mail ftpmail@online.oreilly.com
Subject:
reply-to username@hostname          Where you want files mailed
open
cd /published/oreilly/nutshell/learning_perl2
dir
get README
mode binary
uuencode
get examples.tar.gz
quit
  .
```

A signature at the end of the message is acceptable as long as it appears after "quit."

BITFTP

BITFTP is a mail server for BITNET users. You send it electronic mail messages requesting files, and it sends you back the files by electronic mail. BITFTP currently serves only users who send it mail from nodes that are directly on BITNET, EARN, or NetNorth. BITFTP is a public service of Princeton University. Here's how it works.

To use BITFTP, send mail containing your FTP commands to *BITFTP@PUCC*. For a complete help file, send HELP as the message body.

The following is the message body you should send to BITFTP:

```
FTP  ftp.oreilly.com  NETDATA
USER  anonymous
```

```
PASS  your Internet e-mail address (not your BITNET address)
CD   /published/oreilly/nutshell/perl/learning_perl2
DIR
GET README
GET examples.tar.gz
QUIT
```

Questions about BITFTP can be directed to *MAINT@PUCC* on BITNET.

UUCP

If you or your company has an account with UUNET, you will have a system with a direct UUCP connection to UUNET. Find that system, and type (as one line):

```
uucp uunet\!~/published/oreilly/nutshell/learning_perl2/examples.tar.gz
yourhost\!~/yourname/
```

The backslashes can be omitted if you use the Bourne shell (*sh*) instead of *csh*. The example file should appear some time later (up to a day or more) in the directory */usr/spool/uucppublic/yourname*.

Additional Resources

Perl Manpages

The online documentation for Perl, called *manpages* due to their UNIX origin, has been divided into separate sections so you can easily find what you are looking for without wading through hundreds of pages of text. Since the top-level manpage is simply called *perl*, the UNIX command *man perl* should take you to it.* That page in turn directs you to more specific pages. For example, *man perlre* displays the manpage for Perl's regular expressions. The *perldoc* command may work when the *man*(1) command won't, especially on module documentation that your system administrator may not have felt comfortable installing with the ordinary manpages. On the other hand, your system administrator may have installed the Perl documentation in hypertext markup language (HTML) format, especially on systems other than UNIX. If all else fails, you can always retrieve the Perl documentation from CPAN; look for this information in the section, "How to Get Perl."

---

* If you still get a humongous page when you do that, you're probably picking up the ancient Release 4 manpage. You may need to change your MANPATH environment variable.

Here are the principal manpages included with the 5.004 distribution of Perl:

Manpage	Topic
perl	Overview of documentation
perldelta	Changes since previous version
perlfaq	Frequently asked questions
perldata	Data structures
perlsyn	Syntax
perlop	Operators and precedence
perlre	Regular expressions
perlrun	Execution and options
perlfunc	Built-in functions
perlvar	Predefined variables
perlsub	Subroutines
perlmod	Modules: how they work
perlmodlib	Lib modules: how to write and use
perlform	Formats
perllocale	Locale support
perlref	References
perldsc	Data structures intro
perllol	Data structures: lists of lists
perltoot	Tutorial of object-oriented programming
perlobj	Objects
perltie	Objects hidden behind simple variables
perlbot	Object tricks and examples
perlipc	Interprocess communication
perldebug	Debugging
perldiag	Diagnostic messages
perlsec	Security
perltrap	Traps for the unwary
perlstyle	Style guide
perlpod	Plain old documentation
perlbook	Book information
perlembed	Ways to embed Perl in your C or C++ application
perlapio	Internal IO abstraction interface
perlxs	XS application programming interface
perlxstut	XS tutorial
perlguts	Internal functions for those doing extensions
perlcall	Calling conventions from C

Usenet Newsgroups

The Perl newsgroups are a great, if sometimes cluttered, source of information about Perl. *comp.lang.perl.announce* is a moderated, low-traffic newsgroup for Perl-related announcements. These often deal with new version releases, bug fixes, new extensions and modules, and Frequently Asked Questions (FAQs).

The high-traffic *comp.lang.perl.misc* group discusses everything from technical issues to Perl philosophy to Perl games and Perl poetry. Like Perl itself, *comp.lang.perl.misc* is meant to be useful, and no question is too silly to ask.*

The *comp.lang.perl.tk* group discusses how to use the popular Tk toolkit from Perl. The *comp.lang.perl.modules* group is about the development and use of Perl modules, which are the best way to get reusable code. There may be other *comp.lang.perl.whatever* newsgroups by the time you read this; look around.

One other newsgroup you might want to check out, at least if you're doing CGI programming on the Web, is *comp.infosystems.www.authoring.cgi*. While it isn't strictly speaking a Perl group, most of the programs discussed there are written in Perl. It's the right place to go for web-related Perl issues.

The Perl Home Page

If you have access to the World Wide Web, visit the Perl home page at *http://www.perl.com/perl/*. It tells what's new in the Perl world, and contains source code and ports, documentation, third-party modules, the Perl bugs database, mailing list information, and more. This site also provides the CPAN multiplexer, described later.

Frequently Asked Questions List

The Perl Frequently Asked Questions (FAQ) is a collection of questions and answers that often show up on *comp.lang.perl.misc*. In many respects it's a companion to the available books, explaining concepts that people may not have understood and maintaining up-to-date information about such things as the latest release level and the best place to get the Perl source.

The FAQ is periodically posted to *comp.lang.perl.announce*, and can also be found on the Web at *http://www.perl.com/perl/faq*.

Since the 5.004 release of Perl, the FAQ has been included with the standard distribution's documentation. Here are the main sections, each available as its own manpage:

---

* Of course, some questions are too silly to answer, especially those already answered in the FAQ.

perlfaq
> Structural overview of the FAQ.

perlfaq1
> Very general, high-level information about Perl.

perlfaq2
> Where to find source and documentation to Perl, support and training, and related matters.

perlfaq3
> Programmer tools and programming support.

perlfaq4
> Manipulating numbers, dates, strings, arrays, hashes, and miscellaneous data issues.

perlfaq5
> I/O and the "f" issues: filehandles, flushing, formats, and footers.

perlfaq6
> Pattern matching and regular expressions.

perlfaq7
> General Perl language issues that don't clearly fit into any of the other sections.

perlfaq8
> Interprocess communication (IPC), control over the user-interface: keyboard, screen, and pointing devices.

perlfaq9
> Networking, the Internet, and a few on the Web.

Bug Reports

In the unlikely event that you should encounter a bug that's in Perl proper and not just in your own program, you should try to reduce it to a minimal test case and then report it with the *perlbug* program that comes with Perl.

The Perl Distribution

Perl is distributed under either of two licenses (your choice). The first is the standard GNU Copyleft, which means, briefly, that if you can execute Perl on your system, you should have access to the full source of Perl for no additional charge. Alternately, Perl may also be distributed under the Artistic License, which some people find less threatening than the Copyleft (especially lawyers).

Within the Perl distribution, you will find some example programs in the *eg/* directory. You may also find other tidbits. Poke around in there on some rainy afternoon. Study the Perl source (if you're a C hacker with a masochistic streak). Look at the test suite. See how *Configure* determines whether you have the *mkdir*(2) system call. Figure out how Perl does dynamic loading of C modules. Or whatever else suits your fancy.

Other Books

Programming Perl is the definitive reference book on Perl, whereas this book is more of a tutorial. If you want to learn more about Perl's regular expressions, we suggest *Mastering Regular Expressions*, by Jeffrey E.F. Friedl (also published by O'Reilly & Associates).

Also check out O'Reilly and Associates' *CGI Programming on the World Wide Web* by Shishir Gundavaram; *Web Client Programming with Perl* by Clinton Wong; and *HTML: The Definitive Guide, Second Edition*, by Chuck Musciano and Bill Kennedy.

The AWK Programming Language, by Aho, Kernighan, and Weinberger (published by Addison-Wesley), and *sed & awk*, by Dale Dougherty (published by O'Reilly & Associates), provide an essential background in such things as associative arrays, regular expressions, and the general world view that gave rise to Perl. They also contain many examples that can be translated into Perl by the *awk*-to-*perl* translator, *a2p*, or by the *sed*-to-*perl* translator, *s2p*. These translators won't produce idiomatic Perl, of course, but if you can't figure out how to imitate one of those examples in Perl, the translator output will give you a good place to start.

For webmasters, we recommend the second edition of *How to Setup and Maintain a Web Site*, by Lincoln Stein, M.D., Ph.D. (published by Addison-Wesley). Dr. Stein, renowned author of Perl's CGI.pm module (described in Chapter 19), delivers a professional and comprehensive treatment of all issues related to administering a web site on UNIX, Mac, and Windows platforms.

We also recommend Johan Vromans's convenient and thorough quick reference booklet, called *Perl 5 Desktop Reference*, published by O'Reilly & Associates.

How to Get Perl

The main distribution point for Perl is the *Comprehensive Perl Archive Network*, or CPAN. This archive contains not only the source code, but also just about everything you could ever want that's Perl-related. CPAN is mirrored by dozens of sites all over the world, as well as a few down under. The main site is *ftp.funet.fi* (128.214.248.6). You can find a more local CPAN site by getting the file */pub/*

languages/perl/CPAN/MIRRORS from *ftp.funet.fi*. Or you can use your web browser to access the CPAN multiplex service at *www.perl.com*. Whenever you ask this web server for a file starting with */CPAN/*, it connects you to a CPAN site, which it chooses by looking at your domain name. Here are some popular universal resource locators (URLs) out of CPAN:

> *http://www.perl.com/CPAN/*
> *http://www.perl.com/CPAN/README.html*
> *http://www.perl.com/CPAN/modules/*
> *http://www.perl.com/CPAN/ports/*
> *http://www.perl.com/CPAN/doc/*
> *http://www.perl.com/CPAN/src/latest.tar.gz*

The CPAN multiplex service tries to connect you to a local, fast machine on a large bandwidth hub. This doesn't always work, however, because domain names may not reflect network connections. For example, you might have a hostname ending in *.se*, but you may actually be better connected to North America than to Sweden. If so, you can use the following URL to choose your own site:

> *http://www.perl.com/CPAN*

Note the absence of a slash at the end of the URL. When you omit the trailing slash, the CPAN multiplexer presents a menu of CPAN mirrors from which you can select a site. So long as your web browser supports cookies, the CPAN multiplexer will automatically remember your choice next time.

The following machines should have the Perl source code plus a copy of the CPAN mirror list—both available via anonymous FTP. (Try to use the machine names rather than the numbers, since the numbers may change.)

ftp.perl.com	199.45.129.30
ftp.cs.colorado.edu	128.138.243.20
ftp.funet.fi	128.214.248.6
ftp.cs.ruu.nl	131.211.80.17

The location of the top directory of the CPAN mirror differs on these machines, so look around once you get there. It's often something like */pub/perl/CPAN*.

Where the Files Are

Under the main CPAN directory, you'll see at least the following subdirectories:

authors

> This directory contains numerous subdirectories, one for each contributor of software. For example, if you wanted to find Lincoln Stein's great CGI.pm module, and you knew for a fact that he wrote it, you could look in *authors/*

Lincoln_Stein. If you didn't know he wrote it, you could look in the modules directory explained below.

doc

A directory containing all manner of Perl documentation. This includes all official documentation (manpages) in several formats (such as ASCII text, HTML, PostScript, and Perl's native POD format), plus the FAQs and interesting supplementary documents.

modules

This directory contains unbundled modules written in C, Perl, or both. Extensions allow you to emulate or access the functionality of other software, such as Tk graphical facilities, the UNIX curses library, and math libraries. They also give you a way to interact with databases (Oracle, Sybase, etc.), and to manage HTML files and CGI scripts.

ports

This directory contains the source code and/or binaries for Perl ports to operating systems not directly supported in the standard distribution. These ports are the individual efforts of their respective authors, and may not all function precisely as described in this book.

scripts

A collection of diverse scripts from all over the world. If you need to find out how to do something, or if you just want to see how other people write programs, check this out. The subdirectory *nutshell* contains the examples from this book. (You can also find these sources at the O'Reilly & Associates *ftp.ora.com* site, in */published/oreilly/nutshell/learning_perl2/*.

src

Within this directory you will find the source for the standard Perl distribution. The current production release is always in the file that is called *src/latest.tar.gz.** This large file contains full source and documentation for Perl. Configuration and installation should be relatively straightforward on UNIX and UNIX-like systems, as well as VMS and OS/2. Starting with Version 5.004, Perl also builds on 32-bit Windows systems.

Using Anonymous FTP

In the event you've never used anonymous FTP, here is a quick primer in the form of a sample session with comments. Text in bold typewriter font is what you should type; comments are in italics. The % represents your prompt, and should not be typed.

---

* The trailing *.tar.gz* means that it's in the standard Internet format of a GNU-zipped, *tar* archive.

```
% ftp ftp.CPAN.org (ftp.CPAN.org is not a real site)
Connected to ftp.CPAN.org.
220 CPAN FTP server (Version wu-2.4(1) Fri Dec 1 00:00:00 EST 1995)
ready.
Name (ftp.CPAN.org:CPAN): anonymous
331 Guest login ok, send your complete e-mail address as password.
Password: camel@nutshell.com (Use your username and host here)
230 Guest login ok, access restrictions apply.
ftp> cd pub/perl/CPAN/src 250 CWD command successful.
ftp> binary (You must specify binary transfer for compressed files) 200 Type set to I.
ftp> get latest.tar.gz
200 PORT command successful.
150 Opening BINARY mode data connection for FILE.
226 Transfer complete.
.
.  (repeat this step for each file you want)
.
ftp> quit 221 Goodbye.
%
```

Once you have the files, first unzip and untar them, and then configure, build, and install Perl:

```
% gunzip < latest.tar.gz | tar xvf -
% cd perl5.003 (Use actual directory name)
Now either one of these next two lines:
% sh configure (Lowercase "c" for automatic configuration)
% sh Configure (Capital "C" for manual configuration)
% make (Build all of Perl)
% make test (Make sure it works)
% make install (You should be the superuser for this)
```

Fetching modules

For retrieving and building unbundled Perl modules, the process is slightly different. Let's say you want to build and install a module named CoolMod. You'd first fetch it via *ftp*(1), or you could use your web browser to access the module service from *http://www.perl.com/*, which always retrieves the most up-to-date version of a particular registered module. The address to feed your browser would be similar to:

> *http://www.perl.com/cgi-bin/cpan_mod?module=CoolMod*

Once you've gotten the file, do this:

```
% gunzip < CoolMod-2.34.tar.gz | tar xvf -
% cd CoolMod-2.34
% perl Makefile.PL (Creates the real Makefile)
% make (Build the whole module)
% make test (Make sure it works)
% make install (Probably should be the superuser)
```

When the CoolMod module has been successfully installed (it is automatically placed in your system's Perl library path), your programs can say:

```
use CoolMod;
```

and you should be able to run *man CoolMod* (or maybe *perldoc CoolMod*) to read the module's documentation.

Conventions Used in This Book

The following typographic conventions appear in this book:

Italic

> is used for file and command names. It is also used to highlight comments in command examples, and to define terms the first time they appear.

`Constant Width`

> is used in examples and in regular text to show operators, variables, and the output from commands or programs.

`Constant Bold`

> is used in examples to show the user's actual input at the terminal.

`Constant Italic`

> is used in examples to show variables for which a context-specific substitution should be made. The variable `filename`, for example, would be replaced by some actual filename.

Footnotes

> are used to attach parenthetical notes which you *should not* read on your first reading of this book. Sometimes, lies are spoken to simplify the discussion, and the footnotes restore the lie to truth. Often, the material in the footnote will be advanced information that may not even be discussed anywhere else in the book.

Support

Perl is the child of Larry Wall, and is still being coddled by him. Bug reports and requests for enhancements generally get fixed in later releases, but he is under no obligation to do anything with them. Nevertheless, Larry really does enjoy hearing from all of us, and does truly like to see Perl be useful to the world at large. Direct email generally gets a response (even if it is merely his email answering machine), and sometimes a personal response. These days, Larry is actually acting as an architect to the "Perl 5 Porters" group, a bunch of very clever people that have had a lot to do with the last few Perl releases. If Larry got hit by a bus, everyone would be very sad for a long time, but Perl would still continue to mature under the direction of this group.

If you have a bug, Perl is shipped with a *perlbug* command that gathers pertinent information (including the problem as you see it) and emails it off to *perlbug@perl.com*. At the moment, the Perl 5 Porters read this mail (along with the 20 to 100 messages they send each other every day) and sometimes answer if it really is a bug. If you try to use this address just for support, you'll get flamed, so please keep your table talk to an absolute minimum and refrain from calling out to the performers.

More useful than writing Larry directly, or sending it off as a bug, is the world wide online Perl support group, communicating through the Usenet newsgroup *comp.lang.perl.misc*. If you are emailable to the Internet, but not amenable to Usenet, you can also wire yourself into this group by sending a request to *perl-users-request@cs.orst.edu*, which will reach a human who can connect you to a two-way email gateway into the group and give you guidelines on how it works.

When you subscribe to the newsgroup, you'll find roughly 50 to 200 "postings" a day (at the time of this writing) on all manner of subjects from beginner questions to complicated porting issues and interface problems, and even a fairly large program or two.

The newsgroup is almost constantly monitored by many Perl experts. Most of the time, your question gets answered within minutes of your news article reaching a major Usenet hub. Just try getting *that* level of support from your favorite software vendor for free! If you'd like to purchase a commercial support contract for Perl, see the Perl FAQ (described earlier in "Additional Resources") for directions and availability.

Acknowledgments for the First Edition

First, I wholeheartedly thank Chick Webb and Taos Mountain Software (in Silicon Valley). The folks at TMS offered me an opportunity to write an introductory Perl course for them (with substantial assistance from Chick), and a chance to present their course a few times. From that experience, I gained the motivation and resources to write and repeatedly present a new course of my own, from which this book is derived. Without them, I don't think I'd be doing this, and I wish them continued success at marketing their course. (And if they're looking for a good text for a revision of their course, I just may have a suggestion...)

Thanks also to the reviewers: Perl Godfather Larry Wall (of course), Larry Kistler (Director of Education, Pyramid), fellow Perl trainer Tom Christiansen, and the students of the *Learning Perl* classes I taught at Intel and Pyramid, and—from

O'Reilly & Associates: Tanya Herlick, Lar Kaufman, Lenny Muellner, Linda Mui, and Andy Oram.

This book was created and edited entirely on my personal Apple Macintosh Powerbook (first the 140, and now the 160 model). More often than not, I was away from my office while writing—sometimes in a park, sometimes in a hotel, sometimes waiting for the weather to clear so I could continue to snow-ski, but most often in restaurants. In fact, I wrote a substantial portion of this book at the Beaverton McMenamin's just down the road from my house. The McM's chain of brewpubs make and serve the finest microbrew and best cheesecake and greasiest sandwiches in my hometown area. I consumed many pints of ale and pieces of cheesecake in this ideal work environment, while my Powerbook swallowed many kilowatt hours of electricity at their four tables with power outlets. For the electricity, and the generous hospitality and courtesy (and rent-free booth-office space), I thank the exceptional staff at the Beaverton McM's. I also hacked some early work on the book at the Beaverton Chili's Restaurant, to which I am also grateful. (But they didn't have any outlets near the bar, so I switched when I found McM's, to save the wear and tear on my batteries.)

Thanks to "the Net" (especially the subscribers to *comp.lang.perl*) for their continued support of Larry and me, and their unending curiosity about getting Perl to work for them.

Thanks also to Tim O'Reilly, for Taoistically being.

And especially, a huge personal thanks to my friend Steve Talbott, who guided me through every step of the way (especially suggesting the stroll at the end of the first chapter). His editorial criticisms were always right on, and his incessant talent for beating me over the head ever so gently allowed me to make this book a piece of art with which I'm extremely pleased.

As always, a special thank you to both Lyle and Jack, for teaching me nearly everything I know about writing.

And finally, an immeasurable thank you to my friend and partner, Larry Wall, for giving Perl to us all in the first place.

> A one L Randal wrote a book,
> A two L llama for the look,
> But to whom we owe it all
> Is the three L Larry Wall!

Randal

Acknowledgments for the Second Edition

I'd like to thank Larry Wall for writing Perl, the Perl Porters for their continued maintenance efforts, and the entire Perl community for their helpfulnesss toward one another.

Thanks also to Jon Orwant, Nate Torkington, and Larry Wall for reviewing the CGI chapter.

Tom

We'd Like to Hear from You

We have tested and verified the information in this book to the best of our ability, but you may find that features have changed (or even that we have made mistakes!). Please let us know about any errors you find, as well as your suggestions for future editions, by writing to:

O'Reilly & Associates, Inc.
101 Morris Street
Sebastopol, CA 95472
1-800-998-9938 (in the U.S. or Canada)
1-707-829-0515 (international/local)
1-707-829-0104 (FAX)

To ask technical questions or comment on the book, send email to:

bookquestions@oreilly.com

We have a web site for the book, where we'll list errata and any plans for future editions. You can access this page at:

http://www.oreilly.com/catalog/lperl2/

For more information about our books, conferences, software, Resource Centers, and the O'Reilly Network, see our web site at:

http://www.oreilly.com

In this chapter:
• History of Perl
• Purpose of Perl
• Availability
• Basic Concepts
• A Stroll Through
  Perl

1

Introduction

History of Perl

Perl is short for "*Practical Extraction and Report Language*," although it has also been called a "*Pathologically Eclectic Rubbish Lister*." There's no point in arguing which one is more correct, because both are endorsed by Larry Wall, Perl's creator and chief architect, implementor, and maintainer. He created Perl when he was trying to produce some reports from a Usenet-news-like hierarchy of files for a bug-reporting system, and *awk* ran out of steam. Larry, being the lazy programmer that he is, decided to over-kill the problem with a general-purpose tool that he could use in at least one other place. The result was the first version of Perl.

After playing with this version of Perl a bit, adding stuff here and there, Larry released it to the community of Usenet readers, commonly known as "the Net." The users on this ragtag fugitive fleet of systems around the world (tens of thousands of them) gave him feedback, asking for ways to do this, that, or the other, many of which Larry had never envisioned his little Perl handling.

But as a result, Perl grew, and grew, and grew, at about the same rate as the UNIX operating system. (For you newcomers, the entire UNIX kernel used to fit in 32K! And now we're lucky if we can get it in under a few meg.) It grew in features. It grew in portability. What was once a little language now had over a thousand pages of documentation split across dozens of different manpages, a 600-page Nutshell reference book, a handful of Usenet newsgroups with 200,000 subscribers, and now this gentle introduction.

Larry is no longer the sole maintainer of Perl, but retains his executive title of chief architect. And Perl is still growing.

This book was tested with Perl version 5.0 patchlevel 4 (the most recent release as I write this). Everything here should work with 5.0 and future releases of Perl. In fact, Perl 1.0 programs work rather well with recent releases, except for a few odd changes made necessary in the name of progress.

Purpose of Perl

Perl is designed to assist the programmer with common tasks that are probably too heavy or too portability-sensitive for the shell, and yet too weird or short-lived or complicated to code in C or some other UNIX glue language.

Once you become familiar with Perl, you may find yourself spending less time trying to get shell quoting (or C declarations) right, and more time reading Usenet news and downhill snowboarding, because Perl is a great tool for leverage. Perl's powerful constructs allow you to create (with minimal fuss) some very cool one-up solutions or general tools. Also, you can drag those tools along to your next job, because Perl is highly portable and readily available, so you'll have even *more* time there to read Usenet news and annoy your friends at karaoke bars.

Like any language, Perl can be "write-only"; it's possible to write programs that are impossible to read. But with proper care, you can avoid this common accusation. Yes, sometimes Perl looks like line noise to the uninitiated, but to the seasoned Perl programmer, it looks like checksummed line noise with a mission in life. If you follow the guidelines of this book, your programs should be easy to read and easy to maintain, but they probably won't win any obfuscated Perl contests.

Availability

If you get

```
perl: not found
```

when you try to invoke Perl from the shell, your system administrator hasn't caught the fever yet. But even if it's not on your system, you can get it for free (or nearly so).

Perl is distributed under the GNU Public License,* which says something like, "you can distribute binaries of Perl only if you make the source code available at no cost, and if you modify Perl, you have to distribute the source to your modifications as well." And that's essentially free. You can get the source to Perl for the cost of a blank tape or a few megabytes over a wire. And no one can lock Perl

---

* Or the slightly more liberal Artistic License, found in the distribution sources.

up and sell you just binaries for their particular idea of "supported hardware configurations."

In fact, it's not only free, but it runs rather nicely on nearly everything that calls itself UNIX or UNIX-like and has a C compiler. This is because the package comes with an arcane configuration script called *Configure* that pokes and prods the system directories looking for things it requires, and adjusts the include files and defined symbols accordingly, turning to you for verification of its findings.

Besides UNIX or UNIX-like systems, people have also been addicted enough to Perl to port it to the Amiga, the Atari ST, the Macintosh family, VMS, OS/2, even MS/DOS and Windows NT and Windows 95 and probably even more by the time you read this. The sources for Perl (and many precompiled binaries for non-UNIX architectures) are available from the Comprehensive Perl Archive Network (the CPAN). If you are web-savvy, visit *http://www.perl.com/CPAN* for one of the many mirrors. If you're absolutely stumped, write *bookquestions@oreilly.com* and say "Where can I get Perl?!?!"

Basic Concepts

A shell script is nothing more than a sequence of shell commands stuffed into a text file. The file is then "made executable" by turning on the execute bit (via *chmod +x filename*) and then the name of the file is typed at a shell prompt. Bingo, one shell program. For example, a script to run the *date* command followed by the *who* command can be created and executed like this:

```
% echo date >somescript
% echo who >>somescript
% cat somescript
date
who
% chmod +x somescript
% somescript
[output of date followed by who]
%
```

Similarly, a Perl program is a bunch of Perl statements and definitions thrown into a file. You then turn on the execute bit* and type the name of the file at a shell prompt. However, the file has to indicate that this is a Perl program and not a shell program, so you need an additional step.

Most of the time, this step involves placing the line

```
#!/usr/bin/perl
```

---

* On UNIX systems, that is. For directions on how to render your scripts executable on non-UNIX systems, see the Perl FAQ or your port's release notes.

as the first line of the file. But if your Perl is stuck in some nonstandard place, or your system doesn't understand the #! line, you'll have a little more work to do. Check with your Perl installer about this. The examples in this book assume that you use this common mechanism.

Perl is mostly a free-format language like C—whitespace between tokens (elements of the program, like `print` or +) is optional, unless two tokens put together can be mistaken for another token, in which case whitespace of some kind is mandatory. (Whitespace consists of spaces, tabs, newlines, returns, or formfeeds.) There are a few constructs that require a certain kind of whitespace in a certain place, but they'll be pointed out when we get to them. You can assume that the kind and amount of whitespace between tokens is otherwise arbitrary.

Although nearly any Perl program can be written all on one line, typically a Perl program is indented much like a C program, with nested parts of statements indented more than the surrounding parts. You'll see plenty of examples showing a typical indentation style throughout this book.

Just like a shell script, a Perl program consists of all of the Perl statements of the file taken collectively as one big routine to execute. There's no concept of a "main" routine as in C.

Perl comments are like (modern) shell comments. Anything from an unquoted pound sign (#) to the end of the line is a comment. There are no C-like multiline comments.

Unlike most shells (but like *awk* and *sed*), the Perl interpreter completely parses and compiles the program into an internal format before executing any of it. This means that you can never get a syntax error from the program once the program has started, and that the whitespace and comments simply disappear and won't slow the program down. This compilation phase ensures the rapid execution of Perl operations once it is started, and it provides additional motivation for dropping C as a systems utility language merely on the grounds that C is compiled.

This compilation does take time; it's inefficient to have a voluminous Perl program that does one small quick task (out of many potential tasks) and then exits, because the run-time for the program will be dwarfed by the compile-time.

So Perl is like a compiler and an interpreter. It's a compiler because the program is completely read and parsed before the first statement is executed. It's an interpreter because there is no object code sitting around filling up disk space. In some ways, it's the best of both worlds. Admittedly, a caching of the compiled object code between invocations, or even translation into native machine code, would be nice. Actually, a working version of such a compiler already exists and is currently scheduled to be bundled into the 5.005 release. See the Perl FAQ for current status.

A Stroll Through Perl

We begin our journey through Perl by taking a little stroll. This stroll presents a number of different features by hacking on a small application. The explanations here are extremely brief; each subject area is discussed in *much* greater detail later in this book. But this little stroll should give you a quick taste for the language, and you can decide if you really want to finish this book rather than read some more Usenet news or run off to the ski slopes.

The "Hello, World" Program

Let's look at a little program that actually *does* something. Here is your basic "Hello, world" program:

```
#!/usr/bin/perl -w
print ("Hello, world!\n");
```

The first line is the incantation that says this is a Perl program. It's also a comment for Perl; remember that a comment is anything from a pound sign to the end of that line, as in many interpreter programming languages. Unlike all other comments in the program, the one on the first line is special: Perl looks at that line for any optional arguments. In this case, the -w switch was used. This very important switch tells Perl to produce extra warning messages about potentially dangerous constructs. You should always develop your programs under -w.

The second line is the entire executable part of this program. Here we see a `print` function. The built-in function `print` starts it off, and in this case has just one argument, a C-like text string. Within this string, the character combination \n stands for a newline character. The `print` statement is terminated by a semicolon (;). As in C, all simple statements in Perl are terminated by a semicolon.[*]

When you invoke this program, the kernel fires up a Perl interpreter, which parses the entire program (all two lines of it, counting the first, comment line) and then executes the compiled form. The first and only operation is the execution of the `print` function, which sends its arguments to the output. After the program has completed, the Perl process exits, returning back a successful exit code to the parent shell.

Soon you'll see Perl programs where `print` and other functions are sometimes called with parentheses, other times without them. The rule is simple: in Perl,

---

[*] The semicolon can be omitted when the statement is the last statement of a block or file or `eval`.

parentheses for built-in functions are never required nor forbidden. Their use can
help or hinder clarity, so use your own judgment.

Asking Questions and Remembering the Result

Let's add a bit more sophistication. The `Hello, world` greeting is a touch cold
and inflexible. Let's have the program call you by your name. To do this, we need
a place to hold the name, a way to ask for the name, and a way to get a response.

One kind of place to hold values (like a name) is a *scalar variable*. For this
program, we'll use the scalar variable `$name` to hold your name. We'll go into
more detail in Chapter 2, *Scalar Data*, about what these variables can hold, and
what you can do with them. For now, assume that you can hold a single number
or string (sequence of characters) in a scalar variable.

The program needs to ask for the name. To do that, we need a way to prompt
and a way to accept input. The previous program showed us how to prompt: use
the `print` function. And the way to get a line from the terminal is with the
`<STDIN>` construct, which (as we're using it here) grabs one line of input. We
assign this input to the `$name` variable. This gives us the program:

```
print "What is your name? ";
$name = <STDIN>;
```

The value of `$name` at this point has a terminating newline (`Randal` comes in as
`Randal\n`). To get rid of that, we use the `chomp` function, which takes a scalar
variable as its sole argument and removes the trailing newline (record separator),
if present, from the string value of the variable:

```
chomp ($name);
```

Now all we need to do is say `Hello`, followed by the value of the `$name` variable, which we can do in a shell-like fashion by embedding the variable inside
the quoted string:

```
print "Hello, $name!\n";
```

As with the shell, if we want a dollar sign rather than a scalar variable reference,
we can precede the dollar sign with a backslash.

Putting it all together, we get:

```
#!/usr/bin/perl -w
print "What is your name? ";
$name = <STDIN>;
chomp ($name);
print "Hello, $name!\n";
```

Adding Choices

Now, let's say we have a special greeting for Randal, but want an ordinary greeting for anyone else. To do this, we need to compare the name that was entered with the string `Randal`, and if it's the same, do something special. Let's add a C-like *if-then-else* branch and a comparison to the program:

```
#!/usr/bin/perl
print "What is your name? ";
$name = <STDIN>;
chomp ($name);
if ($name eq "Randal") {
    print "Hello, Randal! How good of you to be here!\n";
} else {
    print "Hello, $name!\n"; # ordinary greeting
}
```

The `eq` operator compares two strings. If they are equal (character-for-character, and have the same length), the result is true. (There's no comparable operator* in C or C++.)

The `if` statement selects which *block* of statements (between matching curly braces) is executed; if the expression is true, it's the first block, otherwise it's the second block.

Guessing the Secret Word

Well, now that we have the name, let's have the person running the program guess a secret word. For everyone except Randal, we'll have the program repeatedly ask for guesses until the person guesses properly. First the program, and then an explanation:

```
#!/usr/bin/perl -w
$secretword = "llama"; # the secret word
print "What is your name? ";
$name = <STDIN>;
chomp $name;
if ($name eq "Randal") {
    print "Hello, Randal! How good of you to be here!\n";
} else {
    print "Hello, $name!\n"; # ordinary greeting
    print "What is the secret word? ";
    $guess = <STDIN>;
    chomp ($guess);
    while ($guess ne $secretword) {
        print "Wrong, try again. What is the secret word? ";
        $guess = <STDIN>;
        chomp ($guess);
    }
}
```

---

* Well, OK, there's a standard `libc` subroutine. But that's not an operator.

First, we define the secret word by putting it into another scalar variable, `$secretword`. After the greeting the (non-Randal) person is asked (with another `print`) for the guess. The guess is compared with the secret word using the `ne` operator, which returns true if the strings are not equal (this is the logical opposite of the `eq` operator). The result of the comparison controls a `while` loop, which executes the block as long as the comparison is true.

Of course, this is not a very secure program, because anyone who is tired of guessing can merely interrupt the program and get back to the prompt, or even look at the source to determine the word. But, we weren't trying to write a security system, just an example for this section.

More than One Secret Word

Let's see how we can modify this to allow more than one valid secret word. Using what we've already seen, we could compare the guess repeatedly against a series of good answers stored in separate scalar variables. However, such a list would be hard to modify or read in from a file or compute based on the day of the week.

A better solution is to store all possible answers in a data structure called a *list*, or (preferably) an *array*. Each *element* of the array is a separate scalar variable that can be independently set or accessed. The entire array can also be given a value in one fell swoop. We can assign a value to the entire array named `@words` so that it contains three possible good passwords:

```
@words = ("camel","llama","alpaca");
```

Array variable names begin with `@`, so they are distinct from scalar variable names. Another way to write this so that we don't have to put all those quote marks there is with the `qw()` operator, like so:

```
@words = qw(camel llama alpaca);
```

These mean exactly the same thing; the `qw` makes it as if we had quoted each of three strings.

Once the array is assigned, we can access each element using a subscript reference. So `$words[0]` is `camel`, `$words[1]` is `llama`, and `$words[2]` is `alpaca`. The subscript can be an expression as well, so if we set `$i` to 2, then `$words[$i]` is `alpaca`. (Subscript references start with `$` rather than `@` because they refer to a single element of the array rather than the whole array.) Going back to our previous example:

```
#!/usr/bin/perl -w
@words = qw(camel llama alpaca);
print "What is your name? ";
$name = <STDIN>;
chomp ($name);
```

```
    if ($name eq "Randal") {
        print "Hello, Randal! How good of you to be here!\n";
    } else {
        print "Hello, $name!\n";          # ordinary greeting
        print "What is the secret word? ";
        $guess = <STDIN>;
        chomp ($guess);
        $i = 0; # try this word first
        $correct = "maybe";               # is the guess correct or not?
        while ($correct eq "maybe") {     # keep checking til we know
            if ($words[$i] eq $guess) {   # right?
                $correct = "yes";         # yes!
            } elsif ($i < 2) {            # more words to look at?
                $i = $i + 1;              # look at the next word next time
            } else {                      # no more words, must be bad
                print "Wrong, try again. What is the secret word?";
                $guess = <STDIN>;
                chomp ($guess);
                $i = 0;                   # start checking at the first word again
            }
        } # end of while not correct
    } # end of "not Randal"
```

You'll notice we're using the scalar variable `$correct` to indicate that we are either still looking for a good password or that we've found one.

This program also shows the `elsif` block of the `if-then-else` statement. This exact construct is not present in all programming languages; it's an abbreviation of the `else` block together with a new `if` condition, but without nesting inside yet another pair of curly braces. It's a very Perl-like thing to compare a set of conditions in a cascaded `if-elsif-elsif-elsif-else` chain. Perl doesn't really have the equivalent of C's "switch" or Pascal's "case" statement, although you can build one yourself without too much trouble. See Chapter 2 of *Programming Perl* or the *perlsyn*(1) manpage for details.

Giving Each Person a Different Secret Word

In the previous program, any person who comes along could guess any of the three words and be successful. If we want the secret word to be different for each person, we'll need a table that matches up people with words:

Person	Secret Word
Fred	camel
Barney	llama
Betty	alpaca
Wilma	alpaca

Notice that both Betty and Wilma have the same secret word. This is fine.

The easiest way to store such a table in Perl is with a *hash*. Each element of the hash holds a separate scalar value (just like the other type of array), but the hashes are referenced by a *key*, which can be any scalar value (any string or number, including noninteger and negative values). To create a hash called `%words` (notice the `%` rather than `@`) with the keys and values given in the table above, we assign a value to `%words` (much as we did earlier with the array):

```
%words = qw(
    fred        camel
    barney      llama
    betty       alpaca
    wilma       alpaca
);
```

Each pair of values in the list represents one key and its corresponding value in the hash. Note that we broke this assignment over many lines without any sort of line-continuation character, because whitespace is generally insignificant in a Perl program.

To find the secret word for Betty, we need to use Betty as the key in a reference to the hash `%words`, via some expression such as `$words{"betty"}`. The value of this reference is `alpaca`, similar to what we had before with the other array. Also as before, the key can be any expression, so setting `$person` to `betty` and evaluating `$words{$person}` gives `alpaca` as well.

Putting all this together, we get a program like this:

```
#!/usr/bin/perl
%words = qw(
    fred        camel
    barney      llama
    betty       alpaca
    wilma       alpaca
);
print "What is your name? ";
$name = <STDIN>;
chomp ($name);
if ($name eq "Randal") {
    print "Hello, Randal! How good of you to be here!\n";
} else {
    print "Hello, $name!\n";      # ordinary greeting
    $secretword = $words{$name}; # get the secret word
    print "What is the secret word? ";
    $guess = <STDIN>;
    chomp ($guess);
    while ($guess ne $secretword) {
        print "Wrong, try again. What is the secret word? ";
        $guess = <STDIN>;
        chomp ($guess);
    }
}
```

Note the lookup of the secret word. If the name is not found, the value of
$secretword will be an empty string,* which we can then check for if we want
to define a default secret word for everyone else. Here's how that looks:

```
[... rest of program deleted ...]
    $secretword = $words{$name}; # get the secret word
    if ($secretword eq "") {      # oops, not found
        $secretword = "groucho"; # sure, why a duck?
    }
    print "What is the secret word? ";
[... rest of program deleted ...]
```

Handling Varying Input Formats

If I enter Randal L. Schwartz or randal rather than Randal, I'm lumped in
with the rest of the users, because the eq comparison is an exact equality. Let's
look at one way to handle that.

Suppose I wanted to look for any string that began with Randal, rather than just
a string that was equal to Randal. I could do this in *sed*, *awk*, or *grep* with a
regular expression: a template that defines a collection of strings that match. As in
sed, *awk*, or *grep*, the regular expression in Perl that matches any string that
begins with Randal is ^Randal. To match this against the string in $name, we
use the match operator as follows:

```
if ($name =~ /^Randal/) {
    ## yes, it matches
} else {
    ## no, it doesn't
}
```

Note that the regular expression is delimited by slashes. Within the slashes, spaces
and other whitespace are significant, just as they are within strings.

This almost does it, but it doesn't handle selecting randal or rejecting Randall.
To accept randal, we add the *ignore-case* option, a small i appended after the
closing slash. To reject Randall, we add a *word boundary* special marker
(similar to *vi* and some versions of *grep*) in the form of \b in the regular expression. This ensures that the character following the first l in the regular expression
is not another letter. This changes the regular expression to be /^randal\b/i,
which means "randal at the beginning of the string, no letter or digit following,
and OK to be in either case."

When put together with the rest of the program, it looks like this:

```
#!/usr/bin/perl
```

---

* Well, OK, it's the undef value, but it looks like an empty string to the eq operator. You'd get a warning
about this if you used -w on the command line, which is why we omitted it here.

```
%words = qw(
    fred        camel
    barney      llama
    betty       alpaca
    wilma       alpaca
);
print "What is your name? ";
$name = <STDIN>;
chomp ($name);
if ($name =~ /^randal\b/i) {
    print "Hello, Randal! How good of you to be here!\n";
} else {
    print "Hello, $name!\n"; # ordinary greeting
    $secretword = $words{$name}; # get the secret word
    if ($secretword eq "") { # oops, not found
        $secretword = "groucho"; # sure, why a duck?
    }
    print "What is the secret word? ";
    $guess = <STDIN>;
    chomp ($guess);
    while ($guess ne $secretword) {
        print "Wrong, try again. What is the secret word? ";
        $guess = <STDIN>;
        chomp ($guess);
    }
}
```

As you can see, the program is a far cry from the simple Hello, world, but it's still very small and workable, and does quite a bit for being so short. This is The Perl Way.

Perl provides every regular expression feature found in every standard UNIX utility (and even some nonstandard ones). Not only that, but the way Perl handles string matching is about the fastest on the planet, so you don't lose performance. (A *grep*-like program written in Perl often beats the vendor-supplied* C-coded *grep* for most inputs. This means that *grep* doesn't even do its one thing very well.)

Making It Fair for the Rest

So, now I can enter Randal or randal or Randal L. Schwartz, but what about everyone else? Barney still has to say exactly barney (not even barney followed by a space).

To be fair to Barney, we need to grab the first word of whatever's entered, and then convert it to lowercase *before* we look up the name in the table. We do this

---

* GNU *egrep* tends to be much faster than Perl at this.

with two operators: the *substitute* operator, which finds a regular expression and replaces it with a string, and the *translate* operator, to put the string in lowercase.

First, the substitute operator: we want to take the contents of $name, find the first nonword character, and zap everything from there to the end of the string. /\W.*/ is the regular expression we are looking for: the \W stands for a nonword character (something besides a letter, digit, or underscore), and .* means any characters from there to the end of the line. Now, to zap these characters away, we need to take whatever part of the string matches this regular expression and replace it with nothing:

```
$name =~ s/\W.*//;
```

We're using the same =~ operator that we did before, but now on the right we have a substitute operator: the letter s followed by a slash-delimited regular expression and string. (The string in this example is the empty string between the second and third slashes.) This operator looks and acts very much like the substitutions of the various editors.

Now, to get whatever's left into lowercase, we translate the string using the tr operator.* It looks a lot like a UNIX *tr* command, taking a list of characters to find and a list of characters to replace them with. For our example, to put the contents of $name in lowercase, we use:

```
$name =~ tr/A-Z/a-z/;
```

The slashes delimit the searched-for and replacement character lists. The dash between A and Z stands for all the characters in between, so we have two lists that are each 26 characters long. When the tr operator finds a character from the string in the first list, the character is replaced with the corresponding character in the second list. So all uppercase A's become lowercase a's, and so on.†

Putting that together with everything else results in:

```
#!/usr/bin/perl
%words = qw(
    fred        camel
    barney      llama
    betty       alpaca
    wilma       alpaca
);
print "What is your name? ";
$name = <STDIN>;
chomp ($name);
```

---

* This doesn't work for characters with accent marks, although the uc function would. See the *perllocale*(1) manpage first distributed with the 5.004 release of Perl for details.

† Experts will note that we could have also constructed something like   s/(\S*).*/\L$1/ to do this all in one fell swoop, but experts probably won't be reading this section.

```
$original_name = $name; #save for greeting
$name =~ s/\W.*//; # get rid of everything after first word
$name =~ tr/A-Z/a-z/; # lowercase everything
if ($name eq "randal") { # ok to compare this way now
    print "Hello, Randal! How good of you to be here!\n";
} else {
    print "Hello, $original_name!\n"; # ordinary greeting
    $secretword = $words{$name}; # get the secret word
    if ($secretword eq "") { # oops, not found
        $secretword = "groucho"; # sure, why a duck?
    }
    print "What is the secret word? ";
    $guess = <STDIN>;
    chomp ($guess);
    while ($guess ne $secretword) {
        print "Wrong, try again. What is the secret word? ";
        $guess = <STDIN>;
        chomp ($guess);
    }
}
```

Notice how the regular expression match for `Randal` became a simple comparison again. After all, both `Randal L. Schwartz` and `Randal` become `randal` after the substitution and translation. And everyone else gets a fair ride, because `Fred` and `Fred Flintstone` both become `fred`; `Barney Rubble` and `Barney, the little guy` become `barney`, and so on.

With just a few statements, we've made the program much more user-friendly. You'll find that expressing complicated string manipulation with a few keystrokes is one of Perl's many strong points.

However, hacking away at the name so that we could compare it and look it up in the table destroyed the name that was entered. So, before the program hacks on the name, it saves it in `$original_name`. (Like C symbols, Perl variable names consist of letters, digits, and underscores and can be of nearly unlimited length.) We can then make references to `$original_name` later.

Perl has many ways to monitor and mangle strings. You'll find out about most of them in Chapter 7, *Regular Expressions*, and Chapter 15, *Other Data Transformation*.

Making It a Bit More Modular

Now that we've added so much to the code, we have to scan through many detailed lines before we can get the overall flow of the program. What we need is to separate the high-level logic (asking for a name, looping based on entered secret words) from the details (comparing a secret word to a known good word). We might do this for clarity, or maybe because one person is writing the high-level part and another is writing (or has already written) the detailed parts.

Perl provides *subroutines* that have *parameters* and *return values*. A subroutine is defined once in a program, and can be used repeatedly by being invoked from within any expression.

For our small-but-rapidly-growing program, let's create a subroutine called good_ word that takes a name and a guessed word, and returns *true* if the word is correct and *false* if not. The definition of such a subroutine looks like this:

```
sub good_word {
    my($somename,$someguess) = @_; # name the parameters
    $somename =~ s/\W.*//; # get rid of everything after first word
    $somename =~ tr/A-Z/a-z/; # lowercase everything
    if ($somename eq "randal") { # should not need to guess
        return 1; # return value is true
    } elsif (($words{$somename} || "groucho") eq $someguess) {
        return 1; # return value is true
    } else {
        return 0; # return value is false
    }
}
```

First, the definition of a subroutine consists of the reserved word sub followed by the subroutine name followed by a block of code (delimited by curly braces). This definition can go anywhere in the program file, though most people put it at the end.

The first line within this particular definition is an assignment that copies the values of the two parameters of this subroutine into two local variables named $somename and $someguess. (The my() defines the two variables as private to the enclosing block—in this case, the entire subroutine—and the parameters are initially in a special local array called @_.)

The next two lines clean up the name, just like the previous version of the program.

The if-elsif-else statement decides whether the guessed word ($some-guess) is correct for the name ($somename). Randal should not make it into this subroutine, but even if it does, whatever word was guessed is OK.

A return statement can be used to make the subroutine immediately return to its caller with the supplied value. In the absence of an explicit return statement, the last expression evaluated in a subroutine is the return value. We'll see how the return value is used after we finish describing the subroutine definition.

The test for the elsif part looks a little complicated; let's break it apart:

```
($words{$somename} || "groucho") eq $someguess
```

The first thing inside the parentheses is our familiar hash lookup, yielding some value from %words based on a key of $somename. The operator between that value and the string `groucho` is the || (logical-or) operator similar to that used in C and *awk* and the various shells. If the lookup from the hash has a value (meaning that the key `$somename` was in the hash), the value of the expression is that value. If the key could not be found, the string of `groucho` is used instead. This is a very Perl-like thing to do: specify some expression, and then provide a default value using || in case the expression turns out to be false.

In any case, whether it's a value from the hash, or the default value `groucho`, we compare it to whatever was guessed. If the comparison is true, we return 1, otherwise we return 0.

So, expressed as a rule, if the name is `randal`, or the guess matches the lookup in `%words` based on the name (with a default of `groucho` if not found), then the subroutine returns 1, otherwise it returns 0.

Now let's integrate all this with the rest of the program:

```
#!/usr/bin/perl
%words = qw(
     fred         camel
     barney       llama
     betty        alpaca
     wilma        alpaca
);
print "What is your name? ";
$name = <STDIN>;
chomp ($name);
if ($name =~ /^randal\b/i) { # back to the other way :-)
     print "Hello, Randal! How good of you to be here!\n";
} else {
     print "Hello, $name!\n"; # ordinary greeting
     print "What is the secret word? ";
     $guess = <STDIN>;
     chomp ($guess);
     while (! good_word($name,$guess)) {
          print "Wrong, try again. What is the secret word? ";
          $guess = <STDIN>;
          chomp ($guess);
     }
}
[... insert definition of good_word() here ...]
```

Notice that we've gone back to the regular expression to check for `Randal`, because now there's no need to pull apart the first name and convert it to lowercase, as far as the main program is concerned.

The big difference is the `while` loop containing the subroutine `good_word`. Here, we see an invocation of the subroutine, passing it two parameters, `$name` and `$guess`. Within the subroutine, the value of `$somename` is set from the first parameter, in this case $name. Likewise, $someguess is set from the second parameter, $guess.

The value returned by the subroutine (either 1 or 0, recalling the definition given earlier) is logically inverted with the prefix ! (logical not) operator. This operator returns true if the expression following is false, and returns false if the expression following is true. The result of this negation controls the while loop. You can read this as "while it's not a good word...". Many well-written Perl programs read very much like English, provided you take a few liberties with either Perl or English. (But you certainly won't win a Pulitzer that way.)

Note that the subroutine assumes that the value of the %words hash is set by the main program.

Such a cavalier approach to global variables doesn't scale very well, of course. Generally speaking, variables not created with my are global to the whole program, while those my creates last only until the block in which they were declared exits. Don't worry: Perl does in fact support a rich variety of other kinds of variables, including those private to a file (or package), as well as variables private to a function that retain their values between invocations, which is what we could really use here. However, at this stage in your Perl education, explaining these would only complicate your life. When you're ready for it, check out what *Programming Perl* has to say about scoping, subroutines, modules, and objects, or see the online documentation in the *perlsub*(1), *perlmod*(1), *perlobj*(1), and *perltoot*(1) manpages.

Moving the Secret Word List into a Separate File

Suppose we wanted to share the secret word list among three programs. If we store the word list as we have done already, we will need to change all three programs when Betty decides that her secret word should be swine rather than alpaca. This can get to be a hassle, especially if Betty changes her mind often.

So, let's put the word list into a file and then read the file to get the word list into the program. To do this, we need to create an I/O channel called a *filehandle*. Your Perl program automatically gets three filehandles called STDIN, STDOUT, and STDERR, corresponding to the three standard I/O channels in most programming environments. We've already been using the STDIN handle to read data from the person running the program. Now, it's just a matter of getting another handle attached to a file of our own choice.

Here's a small chunk of code to do that:

```
sub init_words {
    open (WORDSLIST, "wordslist");
    while ($name = <WORDSLIST>) {
```

```
        chomp ($name);
        $word = <WORDSLIST>;
        chomp ($word);
        $words{$name} = $word;
    }
    close (WORDSLIST);
}
```

We're putting it into a subroutine so that we can keep the main part of the program uncluttered. This also means that at a later time (hint: a few revisions down in this stroll), we can change where the word list is stored, or even the format of the list.

The arbitrarily chosen format of the word list is one item per line, with names and words, alternating. So, for our current database, we'd have something like this:

```
fred
camel
barney
llama
betty
alpaca
wilma
alpaca
```

The `open` function initializes a filehandle named `WORDSLIST` by associating it with a file named `wordslist` in the current directory. Note that the filehandle doesn't have a funny character in front of it as the three variable types do. Also, filehandles are generally uppercase—although they aren't required to be—for reasons detailed later.

The `while` loop reads lines from the `wordslist` file (via the `WORDSLIST` filehandle) one line at a time. Each line is stored into the `$name` variable. At the end of the file, the value returned by the `<WORDSLIST>` operation is the empty string,* which looks false to the `while` loop, and terminates it. That's how we get out at the end.

If you were running with −w, you would have to check that the return value read in was actually defined. The empty string returned by the `<WORDSLIST>` operation isn't merely empty: it's `undef` again. The `defined` function is how you test for `undef` when this matters. When reading lines from a file, you'd do the test this way:

```
    while ( defined ($name = <WORDSLIST>) ) {
```

But if you were being that careful, you'd probably also have checked to make sure that `open` returned a true value. You know, that's probably not a bad idea

---

* Well, technically it's `undef`, but close enough for this discussion.

either. The built-in `die` function is frequently used to exit the program with an error message in case something goes wrong. We'll see an example of it in the next revision of the program.

On the other hand, the normal case is that we've read a line (including the newline) into `$name`. First, off comes the newline using the `chomp` function. Then, we have to read the next line to get the secret word, holding that in the `$word` variable. It, too, gets the newline hacked off.

The final line of the `while` loop puts `$word` into `%words` with a key of `$name`, so that the rest of the program can access it later.

Once the file has been read, the filehandle can be recycled with the `close` function. (Filehandles are automatically closed anyway when the program exits, but we're trying to be tidy. If we were really tidy, we'd even check for a true return value from `close` in case the disk partition the file was on went south, its network filesystem became unreachable, or some other catastrophe occurred. Yes, these things really do happen. Murphy will always be with us.)

This subroutine definition can go after or before the other one. And we invoke the subroutine instead of setting `%words` in the beginning of the program, so one way to wrap up all of this might look like:

```perl
#!/usr/bin/perl
init_words();
print "What is your name? ";
$name = <STDIN>;
chomp $name;
if ($name =~ /^randal\b/i) { # back to the other way :-)
    print "Hello, Randal! How good of you to be here!\n";
} else {
    print "Hello, $name!\n"; # ordinary greeting
    print "What is the secret word? ";
    $guess = <STDIN>;
    chomp ($guess);
    while (! good_word($name,$guess)) {
        print "Wrong, try again. What is the secret word? ";
        $guess = <STDIN>;
        chomp ($guess);
    }
}
## subroutines from here down
sub init_words {
    open (WORDSLIST, "wordslist") ||
                        die "can't open wordlist: $!";
    while ( defined ($name = <WORDSLIST>)) {
        chomp ($name);
        $word = <WORDSLIST>;
        chomp $word;
        $words{$name} = $word;
    }
```

```
        close (WORDSLIST) || die "couldn't close wordlist: $!";
    }
    sub good_word {
        my($somename,$someguess) = @_; # name the parameters
        $somename =~ s/\W.*//;           # delete everything after
                                         # first word
        $somename =~ tr/A-Z/a-z/;        # lowercase everything
        if ($somename eq "randal") {     # should not need to guess
            return 1;                    # return value is true
        } elsif (($words{$somename} || "groucho") eq $someguess) {
            return 1;                    # return value is true
        } else {
            return 0;                    # return value is false
        }
    }
```

Now it's starting to look like a full grown program. Notice the first executable line is an invocation of **init_words()**. The return value is not used in a further calculation, which is good because we didn't return anything remarkable. In this case, it's guaranteed to be a true value (the value 1, in particular), because if the **close** had failed, the **die** would have printed a message to **STDERR** and exited the program. The **die** function is fully explained in Chapter 10, *Filehandles and File Tests*, but because it's essential to check the return values of anything that might fail, we'll get into the habit of using it right from the start. The **$!** variable (also explained in Chapter 10), contains the system error message explaining why the system call failed.

The **open** function is also used to open files for output, or open programs as files (demonstrated shortly). The full scoop on **open** comes much later in this book, however, in Chapter 10.

Ensuring a Modest Amount of Security

"That secret word list has got to change at least once a week!" cries the Chief Director of Secret Word Lists. Well, we can't force the list to be different, but we can at least issue a warning if the secret word list has not been modified in more than a week.

The best place to do this is in the **init_words()** subroutine; we're already looking at the file there. The Perl operator **-M** returns the age in days since a file or filehandle has last been modified, so we just need to see whether this is greater than seven for the **WORDSLIST** filehandle:

```
    sub init_words {
        open (WORDSLIST, "wordslist") ||
                                die "can't open wordlist: $!";
        if (-M WORDSLIST >= 7.0) { # comply with bureaucratic policy
            die "Sorry, the wordslist is older than seven days.";
        }
```

```
        while ($name = <WORDSLIST>) {
            chomp ($name);
            $word = <WORDSLIST>;
            chomp ($word);
            $words{$name} = $word;
        }
        close (WORDSLIST) || die "couldn't close wordlist: $!";
    }
```

The value of -M WORDSLIST is compared to seven, and if greater, bingo, we've violated policy.

The rest of the program remains unchanged, so in the interest of saving a few trees, I won't repeat it here.

Besides getting the age of a file, we can also find out its owner, size, access time, and everything else that the system maintains about a file. More on that in Chapter 10.

Warning Someone When Things Go Astray

Let's see how much we can bog down the system by sending a piece of email each time someone guesses their secret word incorrectly. We need to modify only the good_word() subroutine (thanks to modularity) because we have all the information right there.

The mail will be sent to you if you type your own mail address where the code says "YOUR_ADDRESS_HERE." Here's what we have to do: just before we return 0 from the subroutine, we create a filehandle that is actually a process (*mail*), like so:

```
sub good_word {
    my($somename,$someguess) = @_;  # name the parameters
    $somename =~ s/\W.*//;          # get rid of stuff after
                                    # first word
    $somename =~ tr/A-Z/a-z/;       # lowercase everything
    if ($somename eq "randal") {    # should not need to guess
        return 1;                   # return value is true
    } elsif (($words{$somename}||"groucho") eq $someguess) {
        return 1;                   # return value is true
    } else {
        open MAIL,"|mail YOUR_ADDRESS_HERE";
        print MAIL "bad news: $somename guessed $someguess\n";
        close MAIL;
        return 0;                   # return value is false
    }
}
```

The first new statement here is **open**, which has a pipe symbol (|) at the beginning of its second argument. This is a special indication that we are opening a command rather than a file. Because the pipe is at the beginning of the command, we are opening a command so that we can write to it. (If you put the pipe at the end rather than the beginning, you can read the output of a command instead.)

The next statement, a **print**, shows that a filehandle between the **print** keyword and the values to be printed selects that filehandle for output, rather than **STDOUT**.* This means that the message will end up as the input to the *mail* command.

Finally, we close the filehandle, which starts *mail* sending its data merrily on its way.

To be proper, we could have sent the correct response as well as the error response, but then someone reading over my shoulder (or lurking in the mail system) while I'm reading my mail might get too much useful information.

Perl can also open filehandles, invoke commands with precise control over argument lists, or even fork off a copy of the current program, and execute two (or more) copies in parallel. Backquotes (like the shell's backquotes) give an easy way to grab the output of a command as data. All of this gets described in Chapter 14, *Process Management*, so keep reading.

Many Secret Word Files in the Current Directory

Let's change the definition of the secret word filename slightly. Instead of just the file named **wordslist**, let's look for anything in the current directory that ends in **.secret**. To the shell, we say

```
echo *.secret
```

to get a brief listing of all of these names. As you'll see in a moment, Perl uses a similar wildcard-name syntax.

Pulling out the **init_words()** definition again:

```
sub init_words {
    while ( defined($filename = glob("*.secret")) ) {
    open (WORDSLIST, $filename) ||
                            die "can't open wordlist: $!";
        if (-M WORDSLIST < 7.0) {
            while ($name = <WORDSLIST>) {
                chomp $name;
                $word = <WORDSLIST>;
```

---

* Well, technically, the currently selected filehandle. That's covered much later, though.

```
                    chomp $word;
                    $words{$name} = $word;
            }
        }
        close (WORDSLIST) || die "couldn't close wordlist: $!";
    }
}
```

First, we've wrapped a new **while** loop around the bulk of the routine from the previous version. The new thing here is the **glob** function. This is called a *file-name glob*, for historical reasons. It works much like <STDIN>, in that each time it is accessed, it returns the next value: successive filenames that match the shell pattern, in this case *.secret. When there are no additional filenames to be returned, the filename glob returns an empty string.*

So if the current directory contains **fred.secret** and **barney.secret**, then **$filename** is **barney.secret** on the first pass through the **while** loop (the names come out in alphabetically sorted order). On the second pass, **$filename** is **fred.secret**. And there is no third pass because the glob returns an empty string the third time it is called, perceived by the **while** loop to be false, causing an exit from the subroutine.

Within the **while** loop, we open the file and verify that it is recent enough (less than seven days since the last modification). For the recent-enough files, we scan through as before.

Note that if there are no files that match *.secret and are less than seven days old, the subroutine will exit without having set any secret words into the **%words** array. That means that everyone will have to use the word **groucho**. Oh well. (For *real* code, I would have added some check on the number of entries in **%words** before returning, and **die**'d if it weren't good. See the **keys** function when we get to hashes in Chapter 5, *Hashes*.)

Listing the Secret Words

Well, the Chief Director of Secret Word Lists wants a report of all the secret words currently in use and how old they are. If we set aside the secret word program for a moment, we'll have time to write a reporting program for the Director.

First, let's get all of the secret words, by stealing some code from the **init_words()** subroutine:

```
while ( defined($filename = glob("*.secret")) ) {
open (WORDSLIST, $filename) || die "can't open wordlist: $!";
if (-M WORDSLIST < 7.0) {
```

---

* Yeah, yeah, undef again.

```
        while ($name = <WORDSLIST>) {
            chomp ($name);
            $word = <WORDSLIST>;
            chomp ($word);
### new stuff will go here
            }
        }
        close (WORDSLIST) || die "couldn't close wordlist: $!";
    }
```

At the point marked "new stuff will go here," we know three things: the name of
the file (in $filename), someone's name (in $name), and that person's secret
word (in $word). Here's a place to use Perl's report generating tools. We define a
format somewhere in the program (usually near the end, like a subroutine):

```
format STDOUT =
@<<<<<<<<<<<<<< @<<<<<<<<< @<<<<<<<<<<<
$filename, $name, $word
.
```

The format definition begins with **format STDOUT =**, and ends with a single
period. The two lines between are the format itself. The first line of this format is a
field definition line that specifies the number, length, and type of the fields. For
this format, we have three fields. The line following a field definition line is always
a *field value line*. The value line gives a list of expressions that will be evaluated
when this format is used, and the results of those expressions will be plugged into
the fields defined in the previous line.

We invoke this format with the **write** function, like so:

```
#!/usr/bin/perl
while ( defined($filename = glob("*.secret")) ) {
    open (WORDSLIST, $filename) || die "can't open wordlist: $!";
    if (-M WORDSLIST < 7.0) {
        while ($name = <WORDSLIST>) {
            chomp ($name);
            $word = <WORDSLIST>;
            chomp ($word);
            write; # invoke format STDOUT to STDOUT
        }
    }
    close (WORDSLIST) || die "couldn't close wordlist: $!";
}
format STDOUT =
@<<<<<<<<<<<<<< @<<<<<<<<< @<<<<<<<<<<<
$filename, $name, $word
.
```

When the format is invoked, Perl evaluates the field expressions and generates a
line that it sends to the **STDOUT** filehandle. Because **write** is invoked once each
time through the loop, we'll get a series of lines with text in columns, one line for
each secret word entry.

Hmm. We haven't labeled the columns. That's easy enough. We just need to add a top-of-page format, like so:

```
format STDOUT_TOP =
Page @<<
$%

Filename         Name       Word
================ ========== =============
.
```

This format is named `STDOUT_TOP`, and will be used initially at the first invocation of the `STDOUT` format, and again every time 60 lines of output to `STDOUT` have been generated. The column headings here line up with the columns from the `STDOUT` format, so everything comes out tidy.

The first line of this format shows some constant text (`Page`) along with a three-character field definition. The following line is a field value line, here with one expression. This expression is the `$%` variable,[*] which holds the number of pages printed—a very useful value in top-of-page formats.

The third line of the format is blank. Because this line does not contain any fields, the line following it is not a field value line. This blank line is copied directly to the output, creating a blank line between the page number and the column headers below.

The last two lines of the format also contain no fields, so they are copied as is directly to the output. So this format generates four lines, one of which has a part that changes from page to page.

Just tack this definition onto the previous program to get it to work. Perl notices the top-of-page format automatically.

Perl also has fields that are centered or right-justified, and supports a *filled paragraph area* as well. More on this when we get to formats in Chapter 11, *Formats*.

Making Those Old Word Lists More Noticeable

As we are scanning through the `*.secret` files in the current directory, we may find files that are too old. So far, we are simply skipping over those files. Let's go one step more: we'll rename them to `*.secret.old` so that a directory listing will quickly show us which files are too old, simply by name.

Here's how the `init_words()` subroutine looks with this modification:

```
sub init_words {
```

---

[*] More mnemonic aliases for these predefined scalar variables are available via the English module.

```
while ( defined($filename = glob("*.secret")) ) {
    open (WORDSLIST, $filename) ||
                        die "can't open wordlist: $!";
    if (-M WORDSLIST < 7.0) {
        while ($name = <WORDSLIST>) {
            chomp ($name);
            $word = <WORDSLIST>;
            chomp ($word);
            $words{$name} = $word;
        }
    } else { # rename the file so it gets noticed
        rename ($filename,"$filename.old") ||
            die "can't rename $filename to $filename.old: $!";
    }
    close (WORDSLIST) || die "couldn't close wordlist: $!";
}
```

Notice the new **else** part of the file age check. If the file is older than seven days, it gets renamed with the **rename** function. This function takes two parameters, renaming the file named by the first parameter to the name given in the second parameter.

Perl has a complete range of file manipulation operators; anything you can do to a file from a C program, you can also do from Perl.

Maintaining a Last-Good-Guess Database

Let's keep track of when the most recent correct guess has been made for each user. One data structure that might seem to work at first glance is a hash. For example, the statement

```
$last_good{$name} = time;
```

assigns the current time in internal format (some large integer above 800 million, incrementing one number per second) to an element of **%last_good** that has the name for a key. Over time, this would seem to give us a database indicating the most recent time the secret word was guessed properly for each of the users who had invoked the program.

But, the hash doesn't have an existence between invocations of the program. Each time the program is invoked, a new hash is formed. So at most, we create a one-element hash and then immediately forget it when the program exits.

The **dbmopen** function* maps a hash out into a disk file (actually a pair of disk files) known as a *DBM*. It's used like this:

---

* Or using the more low-level **tie** function on a specific database, as detailed in Chapters 5 and 7 of *Programming Perl*, or in the *perltie*(1) and *AnyDBM_File*(3) manpages.

```
dbmopen (%last_good,"lastdb",0666) ||
                              die "can't dbmopen lastdb: $!";
$last_good{$name} = time;
dbmclose (%last_good) || die "can't dbmclose lastdb: $!";
```

The first statement performs the mapping, using the disk filenames of `lastdb.dir` and `lastdb.pag` (these names are the normal names for a DBM called `lastdb`). The file permissions used for these two files if the files must be created (as they will the first time through) is `0666`.* This mode means that anyone can read or write the files. If you're on a UNIX system, file permission bits are described in the *chmod*(2) manpage. On non-UNIX systems, *chmod*() may or may not work the same way. For example, under MS-DOS, files have no permissions, whereas under WindowsNT, they do. See your port's release notes about this if you're unsure.

The second statement shows that we use this mapped hash just like a normal hash. However, creating or updating an element of the hash automatically updates the disk files that form the DBM. And, when the hash is later accessed, the values within the hash come directly from the disk image. This gives the hash a life beyond the current invocation of the program—a persistence of its own.

The third statement disconnects the hash from the DBM, much like a file `close` operation.

Although the inserted statements maintain the database just fine (and even create it the first time), we don't have any way of examining the information yet. To do that, we can create a separate little program that looks something like this:

```
#!/usr/bin/perl -w
dbmopen (%last_good,"lastdb",0666) ||
                              die "can't dbmopen lastdb: $!";
foreach $name (sort keys (%last_good)) {
    $when = $last_good{$name};
    $hours = (time() - $when) / 3600; # compute hours ago
    write;
}

format STDOUT =
User @<<<<<<<<<<<: last correct guess was @<<< hours ago.
$name, $hours
```

We've got a few new operations here: a `foreach` loop, sorting a list, and getting the keys of an array.

First, the `keys` function takes a hash name as an argument and returns a list of all the keys of that hash in some unspecified order. For the `%words` hash defined

---

* The actual permissions of the files will be the logical AND of 0666 and your process's current umask.

earlier, the result is something like `fred`, `barney`, `betty`, `wilma`, in some unspecified order. For the `%last_good` hash, the result will be a list of all users who have guessed their own secret word successfully.

The `sort` function sorts the list alphabetically (just as if you passed a text file through the *sort* command). This makes sure that the list processed by the `foreach` statement is always in alphabetical order.

Finally, the Perl `foreach` statement is a lot like the C-shell `foreach` statement. It takes a list of values and assigns each one in turn to a scalar variable (here, `$name`) executing the body of the loop (a block) once for each value. So, for five names in the `%last_good` list, we get five passes through the loop, with `$name` being a different value each time.

The body of the `foreach` loop loads up a couple of variables used within the `STDOUT` format and invokes the format. Note that we figure out the age of the entry by subtracting the stored system time (in the array) from the current time (as returned by `time`) and then divide that by 3600 (to convert seconds to hours).

Perl also provides easy ways to create and maintain text-oriented databases (like the Password file) and fixed-length-record databases (like the "last login" database maintained by the *login* program). These are described in Chapter 17, *User Database Manipulation*.

The Final Programs

Here are the programs from this stroll in their final form so you can play with them.

First, the "say hello" program:

```perl
#!/usr/bin/perl
init_words();
print "what is your name? ";
$name = <STDIN>;
chomp($name);
if ($name =~ /^randal\b/i) { # back to the other way :-)
    print "Hello, Randal! How good of you to be here!\n";
} else {
    print "Hello, $name!\n"; # ordinary greeting
    print "What is the secret word? ";
    $guess = <STDIN>;
    chomp $guess;
    while (! good_word($name,$guess)) {
        print "Wrong, try again. What is the secret word? ";
        $guess = <STDIN>;
        chomp $guess;
    }
}
```

```perl
dbmopen (%last_good,"lastdb",0666);
$last_good{$name} = time;
dbmclose (%last_good);
sub init_words {
    while ($filename = <*.secret>) {
        open (WORDSLIST, $filename)||
                            die "can't open $filename: $!";
        if (-M WORDSLIST < 7.0) {
            while ($name = <WORDSLIST>) {
                chomp ($name);
                $word = <WORDSLIST>;
                chomp ($word);
                $words{$name} = $word;
            }
        } else { # rename the file so it gets noticed
            rename ($filename,"$filename.old") ||
                            die "can't rename $filename: $!";
        }
        close WORDSLIST;
    }
}
sub good_word {
    my($somename,$someguess) = @_; # name the parameters
    $somename =~ s/\W.*//; # delete everything after first word
    $somename =~ tr/A-Z/a-z/; # lowercase everything
    if ($somename eq "randal") { # should not need to guess
        return 1; # return value is true
    } elsif (($words{$somename} || "groucho") eq $someguess) {
        return 1; # return value is true
    } else {
        open (MAIL, "|mail YOUR_ADDRESS_HERE");
        print MAIL "bad news: $somename guessed $someguess\n";
        close MAIL;
        return 0; # return value is false
    }
}
```

Next, we have the secret word lister:

```perl
#!/usr/bin/perl
while ($filename = <*.secret>) {
    open (WORDSLIST, $filename) ||
                        die "can't open $filename: $!";

    if (-M WORDSLIST < 7.0) {
        while ($name = <WORDSLIST>) {
            chomp ($name);
            $word = <WORDSLIST>;
            chomp ($word);
            write; # invoke format STDOUT to STDOUT
        }
    }
    close (WORDSLIST);
}
format STDOUT =
```

```
@<<<<<<<<<<<<<< @<<<<<<<<< @<<<<<<<<<<<<
$filename, $name, $word
.

format STDOUT_TOP =
Page @<<
$%

Filename            Name        Word
================ ========== ============
.
```

And finally, the last-time-a-word-was-used display program:

```
#!/usr/bin/perl
dbmopen (%last_good,"lastdb",0666);
foreach $name (sort keys %last_good) {
    $when = $last_good{$name};
    $hours = (time - $when) / 3600; # compute hours ago
    write;
}

format STDOUT =
User @<<<<<<<<<<: last correct guess was @<<< hours ago.
$name, $hours
.
```

Together with the secret word lists (files named *something*.secret in the current directory) and the database lastdb.dir and lastdb.pag, you'll have all you need.

Exercise

Most chapters end with some exercises, for which answers are found in Appendix A, *Exercise Answers*. For this stroll, the answers have already been given above.

1. Type in the example programs, and get them to work. (You'll need to create the secret-word lists as well.) Consult your local Perl guru if you need assistance.

2

Scalar Data

What Is Scalar Data?

A *scalar* is the simplest kind of data that Perl manipulates. A scalar is either a number (like 4 or 3.25e20) or a string of characters (like `hello` or the Gettysburg Address). Although you may think of numbers and strings as very different things, Perl uses them nearly interchangeably, so we'll describe them together.

A scalar value can be acted upon with operators (like plus or concatenate), generally yielding a scalar result. A scalar value can be stored into a scalar variable. Scalars can be read from files and devices and written out as well.

Numbers

Although a scalar is either a number or a string,* it's useful to look at numbers and strings separately for the moment. Numbers first, strings in a minute....

All Numbers Use the Same Format Internally

As you'll see in the next few paragraphs, you can specify both integers (whole numbers, like 17 or 342) and floating-point numbers (real numbers with decimal points, like 3.14, or 1.35 times 10^{25}). But internally, Perl computes only with

---

* Or a reference, but that's an advanced topic.

double-precision floating-point values.* This means that there are no *integer* values internal to Perl; an integer constant in the program is treated as the equivalent floating-point value.† You probably won't notice the conversion (or care much), but you should stop looking for integer operations (as opposed to *floating-point* operations), because there aren't any.

Float Literals

A *literal* is the way a value is represented in the text of the Perl program. You could also call this a *constant* in your program, but we'll use the term *literal*. Literals are the way data is represented in the source code of your program as input to the Perl compiler. (Data that is read from or written to files is treated similarly, but not identically.)

Perl accepts the complete set of floating-point literals available to C programmers. Numbers with and without decimal points are allowed (including an optional plus or minus prefix), as well as tacking on a power-of-10 indicator (exponential notation) with E notation. For example:

```
1.25      # about 1 and a quarter
7.25e45   # 7.25 times 10 to the 45th power (a big number)
-6.5e24   # negative 6.5 times 10 to the 24th
          # (a "big" negative number)
-12e-24   # negative 12 times 10 to the -24th
          # (a very small negative number)
-1.2E-23  # another way to say that
```

Integer Literals

Integer literals are also straightforward, as in:

```
12
15
-2004
3485
```

Don't start the number with a 0, because Perl supports octal and hexadecimal (hex) literals. Octal numbers start with a leading 0, and hex numbers start with a leading 0x or 0X.‡ The hex digits A through F (in either case) represent the conventional digit values of 10 through 15. For example:

```
0377 # 377 octal, same as 255 decimal
-0xff # negative FF hex, same as -255 decimal
```

---

* A "double-precision floating-point value" is whatever the C compiler that compiled Perl used for a `double` declaration.

† Unless you use "integer mode," but that's not on by default.

‡ The "leading zero" indicator works only for literals, not for automatic string-to-number conversion. You can convert a data string that looks like an octal or hex value into a number with `oct` or `hex`.

Strings

Strings are sequences of characters (like `hello`). Each character is an 8-bit value from the entire 256 character set (there's nothing special about the NUL character as in some languages).

The shortest possible string has no characters. The longest string fills all of your available memory (although you wouldn't be able to do much with that). This is in accordance with the principle of "no built-in limits" that Perl follows at every opportunity. Typical strings are printable sequences of letters and digits and punctuation in the ASCII 32 to ASCII 126 range. However, the ability to have any character from 0 to 255 in a string means you can create, scan, and manipulate raw binary data as strings—something with which most other utilities would have great difficulty. (For example, you can patch your operating system by reading it into a Perl string, making the change, and writing the result back out.)

Like numbers, strings have a literal representation (the way you represent the string in a Perl program). Literal strings come in two different flavors: *single-quoted strings* and *double-quoted strings.*[*] Another form that looks rather like these two is the back-quoted string (`` `like this` ``). This isn't so much a literal string as a way to run external commands and get back their output. This is covered in Chapter 14, *Process Management.*

Single-Quoted Strings

A *single-quoted string* is a sequence of characters enclosed in single quotes. The single quotes are not part of the string itself; they're just there to let Perl identify the beginning and the ending of the string. Any character between the quote marks (including newline characters, if the string continues onto successive lines) is legal inside a string. Two exceptions: to get a single quote into a single-quoted string, precede it by a backslash. And to get a backslash into a single-quoted string, precede the backslash by a backslash. In other pictures:

```
'hello'       # five characters: h, e, l, l, o
'don\'t'      # five characters: d, o, n, single-quote, t
''            # the null string (no characters)
'silly\\me'   # silly, followed by backslash, followed by me
'hello\n'     # hello followed by backslash followed by n
'hello
there'        # hello, newline, there (11 characters total)
```

---

[*] There are also the *here* strings, similar to the shell's *here* documents. They are explained in Chapter 19, *CGI Programming.* See also Chapter 2 of *Programming Perl*, and *perldata*(1)

Note that the \n within a single-quoted string is not interpreted as a newline, but as the two characters backslash and n. (Only when the backslash is followed by another backslash or a single quote does it have special meaning.)

Double-Quoted Strings

A *double-quoted string* acts a lot like a C string. Once again, it's a sequence of characters, although this time enclosed in double quotes. But now the backslash takes on its full power to specify certain control characters, or even any character at all through octal and hex representations. Here are some double-quoted strings:

```
"hello world\n"   # hello world, and a newline
"new \177"        # new, space, and the delete character (octal 177)
"coke\tsprite"    # a coke, a tab, and a sprite
```

The backslash can precede many different characters to mean different things (typically called a *backslash escape*). The complete list of double-quoted string escapes is given in Table 2-1.

Table 2-1. Double-Quoted String Representations

Construct	Meaning
\n	Newline
\r	Return
\t	Tab
\f	Formfeed
\b	Backspace
\a	Bell
\e	Escape
\007	Any octal ASCII value (here, 007 = bell)
\x7f	Any hex ASCII value (here, 7f = delete)
\cC	Any "control" character (here, CTRL-C)
\\	Backslash
\"	Double quote
\l	Lowercase next letter
\L	Lowercase all following letters until \E
\u	Uppercase next letter
\U	Uppercase all following letters until \E
\Q	Backslash-quote all nonalphanumerics until \E
\E	Terminate \L , \U, or \Q

Another feature of double-quoted strings is that they are *variable interpolated*, meaning that scalar and array variables within the strings are replaced with their current values when the strings are used. We haven't formally been introduced to what a variable looks like yet (except in the stroll), so I'll get back to this later.

Scalar Operators

An operator produces a new value (the *result*) from one or more other values (the *operands*). For example, + is an operator because it takes two numbers (the operands, like 5 and 6), and produces a new value (11, the result).

Perl's operators and expressions are generally a superset of those provided in most other ALGOL/Pascal-like programming languages, such as C or Java. An operator expects either numeric or string operands (or possibly a combination of both). If you provide a string operand where a number is expected, or vice versa, Perl automatically converts the operand using fairly intuitive rules, which will be detailed in the section "Conversion Between Numbers and Strings," below.

Operators for Numbers

Perl provides the typical ordinary addition, subtraction, multiplication, and division operators, and so on. For example:

```
2 + 3     # 2 plus 3, or 5
5.1 - 2.4 # 5.1 minus 2.4, or approximately 2.7
3 * 12    # 3 times 12 = 36
14 / 2    # 14 divided by 2, or 7
10.2 / 0.3 # 10.2 divided by 0.3, or approximately 34
10 / 3    # always floating point divide, so approximately 3.3333333...
```

Additionally, Perl provides the FORTRAN-like *exponentiation* operator, which many have yearned for in Pascal and C. The operator is represented by the double asterisk, such as 2**3, which is two to the third power, or eight. (If the result can't fit into a double-precision floating-point number, such as a negative number to a noninteger exponent, or a large number to a large exponent, you'll get a fatal error.)

Perl also supports a *modulus* operator. The value of the expression 10 % 3 is the remainder when 10 is divided by 3, which is 1. Both values are first reduced to their integer values, so 10.5 % 3.2 is computed as 10 % 3.

The logical comparison operators are < <= == >= > !=, these compare two values numerically, returning a *true* or *false* value. For example, 3 > 2 returns true because three is greater than two, while 5 != 5 returns false because it's not true that 5 is not equal to 5. The definitions of true and false are covered later, but for now, think of the return values as one for true, and zero for false. (These operators are revisited in Table 2-2.)

You may be wondering about the word "approximately" in the code comments at the start of this section. Don't you get exactly 2.7 when subtracting 2.4 from 5.1? In math class you do, but on computers you usually don't. Instead, you get an approximation that's only accurate to a certain number of decimal places. Computers don't store numbers the same way a mathematician thinks of them. But unless you are doing something extreme, you'll usually see the results you expect to see.

Comparing the following statements, you'll see what the computer really got as the result of the subtraction (the `printf` function is described in Chapter 6, *Basic I/O*):

```
printf("%.51f\n", 5.1 - 2.4)
# 2.6999999999999997335464740899624302983283399658203125

print(5.1 - 2.4, "\n");
# 2.7
```

Don't worry too much about this: the `print` function's default format for printing floating-point numbers usually hides such minor representational inaccuracies. If this ends up being a problem, the Math::BigInt and Math::BigFloat object modules provide infinite-precision arithmetic for integers and floating-point numbers at the cost of somewhat slower execution. For details, see Chapter 7 of *Programming Perl* or the online documentation on these modules.

Operators for Strings

String values can be concatenated with the "." operator. (Yes, that's a single period.) This does not alter either string, any more than 2+3 alters either 2 or 3. The resulting (longer) string is then available for further computation or to be stored into a variable.

```
"hello" . "world"       # same as "helloworld"
'hello world' . "\n"    # same as "hello world\n"
"fred" . " " . "barney" # same as "fred barney"
```

Note that the concatenation must be explicitly called for with the "." operator. You can't just stick the two values close to each other.

Another set of operators for strings are the string comparison operators. These operators are FORTRAN-like, as in `lt` for less-than, and so on. The operators compare the ASCII values of the characters of the strings in the usual fashion. The complete set of comparison operators (for both numbers and strings) is given in Table 2-2.

Table 2-2. Numeric and String Comparison Operators

Comparison	Numeric	String
Equal	==	eq
Not equal	!=	ne
Less than	<	lt
Greater than	>	gt
Less than or equal to	<=	le
Greater than or equal to	>=	ge

You may wonder why there are separate operators for numbers and strings, if numbers and strings are automatically converted back and forth. Consider the two values 7 and 30. If compared as numbers, 7 is obviously less than 30, but if compared as strings, the string "30" comes *before* the string "7" (because the ASCII value for 3 is less than the value for 7), and hence is less. Perl always requires you to specify the proper type of comparison, whether it be numeric or string.

Note that if you come from a UNIX shell programming background, the numeric and string comparisons are roughly opposite of what they are for the UNIX *test* command, which uses -eq for numeric comparison and = for string comparison.

Still another string operator is the *string repetition* operator, consisting of the single lowercase letter **x**. This operator takes its left operand (a string), and makes as many concatenated copies of that string as indicated by its right operand (a number). For example:

```
"fred" x 3        # is "fredfredfred"
"barney" x (4+1)  # is "barney" x 5, or
                  # "barneybarneybarneybarneybarney"
(3+2) x 4         # is 5 x 4, or really "5" x 4, which is "5555"
```

That last example is worth spelling out slowly. The parentheses on (3+2) force this part of the expression to be evaluated first, yielding five. (The parentheses here are working as in standard math.) But the string repetition operator wants a string for a left operand, so the number 5 is converted to the string "5" (using rules described in detail later), a one-character string. This new string is then copied four times, yielding the four-character string 5555. If we had reversed the order of the operands, we would have made five copies of the string 4, yielding 44444. This shows that string repetition is not commutative.

If necessary, the copy count (the right operand) is first truncated to an integer value (4.8 becomes 4) before being used. A copy count of less than one results in an empty (zero-length) string.

Operator Precedence and Associativity

Operator precedence defines how to resolve the ambiguous case where two operators are trying to operate on three operands. For example, in the expression 2+3*4, do we perform the addition first or the multiplication first? If we did the addition first, we'd get 5*4, or 20. But if we did the multiplication first (as we were taught in math class) we'd get 2+12, or 14. Fortunately, Perl chooses the common mathematical definition, performing the multiplication first. Because of this, we say multiplication has a *higher precedence* than addition.

You can override the order defined by precedence using parentheses. Anything in parentheses is completely computed before the operator outside of the parentheses is applied (just as you learned in math class). So if you really want the addition before the multiplication, you can say (2+3)*4, yielding 20. Also, if you want to demonstrate that multiplication is performed before addition, you could add a decorative but functionless set of parentheses in 2+(3*4).

While precedence is intuitive for addition and multiplication,* we start running into problems when faced with, say, string concatenation compared with exponentiation. The proper way to resolve this is to consult the official, accept-no-substitutes Perl operator precedence chart, shown in Table 2-3. (Note that some of the operators have not yet been described, and in fact, may not even appear anywhere in this book, but don't let that scare you from reading about them.) Operators that are also found in C have the same precedence as in C.

Table 2-3. Associativity and Precedence of Operators: Highest to Lowest

Associativity	Operator
Left	The "list" operators (leftward)
Left	-> (method call, dereference)
Nonassociative	++ -- (autoincrement, autodecrement)
Right	** (exponentiation)
Right	! ~ \ + - (logical not, bit-not, reference operator, unary plus, unary minus)
Left	=~ !~ (matches, doesn't match)
Left	* / % x (multiply, divide, modulus, string replicate)

* You recall your high-school algebra class? If not, there's nothing wrong with using parentheses to improve clarity.

Table 2-3. Associativity and Precedence of Operators: Highest to Lowest (continued)

Associativity	Operator
Left	+ − . (add, subtract, string concatenate)
Left	<< >>
Nonassociative	Named unary operators (like chomp)
Nonassociative	< > <= >= lt gt le ge
Nonassociative	== != <=> eq ne cmp
Left	& (bit-and)
Left	| ^ (bit-or, bit-xor)
Left	&& (logical and)
Left	|| (logical or)
Nonassociative	.. ... (noninclusive and inclusive range)
Right	?: (if-then-else)
Right	= += −= *=, etc. (assignment and binary-assignment)
Left	, => (comma and comma-arrow)
Nonassociative	List operators (rightward)
Right	not (logical not)
Left	and (logical and)
Left	or xor (logical or, logical xor)

In the chart, any given operator has higher precedence than those listed below it, and lower precedence than all of the operators listed above it.

Operators at the same precedence level resolve according to rules of *associativity* instead. Just like precedence, associativity resolves the order of operations when two operators of the same precedence compete for three operands:

```
2 ** 3 ** 4   # 2 ** (3 ** 4), or 2 ** 81, or approx 2.41e24
72 / 12 / 3   # (72 / 12) / 3, or 6/3, or 2
30 / 6 * 3    # (30/6)*3, or 15
```

In the first case, the ** operator has right associativity, so the parentheses are implied on the right. Comparatively, the * and / operators have left associativity, yielding a set of implied parentheses on the left.

Conversion Between Numbers and Strings

If a string value is used as an operand for a numeric operator (say, +), Perl automatically converts the string to its equivalent numeric value, as if it had been entered as a decimal floating-point value.* Trailing nonnumerics and leading

---

* Hex and octal values are not supported in this automatic conversion. Use hex and oct to interpret hex and octal values.

whitespace are politely and quietly ignored, so " 123.45fred" (with a leading space) converts to 123.45 with nary a warning.* At the extreme end of this, something that isn't a number at all converts to zero without warning (such as the string fred used as a number).

Likewise, if a numeric value is given when a string value is needed (for the string concatenate operator, for example), the numeric value is expanded into whatever string would have been printed for that number. For example, if you want to concatenate an X followed by the results of 4 multiplied by 5, you can say this simply as:

```
"X" . (4 * 5) # same as "X" . 20, or "X20"
```

(Remember that the parentheses force 4*5 to be computed first, before considering the string concatenation operator.)

In other words, you don't have to worry about whether you have a number or a string (most of the time). Perl performs all the conversions for you.

Scalar Variables

A variable is a name for a container that holds one or more values. The name of the variable is constant throughout the program, but the value or values contained in that variable typically change over and over again throughout the execution of the program.

A scalar variable holds a single scalar value (representing a number, a string, or a reference). Scalar variable names begin with a dollar sign followed by a letter, and then possibly more letters, or digits, or underscores.† Upper- and lowercase letters are distinct: the variable $A is a different variable from $a. And all of the letters, digits, and underscores are significant, so:

```
$a_very_long_variable_that_ends_in_1
```

is different from:

```
$a_very_long_variable_that_ends_in_2
```

You should generally select variable names that mean something regarding the value of the variable. For example, $xyz123 is probably not very descriptive but $line_length is.

---

* Unless you turn on the -w option from the command line, which you should always do for safety's sake.

† Limited to 255 characters, however. We hope that suffices.

Scalar Operators and Functions

The most common operation on a scalar variable is *assignment*, which is the way to give a value to a variable. The Perl assignment operator is the equal sign (much like C or FORTRAN), which takes a variable name on the left side and gives it the value of the expression on the right, like so:

```
$a = 17;     # give $a the value of 17
$b = $a + 3; # give $b the current value of $a plus 3 (20)
$b = $b * 2; # give $b the value of $b multiplied by 2 (40)
```

Notice that last line uses the $b variable twice: once to get its value (on the right side of the =), and once to define where to put the computed expression (on the left side of the =). This is legal, safe, and in fact, rather common. In fact, it's so common that we'll see in a minute that we can write this using a convenient shorthand.

You may have noticed that scalar variables are always specified with the leading $. In shell programming, you use $ to get the value, but leave the $ off to assign a new value. In Java or C, you leave the $ off entirely. If you bounce back and forth a lot, you'll find yourself typing the wrong things occasionally. This is expected. (Our solution was to stop writing shell, *awk*, and C programs, but that may not work for you.)

A scalar assignment may be used as a value as well as an operation, as in C. In other words, $a=3 has a value, just as $a+3 has a value. The value is the value assigned, so the value of $a=3 is 3. Although this may seem odd at first glance, using an assignment as a value is useful if you wish to assign an intermediate value in an expression to a variable, or if you simply wish to copy the same value to more than one variable. For example:

```
$b = 4 + ($a = 3);    # assign 3 to $a, then add 4 to that
                      # resulting in $b getting 7
$d = ($c = 5);        # copy 5 into $c, and then also into $d
$d = $c = 5;          # the same thing without parentheses
```

That last example works because assignment is right-associative.

Binary Assignment Operators

Expressions like $a = $a + 5 (where the same variable appears on both sides of an assignment) occur frequently enough that Perl has a shorthand for the operation of altering a variable: the *binary assignment operator*. Nearly all binary operators that compute a value have a corresponding binary assignment form with an appended equal sign. For example, the following two lines are equivalent:

```
$a = $a + 5; # without the binary assignment operator
$a += 5;     # with the binary assignment operator
```

And so are these:

```
$b = $b * 3;
$b *= 3;
```

In each case, the operator causes the existing value of the variable to be altered in some way, rather than simply overwriting the value with the result of some new expression.

Another common assignment operator is the string concatenate operator:

```
$str = $str . " "; # append a space to $str
$str .= " ";        # same thing with assignment operator
```

Nearly all binary operators are valid this way. For example, a *raise to the power of* operator is written as **=. So, $a **= 3 means "raise the number in $a to the third power, placing the result back in $a".

Like the simple assignment operator, these operators have a value as well: the new value of the variable. For example:

```
$a = 3;
$b = ($a += 4); # $a and $b are both now 7
```

Autoincrement and Autodecrement

As if it weren't already easy enough to add one to $a by saying $a += 1, Perl goes one further and shortens even this up. The ++ operator (called the *autoincrement* operator) adds one to its operand, and returns the incremented value, like so:

```
$a += 1;    # with assignment operator
++$a;       # with prefix autoincrement
$d = 17;
$e = ++$d; # $e and $d are both 18 now
```

Here, the ++ operator is being used as a *prefix* operator; that is, the operator appears to the left of its operand. The autoincrement may also be used in a *suffix* form (to the right of its operand). In this case, the result of the expression is the old value of the variable *before* the variable is incremented. For example:

```
$c = 17;
$d = $c++; # $d is 17, but $c is now 18
```

Because the value of the operand changes, the operand must be a scalar variable, not just an expression. You cannot say ++16 to get 17, nor can you say ++($a+$b) to somehow get one more than the sum of $a and $b.

The autodecrement operator (--) is similar to the autoincrement operator, but subtracts one rather than adding one. Like the autoincrement operator, the autodecrement operator has a prefix and suffix form. For example:

```
$x = 12;
--$x;       # $x is now 11
$y = $x--;  # $y is 11, and $x is now 10
```

The autoincrement and autodecrement operators also work on floating-point values. So autoincrementing a variable with the value 4.2 yields 5.2 as expected.*

The chop and chomp Functions

A useful built-in function is chop. This function takes a single argument within its parentheses—the name of a scalar variable—and removes the last character from the string value of that variable. For example:

```
$x = "hello world";
chop($x); # $x is now "hello worl"
```

Note that the value of the argument is altered here, hence the requirement for a scalar variable, rather than simply a scalar value. It would not make sense, for example, to write chop('suey') to change it to 'sue', because there is no place in which to save the value. Besides, you could have just written 'sue' instead.

The value returned is the discarded character (the letter d in world above). This means that the following code is probably wrong:

```
$x = chop($x);  # WRONG: replaces $x with its last character
chop($x);       # RIGHT: as above, removes the last character
```

If chop is given an empty string, it does nothing, and returns nothing, and doesn't raise an error or even whimper a bit.† Most operations in Perl have sensible boundary conditions; in other words, you can use them right up to the edges (and beyond), frequently without complaint. Some have argued that this is one of Perl's fundamental flaws, while others write screaming programs without having to worry about the fringes. You decide which camp you wish to join.

When you chop a string that has already been chopped, another character disappears off into "bit heaven." For example:

```
$a = "hello world\n";
chop $a; # $a is now "hello world"
chop $a; # oops! $a is now "hello worl"
```

If you're not sure whether the variable has a newline on the end, you can use the slightly safer chomp operator, which removes only a newline character,‡ like so:

---

* Autoincrement even works on strings. See *Programming Perl* or *perlop*(1) for that.

† Unless you are using the sanity-saving -w switch.

‡ Or whatever the input record separator $/ is set to.

```
$a = "hello world\n";
chomp ($a); # $a is now "hello world"
chomp ($a); # aha! no change in $a
```

Interpolation of Scalars into Strings

When a string literal is double-quoted, it is subject to *variable interpolation* (besides being checked for backslash escapes). This means that the string is scanned for possible scalar variable* names—namely, a dollar sign followed by letters, digits, and underscores. When a variable reference is found, it is replaced with its current value (or an empty string if the variable has not yet been assigned a value). For example:

```
$a = "fred";
$b = "some text $a";           # $b is now "some text fred"
$c = "no such variable $what"; # $c is "no such variable "
```

The text that replaces the variable is not rescanned; that is, even if there are dollar signs in the replaced value, no further replacement occurs:

```
$x = '$fred';  # literally a dollar sign followed by "fred"
$y = "hey $x"; # value is 'hey $fred': no double substitution
```

To prevent the substitution of a variable with its value, you must either alter that part of the string so that it appears in single quotes, or precede the dollar sign with a backslash, which turns off the dollar sign's special significance:

```
$fred   = 'hi';
$barney = "a test of " . '$fred'; # literally: 'a test of $fred'
$barney2= "a test of \$fred";     # same thing
```

The variable name will be the longest possible variable name that makes sense at that part of the string. This can be a problem if you want to follow the replaced value immediately with some constant text that begins with a letter, digit, or underscore. As Perl scans for variable names, it would consider those characters to be additional name characters, which is not what you want. Perl provides a delimiter for the variable name. Simply enclose the name of the variable in a pair of curly braces. Or, you can end that part of the string and start another part of the string with a concatenation operator:

```
$fred   = "pay"; $fredday = "wrong!";
$barney = "It's $fredday";        # not payday, but "It's wrong!"
$barney = "It's ${fred}day";      # now, $barney gets "It's payday"
$barney2 = "It's $fred"."day";    # another way to do it
$barney3 = "It's " . $fred . "day"; # and another way
```

The case-shifting string escapes can be used to alter the case of letters brought in with variable interpolation.† For example:

---

* And array variables, but we won't discuss those until Chapter 3, *Arrays and List Data*.

† You may find the uc, ucfirst, lc, and lcfirst functions easier to use.

```
$bigfred   = "\Ufred";                           # $bigfred is "FRED"
$fred      = "fred"; $bigfred = "\U$fred"; # same thing
$capfred   = "\u$fred";                          # $capfred is "Fred"
$barney    = "\LBARNEY";                         # $barney is now "barney"
$capbarney = "\u\LBARNEY";                       # $capbarney is now "Barney"
$bigbarney = "BARNEY"; $capbarney = "\u\L$bigbarney"; # same
```

As you can see, the case-shifting string escapes are remembered within a string until they are used, so even though the first letter of BARNEY doesn't follow the \u, it remains uppercase because of the \u.

The term *variable interpolation* is often used interchangeably with *double-quote interpolation*, because strings that are double-quoted are subject to variable interpolation. So too, are backquoted strings, described in Chapter 14, *Process Management*.

<STDIN> as a Scalar Value

At this point, if you're a typical code hacker, you're probably wondering how to get a value into a Perl program. Here's the simplest way. Each time you use <STDIN> in a place where a scalar value is expected, Perl reads the next complete text line from *standard input* (up to the first newline), and uses that string as the value of <STDIN>. Standard input can mean many things, but unless you do something odd, it means the terminal of the user who invoked your program (probably you). If there's nothing waiting to be read (typically the case, unless you type ahead a complete line), the Perl program will stop and wait for you to enter some characters followed by a newline (return).

The string value of <STDIN> typically has a newline on the end of it. Most often, you'll want to get rid of that newline right away (there's a big difference between hello and hello\n). This is where our friend, the chomp function, comes to the rescue. A typical input sequence goes something like this:

```
$a = <STDIN>;  # get the text
chomp($a);     # get rid of that pesky newline
```

A common abbreviation for these two lines is:

```
chomp($a = <STDIN>);
```

The assignment inside the parentheses continues to refer to $a, even after it has been given a value with <STDIN>. Thus, the chomp function is working on $a. (This is true in general about the assignment operator; an assignment expression can be used wherever a variable is needed, and the actions refer to the variable on the left side of the equal sign.)

Output with print

So, we get things in with `<STDIN>`. How do we get things out? With the `print` function. This function takes the values within its parentheses and puts them out without any embellishment onto standard output. Once again, unless you've done something odd, this will be your terminal. For example:

```
print("hello world\n"); # say hello world, followed by newline
print "hello world\n";  # same thing
```

Note that the second example shows the form of `print` without parentheses. Whether or not to use the parentheses is mostly a matter of style and typing agility, although there are a few cases where you'll need the parentheses to remove ambiguity.

We'll see that you can actually give `print` a *list* of values, in the "Using print for Normal Output" section of Chapter 6, *Basic I/O*, but we haven't talked about lists yet, so we'll put that off for later.

The Undefined Value

What happens if you use a scalar variable before you give it a value? Nothing serious, and definitely nothing fatal. Variables have the `undef` value before they are first assigned. This value looks like a zero when used as a number, or the zero-length empty string when used as a string. You will get a warning under Perl's -w switch, though, which is a good way to catch programming errors.

Many operators return `undef` when the arguments are out of range or don't make sense. If you don't do anything special, you'll get a zero or a null string without major consequences. In practice, this is hardly a problem.

One operation we've seen that returns `undef` under certain circumstances is `<STDIN>`. Normally, this returns the next line that was read; however, if there are no more lines to read (such as when you type CTRL-D at the terminal, or when a file has no more data), `<STDIN>` returns `undef` as a value. In Chapter 6, we'll see how to test for this and take special action when there is no more data available to read.

Exercises

See Appendix A for answers.

1. Write a program that computes the circumference of a circle with a radius of 12.5. The circumference is 2π times the radius, or about 2 times 3.141592654 times the radius.

2. Modify the program from the previous exercise to prompt for and accept a radius from the person running the program.

3. Write a program that prompts for and reads two numbers, and prints out the result of the two numbers multiplied together.

4. Write a program that reads a string and a number, and prints the string the number of times indicated by the number on separate lines. (Hint: use the "**x**" operator.)

3

Arrays and List Data

What Is a List or Array?

A *list* is ordered scalar data. An array is a variable that holds a list. Each *element* of the array is a separate scalar variable with an independent scalar value. These values are ordered; that is, they have a particular sequence from the lowest to the highest element.

Arrays can have any number of elements. The smallest array has no elements, while the largest array can fill all of available memory. Once again, this is in keeping with Perl's philosophy of "no unnecessary limits."

Literal Representation

A *list literal* (the way you represent the value of a list within your program) consists of comma-separated values enclosed in parentheses. These values form the elements of the list. For example:

```
(1,2,3)             # array of three values 1, 2, and 3
("fred",4.5)        # two values, "fred" and 4.5
```

The elements of a list are not necessarily constants; they can be expressions that will be reevaluated each time the literal is used. For example:

```
($a,17);            # two values: the current value of $a, and 17
($b+$c,$d+$e)       # two values
```

The empty list (one of no elements) is represented by an empty pair of parentheses:

```
() # the empty list (zero elements)
```

An item of the list literal can include the *list constructor operator*, indicated by two scalar values separated by two consecutive periods. This operator creates a list of values starting at the left scalar value up through the right scalar value, incrementing by one each time. For example:

```
(1 .. 5)          # same as (1, 2, 3, 4, 5)
(1 ?    5.2)      # same as (1, 2, 3, 4, 5)
(2 .. 6,10,12)    # same as (2,3,4,5,6,10,12)
($a .. $b)        # range determined by current values of $a and $b
```

Having the right scalar less than the left scalar results in an empty list; you can't count down by switching the order of the values. If the final value is not a whole number of steps above the initial value, the list stops just before the next value would have been outside the range:

```
(1.3 .. 6.1) # same as (1, 2, 3, 4, 5, 6)
```

List literals with lots of short text strings start to look pretty noisy with all the quotes and commas:

```
@a = ("fred","barney","betty","wilma"); # ugh!
```

So there's a shortcut: the "quote word" function, which creates a list from the nonwhitespace parts between the parentheses:*

```
@a = qw(fred barney betty wilma); # better!
@a = qw(
    fred
    barney
    betty
    wilma
);                          # same thing
```

One use of a list literal is as arguments to the **print** function introduced earlier. Elements of the list are printed out without any intervening whitespace:

```
print("The answer is ",@a,"\n");
```

This statement prints **The answer is** followed by a space, the value of **@a**, and a newline. Stay tuned for other uses for list literals.

---

* Actually, like the pattern-matching functions we'll learn about later, you could use any nonwhitespace, nonalphanumeric character as the delimiter instead of parentheses.

Variables

An array variable holds a single list value (zero or more scalar values). Array variable names are similar to scalar variable names, differing only in the initial character, which is an at sign (@) rather than a dollar sign ($). For example:

```
@fred # the array variable @fred
@A_Very_Long_Array_Variable_Name
@A_Very_Long_Array_Variable_Name_that_is_different
```

Note that the array variable @fred is unrelated to the scalar variable $fred. Perl maintains separate namespaces for different types of things.

The value of an array variable that has not yet been assigned is ( ), the empty list.

An expression can refer to array variables as a whole, or it can examine and modify individual elements of the array.

Array Operators and Functions

Array functions and operators act on entire arrays. Some return a list, which can then either be used as a value for another array function, or assigned into an array variable.

Assignment

Probably the most important array operator is the array assignment operator, which gives an array variable a value. It is an equal sign, just like the scalar assignment operator. Perl determines whether the assignment is a scalar assignment or an array assignment by noticing whether the assignment is to a scalar or an array variable. For example:

```
@fred = (1,2,3); # The fred array gets a three-element literal
@barney = @fred; # now that is copied to @barney
```

If a scalar value is assigned to an array variable, the scalar value becomes the single element of an array:

```
@huh = 1; # 1 is promoted to the list (1) automatically
```

Array variable names may appear in a list literal list. When the value of the list is computed, Perl replaces the names with the current values of the array, like so:

```
@fred = qw(one two);
@barney = (4,5,@fred,6,7); # @barney becomes
                           # (4,5,"one","two",6,7)
@barney = (8,@barney);     # puts 8 in front of @barney
@barney = (@barney,"last");# and a "last" at the end
                    # @barney is now (8,4,5,"one","two",6,7,"last")
```

Note that the inserted array elements are at the same level as the rest of the literal: a list cannot contain another list as an element.*

If a list literal contains only variable references (not expressions), the list literal can also be treated as a variable. In other words, such a list literal can be used on the left side of an assignment. Each scalar variable in the list literal takes on the corresponding value from the list on the right side of the assignment. For example:

```
($a,$b,$c) = (1,2,3);     # give 1 to $a, 2 to $b, 3 to $c
($a,$b) = ($b,$a);        # swap $a and $b
($d,@fred) = ($a,$b,$c);  # give $a to $d, and ($b,$c) to @fred
($c,@fred) = @fred;       # remove first element of @fred to $e
                          # this makes @fred = ($c) and $e = $b
```

If the number of elements being assigned does not match the number of variables to hold the values, any excess values (on the right side of the equal sign) are silently discarded, and any excess variables (on the left side of the equal sign) are given the value of undef.

An array variable appearing in the array literal list must be last, because the array variable is "greedy" and consumes all remaining values. (Well, you could put other variables after it, but they would just get undef values.)

If an array variable is assigned to a scalar variable, the number assigned is the *length* of the array, as in:

```
@fred = (4,5,6);   # initialize @fred
$a = @fred;        # $a gets 3, the current length of @fred
```

The length is also returned whenever an array variable name is used where a scalar value is needed. (In the upcoming section called "Scalar and List Context," we'll see that this is called using the array name in a *scalar context*.) For example, to get one less than the length of the array, you can use @fred-1, since the scalar subtraction operator wants scalars for both of its operands. Notice the following:

```
$a  = @fred;   # $a gets the length of @fred
($a) = @fred;  # $a gets the first element of @fred
```

The first assignment is a scalar assignment, and so @fred is treated as a scalar, yielding its length. The second assignment is an array assignment (even if only one value is wanted), and thus yields the first element of @fred, silently discarding all the rest.

---

* Although a *list reference* is permitted as a list element, it's not really a list as a list element. Still, it works out to nearly the same thing, allowing for multidimensional arrays. See Chapter 4 of *Programming Perl* or *perllol* (1) for details.

The value of an array assignment is itself a list value, and can be cascaded as you can with scalar assignments. For example:

```
@fred = (@barney =   (2,3,4));    # @fred and @barney get (2,3,4)
@fred = @barney =   (2,3,4);     # same thing
```

Array Element Access

So far, we've been treating the array as a whole, adding and removing values by doing array assignments. Many useful programs are constructed using arrays without ever accessing any specific array element. However, Perl provides a traditional subscripting function to access an array element by numeric index.

For the subscripting function, array elements are numbered using sequential integers, beginning at zero[*] and increasing by one for each element. The first element of the `@fred` array is accessed as `$fred[0]`. Note that the `@` on the array name becomes a `$` on the element reference. This is because accessing an element of the array identifies a scalar variable (part of the array), which can either be assigned to or have its current value used in an expression, like so:

```
@fred = (7,8,9);
$b = $fred[0];  # give 7 to $b (first element of @fred)
$fred[0] = 5;   # now @fred = (5,8,9)
```

Other elements can be accessed with equal ease, as in:

```
$c = $fred[1];                    # give 8 to $c
$fred[2]++;                       # increment the third element of @fred
$fred[1] += 4;                    # add 4 to the second element
($fred[0],$fred[1]) = ($fred[1],$fred[0]); # swap the first two
```

Accessing a list of elements from the same array (as in that last example) is called a *slice*, and occurs often enough that there is a special representation for it:

```
@fred[0,1];                      # same as ($fred[0],$fred[1])
@fred[0,1] = @fred[1,0];         # swap the first two elements
@fred[0,1,2] = @fred[1,1,1];# make all 3 elements like the 2nd
@fred[1,2] = (9,10);             # change the last two values to 9 and 10
```

Note that this slice uses an `@` prefix rather than a `$`. This is because you are creating an array variable by selecting part of the array rather than a scalar variable accessing just one element.

Slices also work on literal lists, or any function that returns a list value:

```
@who = (qw(fred barney betty wilma))[2,3];
# like @x = qw(fred barney betty wilma); @who = @x[2,3];
```

---

[*] It's possible to change the index value of the first element to something else (like "1"). However, doing so has drastic effects, will probably confuse people maintaining your code, and might break the routines you take from other people. Thus, it's highly recommended that you consider this an unusable feature.

The index values in these examples have been literal integers, but the index can also be any expression that returns a number, which is then used to select the appropriate element:

```
@fred = (7,8,9);
$a = 2;
$b = $fred[$a];        # like $fred[2], or the value of 9
$c = $fred[$a-1];      # $c gets $fred[1], or 8
($c) = (7,8,9)[$a-1];  # same thing using slice
```

Perl programs can thus have array accesses similar to many traditional programming languages.

This idea of using an expression for the subscript also works for slices. Remember, however, that the subscript for a slice is a list of values, so the expression is an array expression, rather than a scalar expression.

```
@fred = (7,8,9); # as in previous example
@barney = (2,1,0);
@backfred = @fred[@barney];
# same as @fred[2,1,0], or ($fred[2],$fred[1],$fred[0]), or
# (9,8,7)
```

If you access an array element beyond the end of the current array (that is, an index of greater than the last element's index), the **undef** value is returned without warning. For example:

```
@fred = (1,2,3);
$barney = $fred[7]; # $barney is now undef
```

Assigning a value beyond the end of the current array automatically extends the array (giving a value of **undef** to all intermediate values, if any). For example:

```
@fred = (1,2,3);
$fred[3] = "hi"; # @fred is now (1,2,3,"hi")
$fred[6] = "ho"; # @fred is now (1,2,3,"hi",undef,undef,"ho")
```

You can use **$#fred** to get the index value of the last element of **@fred**. You can even assign this value to change the length of **@fred**, making it grow or shrink, but that's generally unnecessary, because the array grows and shrinks automatically.

A negative subscript on an array counts back from the end. So, another way to get at the last element is with the subscript –1. The second to the last element would be –2, and so on. For example:

```
@fred = ("fred", "wilma", "pebbles", "dino");
print $fred[-1];       # prints "dino"
print $#fred;          # prints 3
print $fred[$#fred];   # prints "dino"
```

The push and pop Functions

One common use of an array is as a stack of information, where new values are added to and removed from the right-hand side of the list. These operations occur often enough to have their own special functions:

```
push(@mylist,$newvalue);     # like @mylist = (@mylist,$newvalue)
$oldvalue = pop(@mylist);    # removes the last element of @mylist
```

The pop function returns **undef** if given an empty list, rather than doing something un-Perl-like such as complaining or generating a warning message.

The push function also accepts a list of values to be pushed. The values are pushed together onto the end of the list. For example:

```
@mylist = (1,2,3);
push(@mylist,4,5,6); # @mylist = (1,2,3,4,5,6)
```

Note that the first argument must be an array variable name; pushing and popping wouldn't make sense on a literal list.

The shift and unshift Functions

The push and pop functions do things to the "right" side of a list (the portion with the highest subscripts). Similarly, the **unshift** and **shift** functions perform the corresponding actions on the "left" side of a list (the portion with the lowest subscripts). Here are a few examples:

```
unshift(@fred,$a);          # like @fred = ($a,@fred);
unshift(@fred,$a,$b,$c);    # like @fred = ($a,$b,$c,@fred);
$x = shift(@fred);          # like ($x,@fred) = @fred;
                            # with some real values
@fred = (5,6,7);
unshift(@fred,2,3,4);       # @fred is now (2,3,4,5,6,7)
$x = shift(@fred);          # $x gets 2, @fred is now (3,4,5,6,7)
```

As with pop, **shift** returns **undef** if given an empty array variable.

The reverse Function

The **reverse** function reverses the order of the elements of its argument, returning the resulting list. For example:

```
@a = (7,8,9);
@b = reverse(@a);    # gives @b the value of (9,8,7)
@b = reverse(7,8,9); # same thing
```

Note that the argument list is unaltered; the **reverse** function works on a copy. If you want to reverse an array "in place," you'll need to assign it back into the same variable:

```
@b = reverse(@b); # give @b the reverse of itself
```

The sort Function

The `sort` function takes its arguments, and sorts them as if they were single strings in ascending ASCII order. It returns the sorted list without altering the original list. For example:

```
@x = sort("small","medium","large");
                # @x gets "large","medium","small"
@y = (1,2,4,8,16,32,64);
@y = sort(@y); # @y gets 1,16,2,32,4,64,8
```

Note that sorting numbers does not happen numerically, but by the string values of each number (1, 16, 2, 32, and so on). In the section "Advanced Sorting," in Chapter 15, *Other Data Transformation*, you'll learn how to sort numerically, or in descending order, or by the third character of each string, or by any other method that you choose.

The chomp Function

The `chomp` function works on an array variable as well as a scalar variable. Each element of the array has its last record separator removed. This can be handy when you've read a list of lines as separate array elements, and you want to remove the newline from each of the lines at once. For example:

```
@stuff = ("hello\n","world\n","happy days");
chomp(@stuff); # @stuff is now ("hello","world","happy days")
```

Scalar and List Context

As you can see, each operator and function is designed to operate on some specified combination of scalars or lists, and returns either a scalar or a list. If an operator or function expects an operand to be a scalar, we say that the operand or argument is being evaluated in a *scalar context*. Similarly, if an operand or argument is expected to be a list value, we say that it is being evaluated in a *list context*.

Normally, this is fairly insignificant. But sometimes you get completely different behavior depending on whether you are within a scalar or a list context. For example, `@fred` returns the contents of the `@fred` array in a list context, but the length of the same array in a scalar context. These subtleties are mentioned when each operator and function is described.

A scalar value used within a list context is promoted to a single-element array.

<STDIN> as an Array

One previously seen operation that returns a different value in a list context is
<STDIN>. As described earlier, <STDIN> returns the next line of input in a scalar
context. However, in a list context, it returns all remaining lines up to end of file.
Each line is returned as a separate element of the list. For example:

```
@a = <STDIN>; # read standard input in a list context
```

If the person running the program types three lines, then presses CTRL-D* (to indicate "end of file"), the array ends up with three elements. Each element will be a
string that ends in a newline, corresponding to the three newline-terminated lines
entered.

Variable Interpolation of Arrays

Like scalars, array values may be interpolated into a double-quoted string. A
single element of an array will be replaced by its value, like so:

```
@fred = ("hello","dolly");
$y = 2;
$x = "This is $fred[1]'s place";      # "This is dolly's place"
$x = "This is $fred[$y-1]'s place";   # same thing
```

Note that the index expression is evaluated as an ordinary expression, as if it
were outside a string. It is not variable interpolated first.

If you want to follow a simple scalar variable reference with a literal left square
bracket, you need to delimit the square bracket so it isn't considered part of the
array, as follows:

```
@fred = ("hello","dolly");  # give value to @fred for testing
$fred = "right";
                            # we are trying to say "this is right[1]"
$x = "this is $fred[1]";    # wrong, gives "this is dolly"
$x = "this is ${fred}[1]";  # right (protected by braces)
$x = "this is $fred"."[1]"; # right (different string)
$x = "this is $fred\[1]";   # right (backslash hides it)
```

Similarly, a list of values from an array variable can be interpolated. The simplest
interpolation is an entire array, indicated by giving the array name (including its
leading @ character). In this case, the elements are interpolated in sequence with
a space character between them, as in:

```
@fred = ("a","bb","ccc",1,2,3);
$all = "Now for @fred here!";
    # $all gets "Now for a bb ccc 1 2 3 here!"
```

---

* Some systems use CTRL-Z to indicate end of file, while others use it to suspend a running process.

You can also select a portion of an array with a slice:

```
@fred = ("a","bb","ccc",1,2,3);
$all = "Now for @fred[2,3] here!";
                                     # $all gets "Now for ccc 1 here!"
$all = "Now for @fred[@fred[4,5]] here!"; # same thing
```

Once again, you can use any of the quoting mechanisms described earlier if you want to follow an array name reference with a literal left bracket rather than an indexing expression.

Exercises

See Appendix A for answers.

1. Write a program that reads a list of strings on separate lines and prints out the list in reverse order. If you're reading the list from the terminal, you'll probably need to delimit the end of the list by pressing your end-of-file character, probably CTRL-D under UNIX or Plan 9; often CTRL-Z elsewhere.

2. Write a program that reads a number and then a list of strings (all on separate lines), and then prints one of the lines from the list as selected by the number.

3. Write a program that reads a list of strings and then selects and prints a random string from the list. To select a random element of @somearray, put

   ```
   srand;
   ```

   at the beginning of your program (this initializes the random-number generator), and then use

   ```
   rand(@somearray)
   ```

   where you need a random value between zero and one less than the length of @somearray.

4

Control Structures

Statement Blocks

A *statement block* is a sequence of statements, enclosed in matching curly braces. It looks like this:

```
{
    first_statement;
    second_statement;
    third_statement;
    ...
    last_statement;
}
```

Perl executes each statement in sequence, from the first to the last. (Later, I'll show you how to alter this execution sequence within a block, but this is good enough for now.)

Syntactically, a block of statements is accepted in place of any single statement, but the reverse is not true.

The final semicolon on the last statement is optional. Thus, you can speak Perl with a C-accent (semicolon present) or Pascal-accent (semicolon absent). To make it easier to add more statements later, we usually suggest omitting the semicolon only when the block is all on one line. Contrast these two `if` blocks for examples of the two styles:

```
if ($ready) { $hungry++ }
if ($tired) {
    $sleepy = ($hungry + 1) * 2;
}
```

The if/unless Statement

Next up in order of complexity is the `if` statement. This construct takes a control expression (evaluated for its truth) and a block. It may optionally have an *else* followed by a block as well. In other words, it looks like this:

```
if (some_expression) {
    true_statement_1;
    true_statement_2;
    true_statement_3;
} else {
    false_statement_1;
    false_statement_2;
    false_statement_3;
}
```

(If you're a C or Java hacker, you should note that the curly braces are required. This eliminates the need for a "confusing dangling else" rule.)

During execution, Perl evaluates the control expression. If the expression is true, the first block (the **true_statement** statements above) is executed. If the expression is false, the second block (the **false_statement** statements above) is executed instead.

But what constitutes true and false? In Perl, the rules are slightly weird, but they give you the expected results. The control expression is evaluated for a *string* value in scalar context (if it's already a string, no change, but if it's a number, it is converted to a string*). If this string is either the empty string (with a length of zero), or a string consisting of the single character `"0"` (the digit zero), then the value of the expression is false. Anything else is true automatically. Why such funny rules? Because it makes it easy to branch on an emptyish versus nonempty string, as well as a zero versus nonzero number, without having to create two versions of interpreting true and false values. Here are some examples of true and false interpretations:

```
0        # converts to "0", so false
1-1      # computes to 0, then converts to "0", so false
1        # converts to "1", so true
""       # empty string, so false
"1"      # not "" or "0", so true
"00"     # not "" or "0", so true (this is weird, watch out)
"0.000"  # also true for the same reason and warning
undef    # evaluates to "", so false
```

Practically speaking, interpretation of values as true or false is fairly intuitive. Don't let us scare you.

---

* Internally, this isn't quite true. But it acts like this is what it does.

Here's an example of a complete `if` statement:

```
print "how old are you? ";
$a = <STDIN>;
chomp($a);
if ($a < 18) {
    print "So, you're not old enough to vote, eh?\n";
} else {
    print "Old enough!  Cool!  So go vote!\n";
    $voter++; # count the voters for later
}
```

You can omit the **else** block, leaving just a "then" part, as in:

```
print "how old are you? ";
$a = <STDIN>;
chomp($a);
if ($a < 18) {
        print "So, you're not old enough to vote, eh?\n";
}
```

Sometimes, you want to leave off the "then" part and have just an **else** part, because it is more natural to say "do that if this is false," rather than "do that if not this is true." Perl handles this with the **unless** variation:

```
print "how old are you? ";
$a = <STDIN>;
chomp($a);
unless ($a < 18) {
    print "Old enough!  Cool!  So go vote!\n";
    $voter++;
}
```

Replacing `if` with **unless** is in effect saying "If the control expression is false, do...." (An **unless** can also have an **else**, just like an **if**.)

If you have more than two possible choices, add an **elsif** branch to the `if` statement, like so:

```
if (some_expression_one) {
    one_true_statement_1;
    one_true_statement_2;
    one_true_statement_3;
} elsif (some_expression_two) {
    two_true_statement_1;
    two_true_statement_2;
    two_true_statement_3;
} elsif (some_expression_three) {
    three_true_statement_1;
    three_true_statement_2;
    three_true_statement_3;
} else {
    all_false_statement_1;
    all_false_statement_2;
    all_false_statement_3;
}
```

Each expression (here, *some_expression_one*, *some_expression_two*, and *some_expression_three*) is computed in turn. If an expression is true, the corresponding branch is executed, and all remaining control expressions and corresponding statement blocks are skipped. If all expressions are false, the `else` branch is executed (if there is one). You don't have to have an `else` block, but it is always a good idea. You may have as many `elsif` branches as you wish.

The while/until Statement

No programming language would be complete without some form of iteration[*] (repeated execution of a block of statements). Perl can iterate using the `while` statement:

```
while (some_expression) {
    statement_1;
    statement_2;
    statement_3;
}
```

To execute this `while` statement, Perl evaluates the control expression (*some_expression* in the example). If its value is true (using Perl's notion of truth), the body of the `while` statement is evaluated once. This is repeated until the control expression becomes false, at which point Perl goes on to the next statement after the `while loop`. For example:

```
print "how old are you? ";
$a = <STDIN>;
chomp($a);
while ($a > 0) {
    print "At one time, you were $a years old.\n";
    $a--;
}
```

Sometimes it is easier to say "until something is true" rather than "while not this is true." Once again, Perl has the answer. Replacing the `while` with `until` yields the desired effect:

```
until (some_expression) {
    statement_1;
    statement_2;
    statement_3;
}
```

Note that in both the `while` and the `until` form, the body statements will be skipped entirely if the control expression is the termination value to begin with.

---

[*] That's why HTML is not a programming language.

For example, if a user enters an age less than zero for the program fragment above, Perl skips over the body of the loop.

It's possible that the control expression never lets the loop exit. This is perfectly legal, and sometimes desired, and thus not considered an error. For example, you might want a loop to repeat as long as you have no error, and then have some error-handling code following the loop. You might use this for a daemon that is meant to run until the system crashes.

The do {} while/until Statement

The `while/until` statement you saw in the previous section tests its condition at the top of every loop, before the loop is entered. If the condition was already false to begin with, the loop won't be executed at all.

But sometimes you don't want to test the condition at the top of the loop. Instead, you want to test it at the bottom. To fill this need, Perl provides the `do {} while` statement, which is just like[*] the regular `while` statement except that it doesn't test the expression until after executing the loop once.

```
do {
    statement_1;
    statement_2;
    statement_3;
} while some_expression;
```

Perl executes the statements in the `do` block.When it reaches the end, it evaluates the expression for truth. If the expression is false, the loop is done. If it's true, then the whole block is executed one more time before the expression is once again checked.

As with a normal `while` loop, you can invert the sense of the test by changing `do {} while` to `do {} until`. The expression is still tested at the bottom, but its sense is reversed. For some cases, especially compound ones, this is the more natural way to write the test.

```
$stops = 0;
do {
    $stops++;
    print "Next stop? ";
    chomp($location = <STDIN>);
} until $stops > 5 || $location eq 'home';
```

---

[*] Well, not quite just like; the loop control directives explained in Chapter 9, *Miscellaneous Control Structures*, don't work for the bottom-testing form.

The for Statement

Another Perl iteration construct is the `for` statement, which looks suspiciously like C or Java's `for` statement and works roughly the same way. Here it is:

```
for ( initial_exp; test_exp; re-init_exp ) {
    statement_1;
    statement_2;
    statement_3;
}
```

Unraveled into forms we've seen before, this turns out as:

```
initial_exp;
while (test_exp) {
    statement_1;
    statement_2;
    statement_3;
    re-init_exp;
}
```

In either case, the *initial_exp* expression is evaluated first. This expression typically assigns an initial value to an iterator variable, but there are no restrictions on what it can contain; in fact, it may even be empty (doing nothing). Then the *test_exp* expression is evaluated for truth or falsehood. If the value is true, the body is executed, followed by the *re-init_exp* (typically, but not solely, used to increment the iterator). Perl then reevaluates the *test_exp*, repeating as necessary.

This example prints the numbers 1 through 10, each followed by a space:

```
for ($i = 1; $i <= 10; $i++) {
    print "$i ";
}
```

Initially, the variable `$i` is set to 1. Then, this variable is compared with 10, which it is indeed less than or equal to. The body of the loop (the single `print` statement) is executed, and then the re-init expression (the autoincrement expression `$i++`) is executed, changing the value in `$i` to 2. Because this is still less than or equal to 10, we repeat the process until the last iteration where the value of 10 in `$i` gets changed to 11. This is then no longer less than or equal to 10, so the loop exits (with `$i` having a value of 11).

The foreach Statement

Yet another iteration construct is the `foreach` statement. This statement takes a list of values and assigns them one at a time to a scalar variable, executing a block of code with each successive assignment. It looks like this:

```
foreach $i (@some_list) {
    statement_1;
    statement_2;
    statement_3;
}
```

Unlike in the C-shell, the original value of the scalar variable is automatically restored when the loop exits; another way to say this is that the scalar variable is local to the loop.

Here's an example of a `foreach`:

```
@a = (1,2,3,4,5);
foreach $b (reverse @a) {
    print $b;
}
```

This program snippet prints 54321. Note that the list used by the `foreach` can be an arbitrary list expression, not just an array variable. (This is typical of all Perl constructs that require a list.)

You can omit the name of the scalar variable, in which case Perl pretends you have specified the $_ variable name instead. You'll find that the $_ variable is used as a default for many of Perl's operations, so you can think of it as a scratch area. (All operations that use $_ by default can also use a normal scalar variable as well.) For example, the `print` function prints the value of $_ if no other value is specified, so the following example works like the previous one:

```
@a = (1,2,3,4,5);
foreach (reverse @a) {
    print;
}
```

See how using the implied $_ variable makes it easier? Once you've learned more functions and operators that default to $_, this construct will become even more useful. This is one case where the shorter construct is more legible than the longer one.

If the list you are iterating over is made of real variables rather than some function returning a list value, then the variable being used for iteration is in fact an alias for each variable in the list instead of being merely a copy of the values. It means that if you change the scalar variable, you are also changing that particular element in the list that the variable is standing in for. For example:

```
@a = (3,5,7,9);
foreach $one (@a) {
    $one *= 3;
}
# @a is now (9,15,21,27)
```

Notice how altering $one in fact altered each element of @a. This is a feature, not a bug.

Exercises

See Appendix A for answers.

1. Write a program that asks for the temperature outside, and prints "too hot" if the temperature is above 72, and "too cold" otherwise.

2. Modify the program from the previous exercise so that it prints "too hot" if the temperature is above 75, "too cold" if the temperature is below 68, and "just right!" if it is between 68 and 75.

3. Write a program that reads a list of numbers (on separate lines) until the number 999 is read, and then prints the total of all the numbers added together. (Be sure not to add in the 999!) For example, if you enter 1, 2, 3, and 999, the program should reply with the answer of 6 (1+2+3).

4. Write a program that reads in a list of strings on separate lines and then prints out the list of strings in reverse order—without using reverse on the list. (Recall that <STDIN> will read a list of strings on separate lines when used in an array context.)

5. Write a program that prints a table of numbers and their squares from zero to 32. Try to come up with a way where you don't need to have all the numbers from 0 to 32 in a list, and then try one where you do. (For nice looking output,

   ```
   printf "%5g %8g\n", $a, $b
   ```

   prints $a as a five-column number and $b as an eight-column number.)

5

Hashes

What Is a Hash?

A hash* is like the array that we discussed earlier, in that it is a collection of scalar data, with individual elements selected by some index value. Unlike a list array, the index values of a hash are not small nonnegative integers, but instead are arbitrary scalars. These scalars (called *keys*) are used later to retrieve the values from the array.

The elements of a hash have no particular order. Consider them instead like a deck of filing cards. The top half of each card is the key, and the bottom half is the value. Each time you put a value into the hash, a new card is created. Later, when you want to modify the value, you give the key, and Perl finds the right card. So, really, the order of the cards is immaterial. In fact, Perl stores the cards (the key-value pairs) in a special internal order that makes it easy to find a specific card, so Perl doesn't have to look through all the pairs to find the right one. You cannot control this order, so don't try.†

Hash Variables

A hash variable name is a percent sign (%) followed by a letter, followed by zero or more letters, digits, and underscores. In other words, the part after the percent is just like what we've had for scalar and array variable names. And, just as there

---

* In older documentation, hashes were called "associative arrays," but we got tired of a seven-syllable word for such a common item, so we replaced it with a much nicer one-syllable word.

† Actually, modules like IxHash and DB_file do provide some ordering, but at the cost of a non-trivial performance penalty.

is no relationship between $fred and @fred, the %fred hash variable is also unrelated to the other two.

Rather than referencing the entire hash, the hash more commonly is created and accessed by referring to its elements. Each element of the hash is a separate scalar variable, accessed by a string index, called the key. Elements of the hash %fred are thus referenced with $fred{$key} where *$key* is any scalar expression. Notice once again that accessing an element of a hash requires different punctuation than when you access the entire hash.

As with arrays, you create new elements merely by assigning to a hash element:

```
$fred{"aaa"} = "bbb"; # creates key "aaa", value "bbb"
$fred{234.5} = 456.7; # creates key "234.5", value 456.7
```

These two statements create two elements in the hash. Subsequent accesses to the same element (using the same key) return the previously stored value:

```
print $fred{"aaa"}; # prints "bbb"
$fred{234.5} += 3;  # makes it 459.7
```

Referencing an element that does not exist returns the undef value, just as with a missing array element or an undefined scalar variable.

Literal Representation of a Hash

You may wish to access the hash as a whole, either to initialize it or to copy it to another hash. Perl doesn't really have a literal representation for a hash, so instead it unwinds the hash as a list. Each pair of elements in the list (which should always have an even number of elements) defines a key and its corresponding value. This unwound representation can be assigned into another hash, which will then recreate the same hash. In other words:

```
@fred_list = %fred;
# @fred_list gets ("aaa","bbb","234.5",456.7)
%barney = @fred_list;  # create %barney like %fred
%barney = %fred;       # a faster way to do the same
%smooth = ("aaa","bbb","234.5",456.7);
# create %smooth like %fred, from literal values
```

The order of the key-value pairs is arbitrary in this unwound representation and cannot be controlled. Even if you swap some of the values around and create the hash as a whole, the returned unwound list is still in whatever order Perl has created for efficient access to the individual elements. You should never rely on any particular ordering.

One quick use of this winding-unwinding is to copy a hash value to another hash variable:

```
%copy = %original; # copy from %original to %copy
```

And you can construct a hash with keys and values swapped using the **reverse** operator, which works well here:

```
%backwards = reverse %normal;
```

Of course, if **%normal** has two identical values, those will end up as only a single element in **%backwards**, so this is best performed only on hashes with unique keys and values.

Hash Functions

This section lists some functions for hashes.

The keys Function

The **keys(** *%hashname* **)** function yields a list of all the current keys in the hash *%hashname*. In other words, it's like the odd-numbered (first, third, fifth, and so on) elements of the list returned by unwinding *%hashname* in an array context, and in fact, returns them in that order. If there are no elements to the hash, then **keys** returns an empty list.

For example, using the hash from the previous examples:

```
$fred{"aaa"} = "bbb";
$fred{234.5} = 456.7;
@list = keys(%fred); # @list gets ("aaa",234.5) or
                     # (234.5,"aaa")
```

As with all other built-in functions, the parentheses are optional: **keys %fred** is like **keys(%fred)**.

```
foreach $key (keys (%fred)) { # once for each key of %fred
    print "at $key we have $fred{$key}\n"; # show key and value
}
```

This example also shows that individual hash elements can be interpolated into double-quoted strings. You cannot interpolate the entire hash, however.[*]

In a scalar context, the **keys** function gives the number of elements (key-value pairs) in the hash. For example, you can find out whether a hash is empty:

```
if (keys(%somehash)) { # if keys() not zero:
    ...; # array is non empty
}
# ... or ...
while (keys(%somehash) < 10) {
```

---

[*] Well, you can, using a slice, but we don't talk about slices here.

```
    ...; # keep looping while we have fewer than 10 elements
}
```

In fact, merely using *%somehash* in a scalar context will reveal whether the hash is empty or not:

```
if (%somehash) { # if true, then something's in it
    # do something with it
}
```

The values Function

The `values(%hashname)` function returns a list of all the current values of the *%hashname*, in the same order as the keys returned by the `keys(%hashname)` function. As always, the parentheses are optional. For example:

```
%lastname = (); # force %lastname empty
$lastname{"fred"} = "flintstone";
$lastname{"barney"} = "rubble";
@lastnames = values(%lastname); # grab the values
```

At this point @lastnames contains either (`"flintstone"`, `"rubble"`) or (`"rubble"`, `"flintstone"`).

The each Function

To iterate over (that is, examine every element of) an entire hash, use `keys`, looking up each returned key to get the corresponding value. Although this method is frequently used, a more efficient way is to use `each(%hashname)`, which returns a key-value pair as a two-element list. On each evaluation of this function for the same hash, the next successive key-value pair is returned until all the elements have been accessed. When there are no more pairs, `each` returns an empty list.

So, for example, to step through the `%lastname` hash from the previous example, do something like this:

```
while (($first,$last) = each(%lastname)) {
    print "The last name of $first is $last\n";
}
```

Assigning a new value to the entire hash resets the `each` function to the beginning. Adding or deleting elements of the hash is quite likely to confuse `each` (and possibly you as well).

The delete Function

So far, with what you know, you can add elements to a hash, but you cannot remove them (other than by assigning a new value to the entire hash). Perl provides the `delete` function to remove hash elements. The operand of `delete` is a hash reference, just as if you were merely looking at a particular value. Perl removes the key-value pair from the hash. For example:

```
%fred = ("aaa","bbb",234.5,34.56); # give %fred two elements
delete $fred{"aaa"};
# %fred is now just one key-value pair
```

Hash Slices

Like an array variable (or list literal), a hash can be sliced to access a collection of elements instead of just one element at a time. For example, consider the bowling scores set individually:

```
$score{"fred"} = 205;
$score{"barney"} = 195;
$score{"dino"} = 30;
```

This seems rather redundant, and in fact can be shortened to:

```
($score{"fred"},$score{"barney"},$score{"dino"}) =
    (205,195,30);
```

But even these seems redundant. Let's use a *hash slice*:

```
@score{"fred","barney","dino"} = (205,195,30);
```

There. Much shorter. We can use a hash slice with variable interpolation as well:

```
@players = qw(fred barney dino);
print "scores are: @score{@players}\n";
```

Hash slices can also be used to merge a smaller hash into a larger one. In this example, the smaller hash takes precedence in the sense that if there are duplicate keys, the value from the smaller hash is used:

```
%league{keys %score} = values %score;
```

Here, the values of `%score` are merged into the `%league` hash. This is equivalent to the much slower operation:

```
%league = (%league, %score); # merge %score into %league
```

Exercises

See Appendix A for answers.

1. Write a program that reads in a string, then prints that string and its mapped value according to the mapping presented in the following table:

Input	Output
red	apple
green	leaves
blue	ocean

2. Write a program that reads a series of words with one word per line until end-of-file, then prints a summary of how many times each word was seen. (For extra challenge, sort the words in ascending ASCII order in the output.)

6

In this chapter:
- *Input from STDIN*
- *Input from the Diamond Operator*
- *Output to STDOUT*
- *Exercises*

Basic I/O

Input from STDIN

Reading from standard input (via the Perl filehandle called STDIN) is easy. We've been doing it already with the <STDIN> operation. Evaluating this in a scalar context gives the next line of input,* or undef if there are no more lines, like so:

```
$a = <STDIN>; # read the next line
```

Evaluating in a list context produces all remaining lines as a list: each element is one line, including its terminating newline. We've seen this before, but as a refresher, it might look something like this:

```
@a = <STDIN>;
```

Typically, one thing you want to do is read all lines one at a time and do something with each line. One common way to do this is:

```
while (defined($line = <STDIN>)) {
    # process $line here
}
```

As long as a line has been read in, <STDIN> evaluates to a defined value, so the loop continues to execute. When <STDIN> has no more lines to read, it returns undef, terminating the loop.

Reading a scalar value from <STDIN> into $_ and using that value as the controlling expression of a loop (as in the previous example) occurs frequently enough that Perl has an abbreviation for it. Whenever a loop test consists solely of the input operator (something like <...>), Perl automatically copies the line that is read into the $_ variable.

---

* Up to a newline, or whatever you've set $/ to.

```
while (<STDIN>) { # like "while(defined($_ = <STDIN>)) {"
    chomp; # like "chomp($_)"
    # other operations with $_ here
}
```

Since the $_ variable is the default for many operations, you can save a noticeable amount of typing this way.

Input from the Diamond Operator

Another way to read input is with the diamond operator: <>. This works like <STDIN> in that it returns a single line in a scalar context (undef if all the lines have been read) or all remaining lines if used in a list context. However, unlike <STDIN>, the diamond operator gets its data from the file or files specified on the command line that invoked the Perl program. For example, you have a program named *kitty*, consisting of

```
#!/usr/bin/perl
while (<>) {
    print $_;
}
```

and you invoke *kitty* with

```
kitty file1 file2 file3
```

then the diamond operator reads each line of file1 followed by each line of file2 and file3 in turn, returning undef only when all of the lines have been read. As you can see, *kitty* works a little like the UNIX command *cat*, sending all the lines of the named files to standard output in sequence. If, like *cat*, you don't specify any filenames on the command line, the diamond operator reads from standard input automatically.

Technically, the diamond operator isn't looking literally at the command-line arguments; it works from the @ARGV array. This array is a special array initialized by the Perl interpreter to the command-line arguments. Each command-line argument goes into a separate element of the @ARGV array. You can interpret this list any way you want.* You can even set this array within your program and have the diamond operator work on that new list rather than the command-line arguments, like so:

```
@ARGV = ("aaa","bbb","ccc");
while (<>) { # process files aaa, bbb, and ccc
    print "this line is: $_ ";
}
```

---

* The standard Perl distribution contains modules for getopt-like parsing of the command-line arguments of a Perl program. See *Programming Perl* or *perlmodlib*(1) for more information on the library.

In Chapter 10, *Filehandles and File Tests*, we'll see how to open and close specific filenames at specific times, but this technique has been used for some of our quick-and-dirty programs.

Output to STDOUT

Perl uses the `print` and `printf` functions to write to standard output. Let's look at how they are used.

Using print for Normal Output

We've already used `print` to display text on standard output. Let's expand on that a bit.

The `print` function takes a list of strings and sends each string to standard output in turn, without any intervening or trailing characters added. What might not be obvious is that `print` is really just a function that takes a list of arguments, and returns a value like any other function. In other words,

```
$a = print("hello ", "world", "\n");
```

would be another way to say `hello world`. The return value of `print` is a true or false value, indicating the success of the `print`. It nearly always succeeds, unless you get some I/O error, so `$a` in this case would usually be 1.

Sometimes you'll need to add parentheses to `print` as shown in the example, especially when the first thing you want to print itself starts with a left parenthesis, as in:

```
print (2+3),"hello";    # wrong! prints 5, ignores "hello"
print ((2+3),"hello");  # right, prints 5hello
print 2+3,"hello";      # also right, prints 5hello
```

Using printf for Formatted Output

You may wish a little more control over your output than `print` provides. In fact, you may be accustomed to the formatted output of C's `printf` function. Fear not: Perl provides a comparable operation with the same name.

The `printf` function takes a list of arguments (enclosed in optional parentheses, like the `print` function). The first argument is a format control string, defining how to print the remaining arguments. If you're not familiar with the standard `printf` function, you should probably check out the manpage for *printf*(3) or *perlfunc*(1), if you have one, or look at the description in Chapter 3 of *Programming Perl*.

As an example, however

```
printf "%15s %5d %10.2f\n", $s, $n, $r;
```

prints $s in a 15-character field, then space, then $n as a decimal integer in a 5-character field, then another space, then $r as a floating-point value with 2 decimal places in a 10-character field, and finally a newline.

Exercises

See Appendix A for answers.

1. Write a program that acts like *cat*, but reverses the order of the lines of all the lines from all the files specified on the command line or all the lines from standard input if no files are specified. (Some systems have a utility like this named *tac*.)

2. Modify the program from the previous exercise so that each file specified on the command line has its lines individually reversed. (Yes, you can do this with only what's been shown to you so far, even excluding the stroll in Chapter 1, *Introduction*.)

3. Write a program that reads a list of strings on separate lines, and prints the strings in a right-justified 20-character column. For example, inputting `hello`, `good-bye` prints `hello` and `good-bye` right-justified in a 20-character column. (Be sure your program is actually using a 20-character column, not a 21-character column. That's a common mistake.)

4. Modify the program from the previous exercise to allow the user to select the column width. For example, entering `20`, `hello`, and `good-bye` should do the same thing as the previous program did, but entering `30`, `hello`, and `good-bye` should justify `hello` and `good-bye` in a 30-character column.

7

Regular Expressions

Concepts About Regular Expressions

A *regular expression* is a pattern—a template—to be matched against a string. Matching a regular expression against a string either succeeds or fails. Sometimes, the success or failure may be all you are concerned about. At other times, you will want to take a matched pattern and replace it with another string, parts of which may depend on exactly how and where the regular expression matched.

Regular expressions are used by many programs, such as the UNIX commands, *grep*, *sed*, *awk*, *ed*, *vi*, *emacs*, and even the various shells. Each program has a different set of (mostly overlapping) template characters. Perl is a semantic superset of all of these tools: any regular expression that can be described in one of these tools can also be written in Perl, but not necessarily using exactly the same characters.

Simple Uses of Regular Expressions

If we were looking for all lines of a file that contain the string abc, we might use the *grep* command:

```
grep abc somefile >results
```

In this case, abc is the regular expression that the *grep* command tests against each input line. Lines that match are sent to standard output, here ending up in the file *results* because of the command-line redirection.

In Perl, we can speak of the string abc as a regular expression by enclosing the string in slashes:

```
if (/abc/) {
    print $_;
}
```

But what is being tested against the regular expression abc in this case? Why, it's our old friend, the $_ variable! When a regular expression is enclosed in slashes (as above), the $_ variable is tested against the regular expression. If the regular expression matches, the *match* operator returns true. Otherwise, it returns false.

For this example, the $_ variable is presumed to contain some text line and is printed if the line contains the characters abc in sequence anywhere within the line—similar to the *grep* command above. Unlike the *grep* command, which is operating on all of the lines of a file, this Perl fragment is looking at just one line. To work on all lines, add a loop, as in:

```
while (<>) {
    if (/abc/) {
        print $_;
    }
}
```

What if we didn't know the number of b's between the a and the c? That is, what if we want to print the line if it contains an a followed by zero or more b's, followed by a c. With *grep*, we'd say:

```
grep "ab*c" somefile >results
```

(The argument containing the asterisk is in quotes because we don't want the shell expanding that argument as if it were a filename wildcard. It has to be passed as-is to *grep* to be effective.) In Perl, we can say exactly the same thing:

```
while (<>) {
    if (/ab*c/) {
        print $_;
    }
}
```

Just like *grep*, this means an a followed by zero or more b's followed by a c.

We'll visit more uses of pattern matching in the section "More on the Matching Operator," later in the chapter, after we talk about all kinds of regular expressions.

Another simple regular expression operator is the *substitute* operator, which replaces the part of a string that matches the regular expression with another string. The substitute operator looks like the s command in the UNIX command *sed* utility, consisting of the letter s, a slash, a regular expression, a slash, a replacement string, and a final slash, looking something like:

```
s/ab*c/def/;
```

The variable (in this case, $_) is matched against the regular expression (ab*c). If the match is successful, the part of the string that matched is discarded and replaced by the replacement string (def). If the match is unsuccessful, nothing happens.

As with the match operator, we'll revisit the myriad options on the substitute operator later, in the section "Substitutions."

Patterns

A regular expression is a pattern. Some parts of the pattern match single characters in the string of a particular type. Other parts of the pattern match multiple characters. First, we'll visit the single-character patterns and then the multiple-character patterns.

Single-Character Patterns

The simplest and most common pattern-matching character in regular expressions is a single character that matches itself. In other words, putting a letter a in a regular expression requires a corresponding letter a in the string.

The next most common pattern matching character is the dot ".". This matches any single character except newline (\n). For example, the pattern /a./ matches any two-letter sequence that starts with a and is not "a\n".

A pattern-matching *character class* is represented by a pair of open and close square brackets and a list of characters between the brackets. One and only one of these characters must be present at the corresponding part of the string for the pattern to match. For example,

```
/[abcde]/
```

matches a string containing any one of the first five letters of the lowercase alphabet, while

```
/[aeiouAEIOU]/
```

matches any of the five vowels in either lower- or uppercase. If you want to put a right bracket (]) in the list, put a backslash in front of it, or put it as the first character within the list. Ranges of characters (like a through z) can be abbreviated by showing the end points of the range separated by a dash (–); to get a literal dash in the list, precede the dash with a backslash or place it at the end. Here are some other examples:

```
[0123456789]     # match any single digit
[0-9]            # same thing
```

```
[0-9\-]              # match 0-9, or minus
[a-z0-9]             # match any single lowercase letter or digit
[a-zA-Z0-9_]         # match any single letter, digit, or underscore
```

There's also a negated character class, which is the same as a character class, but has a leading up-arrow (or caret: ^) immediately after the left bracket. This character class matches any single character that is not in the list. For example:

```
[^0-9]       # match any single non-digit
[^aeiouAEIOU] # match any single non-vowel
[^\^]        # match single character except an up-arrow
```

For your convenience, some common character classes are predefined, as described in Table 7-1.

Table 7-1. Predefined Character Class Abbreviations

Construct	Equivalent Class	Negated Construct	Equivalent Negated Class
\d (a digit)	[0-9]	\D (digits, not!)	[^0-9]
\w (word char)	[a-zA-Z0-9_]	\W (words, not!)	[^a-zA-Z0-9_]
\s (space char)	[\r\t\n\f]	\S (space, not!)	[^ \r\t\n\f]

The \d pattern matches one "digit." The \w pattern matches one "word character," although what it is really matching is any character that is legal in a Perl variable name. The \s pattern matches one "space" (whitespace), here defined as spaces, carriage returns (not often used in UNIX), tabs, line feeds, and form feeds. The uppercase versions match the complements of these classes. Thus, \W matches one character that can't be in an identifier, \S matches one character that is not whitespace (including letter, punctuation, control characters, and so on), and \D matches any single nondigit character.

These abbreviated classes can be used as part of other character classes as well:

```
[\da-fA-F] # match one hex digit
```

Grouping Patterns

The true power of regular expressions comes into play when you can say "one or more of these" or "up to five of those." Let's talk about how this is done.

Sequence

The first (and probably least obvious) grouping pattern is *sequence*. This means that abc matches an a followed by a b followed by a c. Seems simple, but we're giving it a name so we can talk about it later.

Multipliers

We've already seen the asterisk (*) as a grouping pattern. The asterisk indicates zero or more of the immediately previous character (or character class).

Two other grouping patterns that work like this are the plus sign (+), meaning one or more of the immediately previous character, and the question mark (?), meaning zero or one of the immediately previous character. For example, the regular expression `/fo+ba?r/` matches an `f` followed by one or more o's followed by a `b`, followed by an optional `a`, followed by an `r`.

In all three of these grouping patterns, the patterns are greedy. If such a multiplier has a chance to match between five and ten characters, it'll pick the 10-character string every time. For example,

```
$_ = "fred xxxxxxxxx barney";
s/x+/boom/;
```

always replaces all consecutive x's with **boom** (resulting in **fred boom barney**), rather than just one or two x's, even though a shorter set of x's would also match the same regular expression.

If you need to say "five to ten" x's, you could get away with putting five x's followed by five x's each immediately followed by a question mark. But this looks ugly. Instead, there's an easier way: the *general multiplier*. The general multiplier consists of a pair of matching curly braces with one or two numbers inside, as in `/x{5,10}/`. The immediately preceding character (in this case, the letter "x") must be found within the indicated number of repetitions (five through ten here).*

If you leave off the second number, as in `/x{5,}/`, it means "that many or more" (five or more in this case), and if you leave off the comma, as in `/x{5}/`, it means "exactly this many" (five x's). To get five or less x's, you must put the zero in, as in `/x{0,5}/`.

So, the regular expression `/a.{5}b/` matches the letter `a` separated from the letter `b` by any five non-newline characters at any point in the string. (Recall that a period matches any single non-newline character, and we're matching five here.) The five characters do not need to be the same. (We'll learn how to force them to be the same in the next section.)

We could dispense with *, +, and ? entirely, since they are completely equivalent to `{0,}`, `{1,}`, and `{0,1}`. But it's easier to type the equivalent single punctuation character, and more familiar as well.

---

* Of course, `/\d{3}/` doesn't only match three-digit numbers. It would also match any number with more than three digits in it. To match exactly three, you need to use anchors, described later in the section, "Anchoring Patterns."

If two multipliers occur in a single expression, the greedy rule is augmented with "leftmost is greediest." For example:

```
$_ = "a xxx c xxxxxxxx c xxx d";
/a.*c.*d/;
```

In this case, the first ".*" in the regular expression matches all characters up to the second c, even though matching only the characters up to the first c would still allow the entire regular expression to match. Right now, this doesn't make any difference (the pattern would match either way), but later when we can look at parts of the regular expression that matched, it'll matter quite a bit.

We can force any multiplier to be nongreedy (or *lazy*) by following it with a question mark:

```
$_ = "a xxx c xxxxxxxx c xxx d";
/a.*?c.*d/;
```

Here, the a.*?c now matches the fewest characters between the a and c, not the most characters. This means the leftmost c is matched, not the rightmost. You can put such a question-mark modifier after any of the multipliers (?,+,*, and {m,n}).

What if the string and regular expression were slightly altered, say, to:

```
$_ = "a xxx ce xxxxxxxx ci xxx d";
/a.*ce.*d/;
```

In this case, if the .* matches the most characters possible before the next c, the next regular expression character (e) doesn't match the next character of the string (i). In this case, we get automatic *backtracking*: the multiplier is unwound and retried, stopping at someplace earlier (in this case, at the earlier c, next to the e).* A complex regular expression may involve many such levels of backtracking, leading to long execution times. In this case, making that match lazy (with a trailing "?") will actually simplify the work that Perl has to perform, so you may want to consider that.

Parentheses as memory

Another grouping operator is a pair of open and close parentheses around any part pattern. This doesn't change whether the pattern matches, but instead causes the part of the string matched by the pattern to be remembered, so that it may be referenced later. So for example, (a) still matches an a, and ([a-z]) still matches any single lowercase letter.

---

* Well, technically there was a lot of backtracking of the * operator to find the c's in the first place. But that's a little trickier to describe, and it works on the same principle.

To recall a memorized part of a string, you must include a backslash followed by an integer. This pattern construct represents the same sequence of characters matched earlier in the same-numbered pair of parentheses (counting from one). For example,

```
/fred(.)barney\1/;
```

matches a string consisting of **fred**, followed by any single non-newline character, followed by **barney**, followed by that same single character. So, it matches **fredxbarneyx**, but not **fredxbarneyy**. Compare that with

```
/fred.barney./;
```

in which the two unspecified characters can be the same, or different; it doesn't matter.

Where did the 1 come from? It means the first parenthesized part of the regular expression. If there's more than one, the second part (counting the left parentheses from left to right) is referenced as \2, the third as \3, and so on. For example,

```
/a(.)b(.)c\2d\1/;
```

matches an **a**, a character (call it #1), a **b**, another character (call it #2), a **c**, the character #2, a **d**, and the character #1. So it matches **axbycydx**, for example.

The referenced part can be more than a single character. For example,

```
/a(.*)b\1c/;
```

matches an **a**, followed by any number of characters (even zero) followed by **b**, followed by that same sequence of characters followed by **c**. So, it would match **aFREDbFREDc**, or even **abc**, but not **aXXbXXXc**.

Alternation

Another grouping construct is *alternation*, as in **a|b|c**. This means to match exactly one of the alternatives (**a** or **b** or **c** in this case). This works even if the alternatives have multiple characters, as in **/song|blue/**, which matches either **song** or **blue**. (For single character alternatives, you're definitely better off with a character class like **/[abc]/**.)

What if we wanted to match **songbird** or **bluebird**? We could write **/songbird|bluebird/**, but that **bird** part shouldn't have to be in there twice. In fact, there's a way out, but we have to talk about the precedence of grouping patterns, which is covered in the section "Precedence," below.

Anchoring Patterns

Several special notations anchor a pattern. Normally, when a pattern is matched against the string, the beginning of the pattern is dragged through the string from left to right, matching at the first possible opportunity. Anchors allow you to ensure that parts of the pattern line up with particular parts of the string.

The first pair of anchors require that a particular part of the match be located either at a word boundary or not at a word boundary. The \b anchor requires a word boundary at the indicated point for the pattern to match. A word boundary is the place between characters that match \w and \W, or between characters matching \w and the beginning or ending of the string. Note that this has little to do with English words and a lot more to do with C symbols, but that's as close as we get. For example:

```
/fred\b/;      # matches fred, but not frederick
/\bmo/;        # matches moe and mole, but not Elmo
/\bFred\b/;    # matches Fred but not Frederick or alFred
/\b\+\b/;      # matches "x+y" but not "++" or " + "
/abc\bdef/;    # never matches (impossible for a boundary there)
```

Likewise, \B requires that there not be a word boundary at the indicated point. For example:

```
/\bFred\B/; # matches "Frederick" but not "Fred Flintstone"
```

Two more anchors require that a particular part of the pattern be next to an end of the string. The caret (^) matches the beginning of the string if it is in a place that makes sense to match the beginning of the string. For example, ^a matches an a if, and only if, the a is the first character of the string. However, a^ matches the two characters a and ^ anywhere in the string. In other words, the caret has lost its special meaning. If you need the caret to be a literal caret even at the beginning, put a backslash in front of it.

The $, like the ^, anchors the pattern, but to the end of the string, not the beginning. In other words, c$ matches a c only if it occurs at the end of the string.* A dollar sign anywhere else in the pattern is probably going to be interpreted as a scalar value interpretation, so you'll most likely need to backslash it to match a literal dollar sign in the string.

Other anchors are supported, including \A, \Z, and lookahead anchors created via (?=...) and (?!...). These are described fully in Chapter 2 of *Programming Perl* and the *perlre*(1) manpage.

---

* Or just before the newline at the end of the string, for historical simplicity.

Precedence

So what happens when we get `a|b*` together? Is this `a` or `b` any number of times, or is it either a single `a` or any number of `b`'s?

Well, just as operators have precedence, the grouping and anchoring patterns also have precedence. The precedence of patterns from highest to lowest is given in Table 7-2.

Table 7-2. regex Grouping Precedence[a]

Name	Representation
Parentheses	`( )   (?: )`
Multipliers	`?   +   *   {m,n}   ??   +?   *?   {m,n}?`
Sequence and anchoring	`abc   ^   $   \A   \Z   (?= )   (?! )`
Alternation	`|`

[a] Some of these symbols are not described in this book. See *Programming Perl* or *perlre*(1) for details.

According to the table, `*` has a higher precedence than `|`. So `/a|b*/` is interpreted as a single `a`, or any number of `b`'s.

What if we want the other meaning, as in "any number of `a`'s or `b`'s"? We simply throw in a pair of parentheses. In this case, enclose the part of the expression that the `*` operator should apply to inside parentheses, and we've got it, as `(a|b)*`. If you want to clarify the first expression, you can redundantly parenthesize it with `a|(b*)`.

When you use parentheses to affect precedence they also trigger the memory, as shown earlier in this chapter. That is, this set of parentheses counts when you are figuring out whether something is `\2`, `\3`, or whatever. If you want to use parentheses without triggering memory, use the form `(?:...)` instead of `(...)`. This still allows for multipliers, but doesn't throw off your counting by using up `\4` or whatever. For example, `/(?:Fred|Wilma) Flintstone/` does not store anything into `\1`; it's just there for grouping.

Here are some other examples of regular expressions and the effect of parentheses:

```
abc*            # matches ab, abc, abcc, abccc, abcccc, and so on
(abc)*          # matches "", abc, abcabc, abcabcabc, and so on
^x|y            # matches x at the beginning of line, or y anywhere
^(x|y)          # matches either x or y at the beginning of a line
a|bc|d          # a, or bc, or d
(a|b)(c|d)      # ac, ad, bc, or bd
(song|blue)bird # songbird or bluebird
```

More on the Matching Operator

We have already looked at the simplest uses of the matching operator (a regular expression enclosed in slashes). Now let's look at a zillion ways to make this operator do something slightly different.

Selecting a Different Target (the =~ Operator)

Usually the string you'll want to match your pattern against is not within the $_ variable, and it would be a nuisance to put it there. (Perhaps you already have a value in $_ you're quite fond of.) No problem. The =~ operator helps us here. This operator takes a regular expression operator on the right side, and changes the *target* of the operator to something besides the $_ variable—namely, some value named on the left side of the operator. It looks like this:

```
$a = "hello world";
$a =~ /^he/;           # true
$a =~ /(.)\1/;         # also true (matches the double l)
if ($a =~ /(.)\1/) {   # true, so yes...
                       # some stuff
}
```

The target of the =~ operator can be any expression that yields some scalar string value. For example, <STDIN> yields a scalar string value when used in a scalar context, so we can combine this with the =~ operator and a regular expression match operator to get a compact check for particular input, as in:

```
print "any last request? ";
if (<STDIN> =~ /^[yY]/) {             # does the input begin with a y?
    print "And just what might that request be? ";
    <STDIN>;                          # discard a line of standard input
    print "Sorry, I'm unable to do that.\n";
}
```

In this case, <STDIN> yields the next line from standard input, which is then immediately used as the string to match against the pattern ^[yY]. Note that you never stored the input into a variable, so if you wanted to match the input against another pattern, or possibly echo the data out in an error message, you'd be out of luck. But this form frequently comes in handy.

Ignoring Case

In the previous example, we used [yY] to match either a lower- or uppercase y. For very short strings, such as y or fred, this is easy enough, as in [fF][oO][oO]. But what if the string you want to match is the word "procedure" in either lower- or uppercase?

In some versions of *grep*, a `-i` flag indicates "ignore case." Perl also has such an option. You indicate the ignore-case option by appending a lowercase `i` to the closing slash, as in `/`*somepattern*`/i`. This says that the letters of the pattern will match letters in the string in either case. For example, to match the word `proce-dure` in either case at the beginning of the line, use `/^procedure/i`.

Now our previous example looks like this:

```
print "any last request? ";
if (<STDIN> =~ /^y/i) { # does the input begin with a y?
    # yes! deal with it
    ...
}
```

Using a Different Delimiter

If you are looking for a string with a regular expression that contains slash characters (/), you must precede each slash with a backslash (\). For example, you can look for a string that begins with `/usr/etc` like this:

```
$path = <STDIN>; # read a pathname (from "find" perhaps?)
if ($path =~ /^\/usr\/etc/) {
    # begins with /usr/etc...
}
```

As you can see, the backslash-slash combination makes it look like there are little valleys between the text pieces. Doing this for a lot of slash characters can get cumbersome, so Perl allows you to specify a different delimiter character. Simply precede any nonalphanumeric, nonwhitespace character[*] (your selected delimiter) with an `m`, then list your pattern followed by another identical delimiter character, as in:

```
/^\/usr\/etc/      # using standard slash delimiter
m@^/usr/etc@       # using @ for a delimiter
m#^/usr/etc#       # using # for a delimiter (my favorite)
```

You can even use slashes again if you want, as in `m/fred/`. So the common regular-expression matching operator is really the `m` operator; however, the `m` is optional if you choose slash for a delimiter.

Using Variable Interpolation

A regular expression is variable interpolated before it is considered for other special characters. Therefore, you can construct a regular expression from computed strings rather than just literals. For example:

---

[*] If the delimiter happens to be the left character of a left-right pair (parentheses, braces, angle bracket, or square bracket), the closing delimiter is the corresponding right of the same pair. But otherwise, the characters are the same for begin and end.

```
$what = "bird";
$sentence = "Every good bird does fly.";
if ($sentence =~ /\b$what\b/) {
    print "The sentence contains the word $what!\n";
}
```

Here we have used a variable reference to effectively construct the regular expression operator /\bbird\b/.

Here's a slightly more complicated example:

```
$sentence = "Every good bird does fly.";
print "What should I look for? ";
$what = <STDIN>;
chomp($what);
if ($sentence =~ /$what/) { # found it!
    print "I saw $what in $sentence.\n";
} else {
    print "nope... didn't find it.\n";
}
```

If you enter bird, it is found. If you enter scream, it isn't. If you enter [bw]ird, that's also found, showing that the regular expression pattern-matching characters are indeed still significant.

How would you make them insignificant? You'd have to arrange for the non-alphanumeric characters to be preceded by a backslash, which would then turn them into literal matches. That sounds hard, unless you have the \Q quoting escape at your disposal:

```
$what = "[box]";
foreach (qw(in[box] out[box] white[sox])) {
    if (/\Q$what\E/) {
        print "$_ matched!\n";
    }
}
```

Here, the \Q$what\E construct turns into \[box\], making the match look for a literal pair of enclosing brackets, instead of treating the whole thing as a character class.

Special Read-Only Variables

After a successful pattern match, the variables $1, $2, $3, and so on are set to the same values as \1, \2, \3, and so on. You can use this to look at a piece of the match in later code. For example:

```
$_ = "this is a test";
/(\w+)\W+(\w+)/; # match first two words
                 # $1 is now "this" and $2 is now "is"
```

You can also gain access to the same values ($1, $2, $3, and so on) by placing a match in a list context. The result is a list of values from $1 up to the number of memorized things, but only if the regular expression matches. (Otherwise the variables are undefined.) Taking that last example in another way:

```
$_ = "this is a test";
($first, $second) = /(\w+)\W+(\w+)/; # match first two words
        # $first is now "this" and $second is now "is"
```

Other predefined read-only variables include $&, which is the part of the string that matched the regular expression; $`, which is the part of the string before the part that matched; and $', which is the part of the string after the part that matched. For example:

```
$_ = "this is a sample string";
/sa.*le/; # matches "sample" within the string
          # $` is now "this is a "
          # $& is now "sample"
          # $' is now " string"
```

Because these variables are set on each successful match, you should save the values elsewhere if you need them later in the program.*

Substitutions

We've already talked about the simplest form of the substitution operator: `s/old-regex/new-string/`. It's time for a few variations of this operator.

If you want the replacement to operate on all possible matches instead of just the first match, append a `g` to the substitution, as in:

```
$_ = "foot fool buffoon";
s/foo/bar/g; # $_ is now "bart barl bufbarn"
```

The replacement string is variable interpolated, allowing you to specify the replacement string at run-time:

```
$_ = "hello, world";
$new = "goodbye";
s/hello/$new/; # replaces hello with goodbye
```

Pattern characters in the regular expression allow patterns to be matched, rather than just fixed characters:

```
$_ = "this is a test";
s/(\w+)/<$1>/g; # $_ is now "<this> <is> <a> <test>"
```

Recall that $1 is set to the data within the first parenthesized pattern match.

---

* See O'Reilly's *Mastering Regular Expressions* for performance ramifications of using these variables.

An i suffix (either before or after the g if present) causes the regular expression in the substitute operator to ignore case, just like the same option on the match operator described earlier.

As with the match operator, an alternate delimiter can be selected if the slash is inconvenient. Just use the same character three times:*

```
s#fred#barney#; # replace fred with barney, like s/fred/barney/
```

Also as with the match operator, you can specify an alternate target with the =~ operator. In this case, the selected target must be something you can assign a scalar value to, such as a scalar variable or an element of an array. Here's an example:

```
$which = "this is a test";
$which =~ s/test/quiz/;               # $which is now "this is a quiz"
$someplace[$here] =~ s/left/right/; # change an array element
$d{"t"} =~ s/^/x /;                   # prepend "x " to hash element
```

The split and join Functions

Regular expressions can be used to break a string into fields. The `split` function does this, and the `join` function glues the pieces back together.

The split Function

The `split` function takes a regular expression and a string, and looks for all occurrences of the regular expression within that string. The parts of the string that don't match the regular expression are returned in sequence as a list of values. For example, here's something to parse colon-separated fields, such as in UNIX */etc/passwd* files:

```
$line = "merlyn::118:10:Randal:/home/merlyn:/usr/bin/perl";
@fields = split(/:/,$line); # split $line, using : as delimiter
# now @fields is ("merlyn","","118","10","Randal",
#                 "/home/merlyn","/usr/bin/perl")
```

Note how the empty second field became an empty string. If you don't want this, match all of the colons in one fell swoop:

```
@fields = split(/:+/, $line);
```

This matches one or more adjacent colons together, so there is no empty second field.

---

* Or two matching pairs if a left-right pair character is used.

One common string to split is the `$_` variable, and that turns out to be the default:

```
$_ = "some string";
@words = split(/ /); # same as @words = split(/ /, $_);
```

For this split, consecutive spaces in the string to be split will cause null fields (empty strings) in the result. A better pattern would be `/ +/`, or ideally `/\s+/`, which matches one or more whitespace characters together. In fact, this pattern is the default pattern,* so if you're splitting the `$_` variable on whitespace, you can use all the defaults and merely say:

```
@words = split; # same as @words = split(/\s+/, $_);
```

Empty trailing fields do not normally become part of the list. This is not generally a concern. A solution like this,

```
$line = "merlyn::118:10:Randal:/home/merlyn:";
($name,$password,$uid,$gid,$gcos,$home,$shell) =
    split(/:/,$line); # split $line, using : as delimiter
```

simply gives `$shell` a null (`undef`) value if the line isn't long enough or if it contains empty values in the last field. (Extra fields are silently ignored, because list assignment works that way.)

The join Function

The `join` function takes a list of values and glues them together with a glue string between each list element. It looks like this:

```
$bigstring = join($glue,@list);
```

For example, to rebuild the password line, try something like:

```
$outline = join(":", @fields);
```

Note that the glue string is not a regular expression—just an ordinary string of zero or more characters.

If you need to get glue ahead of every item instead of just between items, a simple cheat suffices:

```
$result = join ("+", "", @fields);
```

Here, the extra `""` is treated as an empty element, to be glued together with the first data element of `@fields`. This results in glue ahead of every element. Similarly, you can get trailing glue with an empty element at the end of the list, like so:

```
$output = join ("\n", @data, "");
```

---

* Actually, the `" "` string is the default pattern, and this will cause leading whitespace to be ignored, but that's still close enough for this discussion.

Exercises

See Appendix A for answers.

1. Construct a regular expression that matches:

    a. at least one **a** followed by any number of **b**'s

    b. any number of backslashes followed by any number of asterisks (any number might be zero)

    c. three consecutive copies of whatever is contained in $whatever

    d. any five characters, including newline

    e. the same word written two or more times in a row (with possibly varying intervening whitespace), where "word" is defined as a nonempty sequence of nonwhitespace characters

2. a. Write a program that accepts a list of words on STDIN and looks for a line containing all five vowels (a, e, i, o, and u). Run this program on /usr/dict/words* and see what shows up. In other words, enter:

    ```
    $ myprogram </usr/dict/words
    ```

    (This presumes you name your program *myprogram*.)

    b. Modify the program so that the five vowels have to be in order and intervening letters don't matter.

    c. Modify the program so that all vowels must be in an increasing order, so all five vowels have to be present, and no "e" can occur before an "a", no "i" can occur before an "e", and so on.

3. Write a program that looks through /etc/passwd† (on STDIN), printing the login name and real name of each user. (Hint: use split to break the line up into fields, then s/// to get rid of the parts of the comment field that are after the first comma.)

4. Write a program that looks through /etc/passwd (on STDIN) for two users with the same first name, and prints those names. (Hint: after extracting the first name, create a hash with the name for a key and the number of times it was seen as the value. When the last line of STDIN has been read, look through the associative array for counts of greater than one.)

5. Repeat the last exercise, but report the login names of all users with the same first name. (Hint: instead of storing a count, store a list of login names separated by spaces. When finished, look through the values for ones that contain a space.)

---

* Your system's dictionary may be somewhere other than */usr/dict/words*; check the *spell*(1) manpage.

† If using NIS, your system may have little data in */etc/passwd*. See if ypcat passwd gives more information.

8

Functions

We've already seen and used built-in functions, such as `chomp`, `print`, and so on. Now, let's take a look at functions that you define for yourself.

Defining a User Function

A user function, more commonly called a *subroutine* or just a *sub*, is defined in your Perl program using a construct like this:

```
sub subname {
    statement_1;
    statement_2;
    statement_3;
}
```

The *subname* is the name of the subroutine, which is any name like the names we've had for scalar variables, arrays, and hashes. Once again, these come from a different namespace, so you can have a scalar variable `$fred`, an array `@fred`, a hash `%fred`, and now a subroutine `fred`.*

The block of statements following the subroutine name becomes the definition of the subroutine. When the subroutine is invoked (described shortly), the block of statements that makes up the subroutine is executed, and any return value (described later) is returned to the caller.

Here, for example, is a subroutine that displays that famous phrase:

---

* Technically, the subroutine's name is `&fred`, but you seldom need to call it that.

```
sub say_hello {
    print "hello, world!\n";
}
```

Subroutine definitions can be anywhere in your program text (they are skipped on execution), but we like to put them at the end of the file, so that the main part of the program appears at the beginning of the file. (If you like to think in Pascal terms, you can put your subroutines at the beginning and your executable statements at the end, instead. It's up to you.)

Subroutine definitions are global;* there are no local subroutines. If you have two subroutine definitions with the same name, the later one overwrites the earlier one without warning.†

Within the subroutine body, you may access or give values to variables that are shared with the rest of the program (a *global* variable). In fact, by default, any variable reference within a subroutine body refers to a global variable. We'll tell you about the exceptions in the upcoming section "Private Variables in Functions." In the following example,

```
sub say_what {
    print "hello, $what\n";
}
```

$what refers to the global $what, shared with the rest of the program.

Invoking a User Function

You invoke a subroutine from within any expression by following the subroutine name with parentheses, as in:

```
say_hello();           # a simple expression
$a = 3 + say_hello(); # part of a larger expression
for ($x = start_value(); $x < end_value(); $x += increment()) {
    ...
}                      # invoke three subroutines to define values
```

A subroutine can invoke another subroutine, and that subroutine can in turn invoke another subroutine, and so on, until all available memory is filled with return addresses and partially computed expressions. (No mere 8 or 32 levels could satisfy a real programmer.)

---

* Global to the current package, actually, but since this book doesn't really deal with separate packages, you may think of subroutine definitions as global to the whole program.

† Unless you are running with the -w switch.

Return Values

A subroutine is always part of some expression. The value of the subroutine invocation is called the *return value*. The return value of a subroutine is the value of the *return* statement or of the last expression evaluated in the subroutine.

For example, let's define this subroutine:

```
sub sum_of_a_and_b {
    return $a + $b;
}
```

The last expression evaluated in the body of this subroutine (in fact, the only expression evaluated) is the sum of $a and $b, so the sum of $a and $b will be the return value. Here's that in action:

```
$a = 3; $b = 4;
$c = sum_of_a_and_b();      # $c gets 7
$d = 3 * sum_of_a_and_b(); # $d gets 21
```

A subroutine can also return a list of values when evaluated in a list context. Consider this subroutine and invocation:

```
sub list_of_a_and_b {
    return($a,$b);
}
$a = 5; $b = 6;
@c = list_of_a_and_b(); # @c gets (5,6)
```

The last expression evaluated really means the last expression evaluated, rather than the last expression defined in the body of the subroutine. For example, this subroutine returns $a if $a > 0; otherwise it returns $b:

```
sub gimme_a_or_b {
    if ($a > 0) {
        print "choosing a ($a)\n";
        returns $a;
    } else {
        print "choosing b ($b)\n";
        return $b;
    }
}
```

These are all rather trivial examples. It gets better when we can pass values that are different for each invocation into a subroutine instead of relying on global variables. In fact, that's coming right up.

Arguments

Although subroutines that have one specific action are useful, a whole new level of usefulness becomes available when you can pass *arguments* to a subroutine.

In Perl, the subroutine invocation is followed by a list within parentheses, causing the list to be automatically assigned to a special variable named @_ for the duration of the subroutine. The subroutine can access this variable to determine the number of arguments and the value of those arguments. For example:

```
sub say_hello_to {
    print "hello, $_[0]!\n"; # first parameter is target
}
```

Here, we see a reference to $_[0], which is the first element of the @_ array. Special note: as similar as they look, the $_[0] value (the first element of the @_ array) has nothing whatsoever to do with the $_ variable (a scalar variable of its own). Don't confuse them! From the code, it appears to say hello to whomever we pass as the first parameter. That means we can invoke it like this:

```
say_hello_to("world");                  # gives hello, world!
$x = "somebody";
say_hello_to($x);                       # gives hello, somebody!
say_hello_to("me")+say_hello_to("you"); # and me and you
```

Note that in the last line, the return values weren't really used. But in evaluating the sum, Perl has to evaluate all of its parts, so the subroutine was invoked twice.

Here's an example using more than one parameter:

```
sub say {
    print "$_[0], $_[1]!\n";
}

say("hello","world");        # hello world, once again
say("goodbye","cruel world"); # silent movie lament
```

Excess parameters are ignored: if you never look at $_[3], Perl doesn't care. And insufficient parameters are also ignored; you simply get **undef** if you look beyond the end of the @_ array, as with any other array.

The @_ variable is *private* to the subroutine; if there's a global value for @_, it is saved away before the subroutine is invoked and restored to its previous value upon return from the subroutine. This also means that a subroutine can pass arguments to another subroutine without fear of losing its own @_ variable; the nested subroutine invocation gets its own @_ in the same way.

Let's revisit that "add a and b" routine from the previous section. Here's a subroutine that adds any two values, specifically, the two values passed to the subroutine as parameters:

```
sub add_two {
    return $_[0] + $_[1];
}
print add_two(3,4); # prints 7
$c = add_two(5,6);  # $c gets 11
```

Now let's generalize this subroutine. What if we had 3, 4, or 100 values to add together? We could do it with a loop, like so:

```
sub add {
    $sum = 0;           # initialize the sum
    foreach $_ (@_) {
        $sum += $_;     # add each element
    }
    return $sum;        # last expression evaluated: sum of all elements
}
$a = add(4,5,6);        # adds 4+5+6 = 15, and assigns to $a
print add(1,2,3,4,5);   # prints 15
print add(1..5);        # also prints 15, because 1..5 is expanded
```

What if we had a variable named $sum when we called add? We just clobbered it. In the next section, we see how to avoid this.

Private Variables in Functions

We've already talked about the @_ variable and how a local copy gets created for each subroutine invoked with parameters. You can create your own scalar, array, and hash variables that work the same way. You do this with the my operator, which takes a list of variable names and creates local versions of them (or *instantiations*, if you like bigger words). Here's that add function again, this time using my:

```
sub add {
    my ($sum);          # make $sum a local variable
    $sum = 0;           # initialize the sum
    foreach $_ (@_) {
        $sum += $_;     # add each element
    }
    return $sum;        # last expression evaluated: sum of all elements
}
```

When the first body statement is executed, any current value of the global variable $sum is saved away, and a brand new variable named $sum is created (with the value undef). When the subroutine exits, Perl discards the local variable and restores the previous (global) value. This works even if the $sum variable is currently a local variable from another subroutine (a subroutine that invokes this one, or one that invokes one that invokes this one, and so on). Variables can have many nested local versions, although you can access only one at a time.

Here's a way to create a list of all the elements of an array greater than 100:

```
sub bigger_than_100 {
    my (@result);            # temporary for holding the return value
    foreach $_ (@_) {        # step through the arg list
        if ($_ > 100) {      # is it eligible?
            push(@result,$_); # add it
```

```
        }
    }
    return @result;              # return the final list
}
```

What if we wanted all elements greater than 50 rather than greater than 100? We'd have to edit the program, changing the 100's to 50's. But what if we needed both? Well, we can replace the 50 or 100 with a variable reference instead. This makes it look like:

```
sub bigger_than {
    my($n,@values);             # create some local variables
    ($n,@values) = @_;          # split args into limit and values
    my(@result);                # temporary for holding the return value
    foreach $_ (@values) {      # step through the arg list
        if ($_ > $n) {          # is it eligible?
            push(@result,$_);   # add it
        }
    }
    return @result;                 # return the final list
}
                                # some invocations:
@new = bigger_than(100,@list);      # @new gets all @list > 100
@this = bigger_than(5,1,5,15,30);   # @this gets (15,30)
```

Notice that this time we used two additional local variables to give names to arguments. This is fairly common in practice; it's much easier to talk about $n and @values than to talk about $_[0] and @_[1..$#], and safer, too.

The result of **my** is an assignable list, meaning that it can be used on the left side of an array assignment operator. This list can be given initial values for each of the newly created variables. (If you don't give values to the list, the new variables start with a value of **undef**, just like any other new variable.) This means we can combine the first two statements of this subroutine, replacing:

```
my($n,@values);
($n,@values) = @_; # split args into limit and values
```

with:

```
my($n,@values)= @_;
```

This is, in fact, a very common Perl-ish thing to do. Local nonargument variables can be given literal values in the same way, such as:

```
my($sum) = 0; # initialize local variable
```

Be warned that despite its appearances as a declaration, **my** is really an executable operator. Good Perl hacking strategy suggests that you bunch all your **my** operators at the beginning of the subroutine definition, before you get into the meat of the routine.

Semiprivate Variables Using local

Perl gives you a second way to create "private" variables, using the `local` function. It is important to understand the differences between `my` and `local`. For example:

```
$value = "original";

tellme();
spoof();
tellme();

sub spoof {
    local ($value) = "temporary";
    tellme();
}

sub tellme {
    print "Current value is $value\n";
}
```

This prints out:

```
Current value is original
Current value is temporary
Current value is original
```

If `my` had been used instead of `local`, the private reading of `$value` would be available only within the `spoof()` subroutine. But with `local`, as the output shows, the private value is not quite so private; it is also available within any subroutines called from `spoof()`. The general rule is that `local` variables are visible to functions called from within the block in which those variables are declared.

Whereas `my` can be used only to declare simple scalar, array, or hash variables with alphanumeric names, `local` suffers no such restrictions. Also, Perl's built-in variables, such as `$_`, `$1`, and `@ARGV`, cannot be declared with `my`, but work fine with `local`. Because `$_` is so often used throughout most Perl programs, it's probably prudent to place a

```
local $_;
```

at the top of any function that uses `$_` for its own purposes. This assures that the previous value will be preserved and automatically restored when the function exits.

In your more advanced programming you may eventually need to know that `local` variables are really global variables in disguise. That is, the value of the global variable is saved and temporarily replaced with the locally declared value.

By and large, you should prefer to use `my` over `local` because it's faster and safer.

File-Level my() Variables

The `my()` operator can also be used at the outermost level of your program, outside of any subroutines or blocks. While this isn't really a "local" variable in the sense defined above, it's actually rather useful, especially when used in conjunction with a Perl *pragma:**

```
use strict;
```

If you place this pragma at the beginning of your file, you will no longer be able to use variables (scalars, arrays, and hashes) until you have first "declared" them. And you declare them with `my()`, like so:

```
use strict;
my $a;                           # starts as undef
my @b = qw(fred barney betty);   # give initial value
...
push @b, qw(wilma);              # cannot leave her out
@c = sort @b;                    # WILL NOT COMPILE
```

That last statement will be flagged at compile time as an error, because it referred to a variable that had not previously been declared with `my` (that is, `@c`). In other words, your program won't even start running unless every single variable being used has been declared.

The advantages of forcing variable declarations are twofold:

1. Your programs will run slightly faster (variables created with `my` are accessed slightly faster than ordinary variables†).

2. You'll catch mistakes in typing much faster, because you'll no longer be able to accidentally reference a nonexisting variable named `$freed` when you wanted `$fred`.

Because of this, many Perl programmers automatically begin every new Perl program with `use strict`.

---

* A pragma is a compiler directive. Other directives include those to set up integer arithmetic, overload numeric operators, or request more verbose warnings and error messages. These are documented in Chapter 7 of *Programming Perl* and the *perlmodlib*(1) manpage.

† In this case, "ordinary variable" is really a package variable (so `$x` is really `$main::x`). Variables created with `my()` are not found in any package.

Exercises

See Appendix A for answers.

1. Write a subroutine to take a numeric value from 1 to 9 as an argument and return the English name (such as one, two, or nine). If the value is out of range, return the original number as the name instead. Test it with some input data; you'll probably have to write some sort of code to call the subroutine. (Hint: the subroutine should *not* perform any I/O.)

2. Taking the subroutine from the previous exercise, write a program to take two numbers and add them together, displaying the result as Two plus two equals four. (Don't forget to capitalize the initial word!)

3. Extend the subroutine to return negative nine through negative one and zero. Try it in a program.

9

Miscellaneous Control Structures

The last Statement

In some of the previous exercises you may have thought, "If I just had a C break statement here, I'd be done." Even if you didn't think that, let me tell you about Perl's equivalent for getting out of a loop early: the last statement.

The last statement breaks out of the innermost enclosing loop block,* causing execution to continue with the statement immediately following the block. For example:

```
while (something) {
    something;
    something;
    something;
    if (somecondition) {
        somethingorother;
        somethingorother;
        last; # break out of the while loop
    }
    morethings;
    morethings;
}
# last comes here
```

If *somecondition* is true, the *somethingorother*'s are executed, and then last forces the while loop to terminate.

The last statement counts only looping blocks, not other blocks that are needed to make up some syntactic construct. This means that the blocks for the if and

---

* Note that the do { } while/until construct does not count as a loop for purposes of next, last, and redo.

else statements, as well as the ones for do {} while/until, do not count;
only the blocks that make up the for, foreach, while, until, and "naked"
blocks count. (A naked block is a block that is not part of a larger construct such
as a loop, subroutine, or an if/then/else statement.)

Suppose we wanted to see whether a mail message that had been saved in a file
was from merlyn. Such a message might look like this:

```
From: merlyn@stonehenge.com (Randal L. Schwartz)
To: stevet@ora.com
Date: 01-DEC-94 08:16:24 PM PDT -0700
Subject: A sample mail message

Here's the body of the mail message. And
here is some more.
```

We'd have to look through the message for a line that begins with From: and
then notice whether the line also contains the login name, merlyn.

We could do it like this:

```
while (<STDIN>) { # read the input lines
    if (/^From: /) { # does it begin with From:? If yes...
        if (/merlyn/) { # it's from merlyn!
            print "Email from Randal! It's about time!\n";
        }
        last; # no need to keep looking for From:, so exit
    } # end "if from:"
    if (/^$/) { # blank line?
        last; # if so, don't check any more lines
    }
} # end while
```

Once the line starting with From: is found, we exit the main loop because we
want to see only the first From: line. Also because a mail message header ends
at the first blank line, we can exit the main loop there as well.

The next Statement

Like last, next alters the ordinary sequential flow of execution. However,
next causes execution to skip past the rest of the innermost enclosing looping
block without terminating the block.* It is used like this:

```
while (something) {
    firstpart;
    firstpart;
    firstpart;
    if (somecondition) {
```

---

* If there's a continue block for the loop, which we haven't discussed, next goes to the beginning of
the continue block rather than the end of the block. Pretty close.

```
            somepart;
            somepart;
            next;
    }
    otherpart;
    otherpart;
    # next comes here
}
```

If *somecondition* is true, then *somepart* is executed, and *otherpart* is skipped around.

Once again, the block of an `if` statement doesn't count as a looping block.

The redo Statement

The third way you can jump around in a looping block is with `redo`. This construct causes a jump to the beginning of the current block (without reevaluating the control expression), like so:

```
while (somecondition) {
    # redo comes here
    something;
    something;
    something;
    if (somecondition) {
        somestuff;
        somestuff;
        redo;
    }
    morething;
    morething;
    morething;
}
```

Once again, the `if` block doesn't count: just the looping blocks.

With `redo` and `last` and a naked block, you can make an infinite loop that exits out of the middle, like so:

```
{
    startstuff;
    startstuff;
    startstuff;
    if (somecondition) {
        last;
    }
    laterstuff;
    laterstuff;
    laterstuff;
    redo;
}
```

This would be appropriate for a `while`-like loop that needed to have some part of the loop executed as initialization before the first test. (In the upcoming section "Expression Modifiers," we'll show you how to write that `if` statement with fewer punctuation characters.)

Labeled Blocks

What if you want to jump out of the block that contains the innermost block, or to put it another way, exit from two nested blocks at once? In C, you'd resort to that much maligned `goto` to get you out. No such kludge is required in Perl; you can use `last`, `next`, and `redo` on any enclosing block by giving the block a name with a *label*.

A label is yet another type of name from yet another namespace following the same rules as scalars, arrays, hashes, and subroutines. As we'll see, however, a label doesn't have a special prefix punctuation character (like $ for scalars, & for subroutines, and so on), so a label named `print` conflicts with the reserved word `print` and would not be allowed. For this reason, you should choose labels that consist entirely of uppercase letters and digits, which will never be chosen for a reserved word in the future. Besides, using all uppercase stands out better within the text of a mostly lowercase program.

Once you've chosen your label, place it immediately in front of the statement containing the block followed by a colon, like this:

```
SOMELABEL: while (condition) {
    statement;
    statement;
    statement;
    if (nuthercondition) {
        last SOMELABEL;
    }
}
```

We added `SOMELABEL` as a parameter to `last`. This tells Perl to exit the block named `SOMELABEL`, rather than just the innermost block. In this case, we don't have anything but the innermost block. But suppose we had nested loops:

```
OUTER: for ($i = 1; $i <= 10; $i++) {
    INNER: for ($j = 1; $j <= 10; $j++) {
        if ($i * $j == 63) {
            print "$i times $j is 63!\n";
            last OUTER;
        }
        if ($j >= $i) {
            next OUTER;
        }
    }
}
```

This set of statements tries all successive values of two small numbers multiplied together until it finds a pair whose product is 63 (7 and 9). Once the pair is found, there's no point in testing other numbers, so the first `if` statement exits both `for` loops using `last` with a label. The second `if` ensures that the bigger of the two numbers will always be the first one by skipping to the next iteration of the outer loop as soon as the condition would no longer hold. This means that the numbers will be tested with (`$i`, `$j`) being (1,1), (2,1), (2,2), (3,1), (3,2), (3,3), (4,1), and so on.

Even if the innermost block is labeled, the `last`, `next`, and `redo` statements without the optional parameter (the label) still operate with respect to that innermost block. Also, you can't use labels to jump into a block—just out of a block. The `last`, `next`, or `redo` has to be within the block.

Expression Modifiers

As Yet Another Way to indicate "if this, then that," Perl allows you to tag an *if* modifier onto an expression that is a standalone statement, like this:

```
some_expression if control_expression;
```

In this case, *control_expression* is evaluated first for its truth value (using the same rules as always), and if true, *some_expression* is evaluated next. This is roughly equivalent to

```
if (control_expression) {
    some_expression;
}
```

except that you don't need the extra punctuation, the statement reads backwards, and the expression must be a simple expression (not a block of statements). Many times, however, this inverted description turns out to be the most natural way to state the problem. For example, here's how you can exit from a loop when a certain condition arises:

```
LINE: while (<STDIN>) {
    last LINE if /^From: /;
}
```

See how much easier that is to write? And you can even read it in a normal English way: "last line if it begins with From."

Other parallel forms include the following:

```
exp2 unless exp1; # like: unless (exp1) { exp2; }
exp2 while exp1;  # like: while (exp1) { exp2; }
exp2 until exp1;  # like: until (exp1) { exp2; }
```

All of these forms evaluate *exp1* first, and based on that, do or don't do something with *exp2*.

For example, here's how to find the first power of two greater than a given number:

```
chomp($n = <STDIN>);
$i = 1;                  # initial guess
$i *= 2 until $i > $n;   # iterate until we find it
```

Once again, we gain some clarity and reduce the clutter.

These forms don't nest: you can't say *exp3* while *exp2* if *exp1*. This is because the form *exp2* if *exp1* is no longer an expression, but a full-blown statement, and you can't tack one of these modifiers on after a statement.

&& and || as Control Structures

These look like punctuation characters or parts of expressions. Can they really be considered control structures? Well, in Perl-think, almost anything is possible, so let's see what we're talking about here.

Often, you run across "if this, then that." We've previously seen these two forms:

```
if (this) { that; } # one way
that if this;       # another way
```

Here's a third (and believe it or not, there are still others):

```
this && that;
```

Why does this work? Isn't that the logical-and operator? Check out what happens when *this* takes on each value of true or false:

- If *this* is true, then the value of the entire expression is still not known, because it depends on the value of *that*. So *that* has to be evaluated.

- If *this* is false, there's no point in looking at *that*, because the value of the whole expression has to be false. Since there's no point to evaluating *that*, we might as well skip it.

And in fact, this is what Perl does. Perl evaluates *that* only when *this* is true, making it equivalent to the previous two forms.

Likewise, the logical-or works like the **unless** statement (or **unless** modifier). So you can replace:

```
unless (this) { that; }
```

with:

```
this || that;
```

If you're familiar with using these operators in shell programming to control conditional execution commands, you'll see that they work similarly in Perl.

Which one should you use? It depends on your mood, sometimes, or how big each of the expression parts are, or whether you need to parenthesize the expressions because of precedence conflicts. Look at other people's programs, and see what they do. You'll probably see a little of each. Larry suggests that you put the most important part of the expression first, so that it stands out.

Exercises

See Appendix A for the answers.

1. Extend the problem from the last chapter to repeat the operation until the word **end** is entered for one of the values. (Hint: use an infinite loop, and then do a `last` if either value is **end**.)

2. Rewrite the exercise from Chapter 4, *Control Structures*, summing numbers up to 999, using a loop that exits from the middle. (Hint: use a naked block with a `redo` at the end to get an infinite loop and a `last` in the middle based on a condition.)

10

Filehandles and File Tests

What Is a Filehandle?

A *filehandle* in a Perl program is the name for an I/O connection between your Perl process and the outside world. We've already seen and used filehandles implicitly: STDIN is a filehandle, naming the connection between the Perl process and the UNIX standard input. Likewise, Perl provides STDOUT (for standard output) and STDERR (for standard error output). These names are the same as those used by the C and C++ "standard I/O" library package, which Perl uses for most of its I/O.

Filehandle names are like the names for labeled blocks, but they come from yet another namespace (so you can have a scalar $fred, an array @fred, a hash %fred, a subroutine &fred, a label fred, and now a filehandle fred). Like block labels, filehandles are used without a special prefix character, and thus might be confused with present or future reserved words. Once again, the recommendation is that you use ALL UPPERCASE letters in your filehandle; not only will it stand out better, but it will also guarantee that your program won't fail when a future reserved word is introduced.

Opening and Closing a Filehandle

Perl provides three filehandles, STDIN, STDOUT, and STDERR, which are automatically open to files or devices established by the program's parent process (probably the shell). You use the open function to open additional filehandles. The syntax looks like this:

```
open(FILEHANDLE, "somename");
```

where *FILEHANDLE* is the new filehandle and *somename* is the external filename (such as a file or a device) that will be associated with the new filehandle. This invocation opens the filehandle for reading. To open a file for writing, use the same **open** function, but prefix the filename with a greater-than sign (as in the shell):

```
open(OUT, ">outfile");
```

We'll see how to use this filehandle in the upcoming section "Using Filehandles." Also, as in the shell, you can open a file for appending by using two greater-than signs for a prefix, as in:

```
open(LOGFILE, ">>mylogfile");
```

All forms of **open** return true for success and false for failure. (Opening a file for input fails, for example, if the file is not there or cannot be accessed because of permissions; opening a file for output fails if the file is write-protected, or if the directory is not writable or accessible.)

When you are finished with a filehandle, you may close it with the **close** operator, like so:

```
close(LOGFILE);
```

Reopening a filehandle also closes the previously open file automatically, as does exiting the program. Because of this, many Perl programs don't bother with **close**. But it's there if you want to be tidy or make sure that all of the data is flushed out sometime earlier than program termination. A **close** call could also fail if the disk filled up, the remote server that held the file became inaccessible, or any of various other esoteric problems occurred. It's a good idea to check the return values of all system calls.

A Slight Diversion: die

Consider this a large footnote, in the middle of the page.

A filehandle that has not been successfully opened can still be used without even so much as a warning* throughout the program. If you read from the filehandle, you'll get end-of-file right away. If you write to the filehandle, the data is silently discarded (like last year's campaign promises).

Typically you'll want to check the result of the **open** and report an error if the result is not what you expect. Sure, you can pepper your program with stuff like:

```
unless (open (DATAPLACE,">/tmp/dataplace")) {
    print "Sorry, I couldn't create /tmp/dataplace\n";
```

---

* Unless you are running with the -w switch enabled.

```
} else {
    # the rest of your program
}
```

But that's a lot of work. And it happens often enough for Perl to offer a bit of a shortcut. The `die` function takes a list within optional parentheses, spits out that list (like `print`) on the standard error output, and then ends the Perl process (the one running the Perl program) with a nonzero exit status (generally indicating that something unusual happened[*]). So, rewriting the chunk of code above turns out to look like this:

```
unless (open DATAPLACE,">/tmp/dataplace") {
    die "Sorry, I couldn't create /tmp/dataplace\n";
}
# rest of program
```

But we can go even one step further. Remember that we can use the `||` (logical-or) operator to shorten this up, as in:

```
open(DATAPLACE,">/tmp/dataplace") ||
    die "Sorry, I couldn't create /tmp/dataplace\n";
```

So the `die` gets executed only when the result of the `open` is false. The common way to read this is "open that file or die!" And that's an easy way to remember whether to use the logical-and or logical-or.

The message at death (built from the argument to `die`) has the Perl program name and line number automatically attached, so you can easily identify which `die` was responsible for the untimely exit. If you don't like the line number or file revealed, make sure that the death text has a newline on the end. For example,

```
die "you gravy-sucking pigs";
```

prints the file and line number, while

```
die "you gravy-sucking pigs\n";
```

does not.

Another handy thing inside `die` strings is the `$!` variable, which contains the error string describing the most recent operating system error. It's used like this:

```
open(LOG, ">>logfile") || die "cannot append: $!";
```

This might end up saying "`cannot append: Permission denied`" as part of the message.

---

[*] Actually, `die` merely raises an exception, but since you aren't being shown how to trap exceptions, it behaves as described. See `eval` in Chapter 3 of *Programming Perl* or *perlfunc*(1) for details.

There's also the "close call" function, which most people know as **warn**. It does everything **die** does, just short of actually dying. Use it to give error messages on standard error without a lot of extra hassle:

```
open(LOG,">>log") || warn "discarding logfile output\n";
```

Using Filehandles

Once a filehandle is open for reading, you can read lines from it just as you can read from standard input with **STDIN**. So, for example, to read lines from the password file:

```
open (EP,"/etc/passwd");
while (<EP>) {
    chomp;
    print "I saw $_ in the password file!\n";
}
```

Note that the newly opened filehandle is used inside the angle brackets, just as we have used **STDIN** previously.

If you have a filehandle open for writing or appending, and if you want to **print** to it, you must place the filehandle immediately after the **print** keyword and before the other arguments. No comma should occur between the filehandle and the rest of the arguments:

```
print LOGFILE "Finished item $n of $max\n";
print STDOUT "hi, world!\n"; # like print "hi, world!\n"
```

In this case, the message beginning with **Finished** goes to the **LOGFILE** file-handle, which presumably was opened earlier in the program. And **hi, world** still goes to standard output, just as when you didn't specify the filehandle. We say that **STDOUT** is the *default filehandle* for the **print** statement.

Here's a way to copy data from a file specified in **$a** into a file specified in **$b**. It illustrates nearly everything we've learned in the last few pages:[*]

```
open(IN,$a) || die "cannot open $a for reading: $!";
open(OUT,">$b") || die "cannot create $b: $!";
while (<IN>) {      # read a line from file $a into $_
    print OUT $_;   # print that line to file $b
}
close(IN) || die "can't close  $a: $!";
close(OUT) || die "can't close  $b: $!";
```

---

[*] Although it's entirely redundant with the **File::Copy** module.

The -x File Tests

Now you know how to open a filehandle for output, overwriting any existing file with the same name. Suppose you wanted to make sure that there wasn't a file by that name (to keep you from accidentally blowing away your spreadsheet data or that important birthday calendar). If you were writing a shell script, you'd use something like -e *filename* to test if the file exists. Similarly, Perl uses -e *$filevar* to test for the existence of the file named by the scalar value in *$filevar*. If this file exists, the result is true; otherwise it is false.* For example:

```
$name = "index.html";
if (-e $name) {
    print "I see you already have a file named $name\n";
} else {
    print "Perhaps you'd like to make a file called $name\n";
}
```

The operand of the -e operator is really just any scalar expression that evaluates to some string, including a string literal. Here's an example that checks to see whether both *index.html* and *index.cgi* exist in the current directory:

```
if (-e "index.html" && -e "index.cgi") {
    print "You have both styles of index files here.\n";
}
```

Other operators are defined as well. For example, -r *$filevar* returns true if the file named in *$filevar* exists and is readable. Similarly, -w *$filevar* tests whether it is writable. Here's an example that tests a user-specified filename for both readability and writability:

```
print "where? ";
$filename = <STDIN>;
chomp $filename; # toss pesky newline
if (-r $filename && -w $filename) {
    # file exists, and I can read and write it
    ...
}
```

Many more file tests are available. Table 10-1 gives the complete list.

Table 10-1. File Tests and Their Meanings

File Test	Meaning
-r	File or directory is readable
-w	File or directory is writable

---

* This isn't good enough if you are managing lock files, or if files are appearing and disappearing quickly. In that case, you need to look into the sysopen and flock functions described in *Programming Perl* or see the examples in Chapter 19, *CGI Programming*.

Table 10-1. File Tests and Their Meanings (continued)

File Test	Meaning
-x	File or directory is executable
-o	File or directory is owned by user
-R	File or directory is readable by real user, not effective user (differs from -r for setuid programs)
-W	File or directory is writable by real user, not effective user (differs from -w for setuid programs)
-X	File or directory is executable by real user, not effective user (differs from -x for setuid programs)
-O	File or directory is owned by real user, not effective user (differs from -o for setuid programs)
-e	File or directory exists
-z	File exists and has zero size (directories are never empty)
-s	File or directory exists and has nonzero size (the value is the size in bytes)
-f	Entry is a plain file
-d	Entry is a directory
-l	Entry is a symlink
-S	Entry is a socket
-p	Entry is a named pipe (a "fifo")
-b	Entry is a block-special file (like a mountable disk)
-c	Entry is a character-special file (like an I/O device)
-u	File or directory is setuid
-g	File or directory is setgid
-k	File or directory has the sticky bit set
-t	isatty() on the filehandle is true
-T	File is "text"
-B	File is "binary"
-M	Modification age in days
-A	Access age in days
-C	Inode-modification age in days

Most of these tests return a simple true-false condition. A few don't, so let's talk about them.

The -s operator does return true if the file is nonempty, but it's a particular kind of true. It's the length in bytes of the file, which evaluates as true for a nonzero number.

The age operators –M, –A, and –C (yes, they're uppercase) return the number of days since the file was last modified, accessed, or had its inode changed.* (The inode contains all of the information about the file except for its contents: see the stat system call manpage for details.) This age value is fractional with a resolution of one second: 36 hours is returned as 1.5 days. If you compare the age with a whole number (say three), you'll get only the files that were changed exactly that many days ago, not one second more or less. This means you'll probably want a range comparison† rather than an exact comparison to get files that are between three and four days old.

These operators can operate on filehandles as well as filenames. Giving a filehandle for the operand is all it takes. So to test whether the file opened as SOMEFILE is executable, you can use:

```
if (-x SOMEFILE) {
    # file open on SOMEFILE is executable
}
```

If you leave the filename or filehandle parameter off (that is, you have just –r or –s), the default operand is the file named in the $_ variable (there it is again!). So, to test a list of filenames to see which ones are readable, it's as simple as this:

```
foreach (@some_list_of_filenames) {
    print "$_ is readable\n" if -r; # same as -r $_
}
```

The stat and lstat Functions

While these file tests are fine for testing various attributes regarding a particular file or filehandle, they don't tell the whole story. For example, there's no file test that returns the number of links to a file. To get at the remaining information about a file, merely call the stat function, which returns pretty much everything that the stat POSIX system call returns (hopefully more than you want to know).

The operand to stat is a filehandle or an expression that evaluates to a filename. The return value is either undef, indicating that the stat failed, or a 13-element list,‡ most easily described using the following list of scalar variables:

```
($dev,$ino,$mode,$nlink,$uid,$gid,$rdev,
 $size,$atime,$mtime,$ctime,$blksize,$blocks) = stat(...)
```

---

* The age is measured relative to the time the program started, as captured in system time format in the $^T variable. It's possible to get negative numbers for these ages if the queried value refers to an event that happened after the program began.

† Or the int operator.

‡ If you have a hard time remembering the order of stat's return values, you might look at the File::stat module, first introduced in release 5.004 of Perl. It provides access such as:

```
$file_owner = stat($filename)->uid;
```

The names here refer to the parts of the stat structure, described in detail in your
stat(2) manpage. You should probably look there for the detailed descriptions.

For example, to get the user ID and the group ID of the password file, let's try:

```
($uid, $gid) = (stat("/etc/passwd"))[4,5];
```

And that's the way it goes.

Invoking the `stat` function on the name of a symbolic link returns information
on what a symbolic link points at, not information about the symbolic link itself
(unless the link just happens to be pointing at nothing currently accessible). If
you need the (mostly useless) information about the symbolic link itself, use
`lstat` rather than `stat` (which returns the same information in the same order).
The `lstat` function works like `stat` on things that aren't symbolic links.

Like the file tests, the operand of `stat` or `lstat` defaults to `$_`, meaning that
the stat will be performed on the file named by the scalar variable `$_`.

Exercises

See Appendix A for answers.

1. Write a program to read in a filename from `STDIN`, then open that file and
   display its contents with each line preceded by the filename and a colon. For
   example, if `fred` was read in, and the file *fred* consisted of the three lines
   `aaa`, `bbb`, and `ccc`, you would see `fred: aaa`, `fred: bbb`, and `fred:
   ccc`.

2. Write a program that prompts for an input filename, an output filename, a
   search pattern, and a replacement string, and replaces all occurrences of the
   search pattern with the replacement string while copying the input file to the
   output file. Try it on some files. Can you overwrite an existing file (don't try it
   with anything important!)? Can you use regular expression characters in the
   search string? Can you use `$1` in the replacement string?

3. Write a program to read in a list of filenames and then display which of the
   files are readable, writable, and/or executable, and which ones don't exist.
   (You can perform each test for each filename as you read them, or on the
   entire set of names when you've read them all. Don't forget to remove the
   newline at the end of each filename you have read in.)

4. Write a program to read in a list of filenames and find the oldest file among
   them. Print out the name of the file and the age of that file in days.

11

Formats

What Is a Format?

Perl stands, among other things, for "practical extraction and report language." It's time to learn about that "...report language" business.

Perl provides the notion of a simple report writing template, called a *format*. A format defines a constant part (the column headers, labels, fixed text, or whatever) and a variable part (the current data you're reporting). The shape of the format is very close to the shape of the output, similar to formatted output in COBOL or the `print using` clauses of some BASICs.

Using a format consists of doing three things:

1. Defining a format
2. Loading up the data to be printed into the variable portions of the format (fields)
3. Invoking the format

Most often, the first step is done once (in the program text so that it gets defined at compile-time),* and the other two steps are performed repeatedly.

---

* You can also create formats at run-time using the `eval` function, as described in *Programming Perl* and in the *perlform*(1) manpage.

Defining a Format

A format is defined using a format definition. This format definition can appear anywhere in your program text, like a subroutine. A format definition looks like this:

```
format someformatname =
fieldline
value_one, value_two, value_three
fieldline
value_one, value_two
fieldline
value_one, value_two, value_three
.
```

The first line contains the reserved word `format`, followed by the format name and then an equal sign (=). The format name is chosen from yet another namespace, and follows the same rule as everything else. Because format names are never used within the body of the program (except within string values), you can safely use names that are identical to reserved words. As you'll see in the next section, "Invoking a Format," most of your format names will probably be the same as filehandle names (which then makes them *not* the same as reserved words... oh well).

Following the first line comes the *template* itself, spanning zero or more text lines. The end of the template is indicated by a line consisting of a single dot by itself.[*] Templates are sensitive to whitespace; this is one of the few places where the kind and amount of whitespace (space, newline, or tab) matters in the text of a Perl program.

The template definition contains a series of *fieldlines*. Each fieldline may contain fixed text—text that will be printed out literally when the format is invoked. Here's an example of a fieldline with fixed text:

```
Hello, my name is Fred Flintstone.
```

Fieldlines may also contain *fieldholders* for variable text. If a line contains fieldholders, the following line of the template (called the *value* line) dictates a series of scalar values —one per fieldholder—that provide the values that will be plugged into the fields. Here's an example of a fieldline with one fieldholder and the value line that follows:

```
Hello, my name is @<<<<<<<<<<
$name
```

---

[*] In text files, the last line needs to end with a newline to work properly.

The fieldholder is the @<<<<<<<<<, which specifies a left-justified text field with 11 characters. More complete details about fieldholders will be given in the upcoming section, "More About the Fieldholders."

If the fieldline has multiple fieldholders, it needs multiple values, so the values are separated on the value line by commas:

```
Hello, my name is @<<<<<<<<<< and I'm @<< years old.
$name, $age
```

Putting all this together, we can create a simple format for an address label:

```
format ADDRESSLABEL =
===============================
| @<<<<<<<<<<<<<<<<<<<<<<<<<< |
$name
| @<<<<<<<<<<<<<<<<<<<<<<<<<< |
$address
| @<<<<<<<<<<<<<<, @< @<<<< |
$city,          $state, $zip
===============================
```

Note that the lines of equal signs at the top and bottom of the format have no fields and thus have no value lines following. (If you put a value line following such a fieldline, it will be interpreted as another fieldline, probably not doing what you want.)

Whitespace within the value line is ignored. Some people choose to use additional whitespace in the value line to line up the variable with the fieldholder on the preceding line (such as putting `$zip` underneath the third field of the previous line in this example), but that's just for looks. Perl doesn't care, and it doesn't affect your output.

Text after the first newline in a value is discarded (except in the special case of multiline fieldholders, described later).

A format definition is like a subroutine definition. It doesn't contain immediately executed code, and can therefore be placed anywhere in the file with the rest of the program. We tend to put ours toward the end of the file, ahead of our subroutine definitions.

Invoking a Format

You invoke a format with the `write` function. This function takes the name of a filehandle and generates text for that filehandle using the current format for that filehandle. By default, the current format for a filehandle is a format with the same name (so for the STDOUT filehandle, the STDOUT format is used), but we'll soon see that you can change it.

```
format ADDRESSLABEL =
=================================
| @<<<<<<<<<<<<<<<<<<<<<<<<< |
$name
| @<<<<<<<<<<<<<<<<<<<<<<<<< |
$address
| @<<<<<<<<<<<<<<<, @< @<<<< |
$city,           $state, $zip
=================================
.


open(ADDRESSLABEL,">labels-to-print") || die "can't create";
open(ADDRESSES,"addresses") || die "cannot open addresses";
while (<ADDRESSES>) {
    chomp; # remove newline
    ($name,$address,$city,$state,$zip) = split(/:/);
        # load up the global variables
    write (ADDRESSLABEL); # send the output
}
```

Here we see our previous format definition, but now we also have some executable code. First, we open a filehandle onto an output file, which is called `labels-to-print`. Note that the filehandle name (`ADDRESSLABEL`) is the same as the name of the format. This is important. Next, we open a filehandle on an address list. The format of the address list is presumed to be something like this:

```
Stonehenge:4470 SW Hall Suite 107:Beaverton:OR:97005
Fred Flintstone:3737 Hard Rock Lane:Bedrock:OZ:999bc
```

In other words, five colon-separated fields, which our code parses as described below.

The `while` loop in the program reads each line of the address file, gets rid of the newline, and then splits the remainder into five variables. Note that the variable names are the same names as the ones we used when we defined the format. This, too, is important.

Once we have all of the variables loaded up (so that the values used by the format are correct), the `write` function invokes the format. Note that the parameter to `write` is the filehandle to be written to, and by default, the format of the same name is also used.

Each field in the format is replaced with the corresponding value from the next line of the format. After the two sample records given above are processed, the file `labels-to-print` contains:

```
================================
| Stonehenge                   |
| 4470 SW Hall Suite 107       |
| Beaverton        , OR 97005  |
================================
================================
| Fred Flintstone             |
| 3737 Hard Rock Lane         |
| Bedrock          , OZ 999bc |
================================
```

More About the Fieldholders

So far, by example, you know that the fieldholder @<<<< means a five-character left-justified field and that @<<<<<<<<<< means an 11-character left-justified field. Here's the whole scoop, as promised earlier.

Text Fields

Most fieldholders start with @. The characters following the @ indicate the type of field, while the number of characters (including the @) indicates the field width.

If the characters following the @ are left-angle brackets (<<<<), you get a left-justified field; that is, the value will be padded on the right with spaces if the value is shorter than the field width. (If a value is too long, it's truncated automatically; the layout of the format is always preserved.)

If the characters following the @ are right-angle brackets (>>>>), you get a right-justified field—that is, if the value is too short, it gets padded on the left with spaces.

Finally, if the characters following the @ are vertical bars (||||), you get a centered field: if the value is too short, it gets padded on both sides with spaces, enough on each side to make the value mostly centered within the field.

Numeric Fields

Another kind of fieldholder is a fixed-precision numeric field, useful for those big financial reports. This field also begins with @, and is followed by one or more #'s with an optional dot (indicating a decimal point). Once again, the @ counts as one of the characters of the field. For example:

```
format MONEY =
Assets: @#####.## Liabilities: @#####.## Net: @#####.##
$assets, $liabilities, $assets-$liabilities
.
```

The three numeric fields allow for six places to the left of the decimal place, and two to the right (useful for dollars and cents). Note the use of an expression in the format—perfectly legal and frequently used.

Perl provides nothing fancier than this; you can't get floating currency symbols or brackets around negative values or anything interesting. To do that, you have to write your own spiffy subroutine, like so:

```
format MONEY =
Assets: @<<<<<<<<< Liabilities @<<<<<<<< Net: @<<<<<<<<<
&pretty($assets,10), &pretty($liab,9), &pretty($assets-$liab,10)
.

sub pretty {
    my($n,$width) = @_;
    $width -= 2; # back off for negative stuff
    $n = sprintf("%.2f",$n); # sprintf is in later chapter
    if ($n < 0) {
        return sprintf("[%$width.2f]", -$n);
            # negative numbers get brackets
    } else {
        return sprintf(" %$width.2f ", $n);
            # positive numbers get spaces instead
    }
}

## body of program:
$assets = 32125.12;
$liab = 45212.15;
write (MONEY);
```

Multiline Fields

As mentioned earlier, Perl normally stops at the first newline of a value when placing the result into the output. One kind of fieldholder, the multiline fieldholder, allows you to include a value that may have many lines of information. This fieldholder is denoted by @* on a line by itself: as always, the following line defines the value to be substituted into the field, which in this case may be an expression that results in a value containing many newlines.

The substituted value will look just like the original text: four lines of value become four lines of output. For example:

```
format STDOUT =
Text Before.
@*
$long_string
Text After.
.

$long_string = "Fred\nBarney\nBetty\nWilma\n";
write;
```

generates the output:

```
Text Before.
Fred
Barney
Betty
Wilma
Text After.
```

Filled Fields

Another kind of fieldholder is a filled field. This fieldholder allows you to create a filled paragraph, breaking the text into conveniently sized lines at word boundaries, wrapping the lines as needed. There are a few parts that work together here, but let's look at them separately.

First, a filled field is denoted by replacing the @ marker in a text fieldholder with a caret (so you get ^<<<, for example). The corresponding value for a filled field (on the following line of the format) must be a scalar variable* containing text, rather than an expression that returns a scalar value. The reason for this is that Perl will alter the variable while filling the filled field, and it's pretty hard to alter an expression.

When Perl is filling the filled field, it takes the value of the variable and grabs as many words (using a reasonable definition of "word")† as will fit into the field. These words are actually ripped out of the variable; the value of the variable after filling this field is whatever is left over after removing the words. You'll see why in a minute.

So far, this isn't much different from how a normal text field works; we're printing only as much as will fit (except that we're respecting a word boundary rather than just cutting it off at the field width). The beauty of this filled field appears when you have multiple references to the same variable in the same format. Take a look at this:

```
format PEOPLE =
Name: @<<<<<<<<<<<< Comment: ^<<<<<<<<<<<<<<<<<<<<<<<<<<<<
      $name,                 $comment
                             ^<<<<<<<<<<<<<<<<<<<<<<<<<<<<
                             $comment
                             ^<<<<<<<<<<<<<<<<<<<<<<<<<<<<
                             $comment
                             ^<<<<<<<<<<<<<<<<<<<<<<<<<<<<
                             $comment
```

---

* Including a single scalar element of an array or hash, like $a[3] or $h{"fred"}.

† The word separator characters are defined by the $: variable.

Note that the variable $comment appears four times. The first line (the one with the name field) prints the person's name and the first few words of the value in $comment. But in the process of computing this line, $comment is altered so that the words disappear. The second line once again refers to the same variable ($comment), and so will take the next few words from the same variable. This is also true for the third and fourth lines. Effectively, what we've created is a rectangle in the output that will be filled as best it can with the words from $comment spread over four lines.

What happens if the complete text occupies less than four lines? Well, you'll get a blank line or two. This is probably OK if you are printing out labels and need exactly the same number of lines for each entry to match them up with the labels. But if you are printing out a report, many blank lines merely use up your printer paper budget.

To fix this, use the suppression indicator. Any line that contains a tilde (~) character is suppressed (not output) if the line would have otherwise printed blank (just whitespace). The tilde itself always prints as a blank and can be placed anywhere a space could have been placed in the line. Rewriting that last example:

```
format PEOPLE =
Name: @<<<<<<<<<<<< Comment: ^<<<<<<<<<<<<<<<<<<<<<<<<<<<<<
      $name,                  $comment
~                             ^<<<<<<<<<<<<<<<<<<<<<<<<<<<<
                              $comment
~                             ^<<<<<<<<<<<<<<<<<<<<<<<<<<<<
                              $comment
~                             ^<<<<<<<<<<<<<<<<<<<<<<<<<<<<
                              $comment
.
```

Now, if the comment covers only two lines, the third and fourth lines are automatically suppressed.

What if the comment is more than four lines? Well, we could make about 20 copies of the last two lines of that format, hoping that 20 lines will cover it. But that goes against the idea that Perl helps you to be lazy, so there's a lazy way to do it. Any line that contains two consecutive tildes will be repeated automatically until the result is a completely blank line. (The blank line is suppressed.) This changes our format to look like this:

```
format PEOPLE =
Name: @<<<<<<<<<<<< Comment: ^<<<<<<<<<<<<<<<<<<<<<<<<<<<<<
      $name,                  $comment
~~                            ^<<<<<<<<<<<<<<<<<<<<<<<<<<<<
                              $comment
.
```

This way, if the comment takes one line, two lines, or 20 lines, we are still OK.

Note that the criterion for stopping the repeated line requires the line to be blank at some point. That means you probably don't want any constant text (other than blanks or tildes) on the line, or else it will never become blank.

The Top-of-Page Format

Many reports end up on some hardcopy device, like a printer. Printer paper is generally clipped into page-size chunks, because most of us stopped reading paper in scrolls a long time ago. So the text being fed to a printer typically has to take page boundaries into consideration by putting in blank lines or formfeed characters to skip across the perforations. Now, you could take the output of a Perl program and feed it through some utility (maybe even one written in Perl) that does this pagination, but there's an easier way.

Perl allows you to define a top-of-page format that triggers a page-processing mode. Perl counts each line of output generated by any format invocation to a particular filehandle. When the next format output cannot fit on the remainder of the current page, Perl spits out a formfeed followed by an automatic invocation of the top-of-page format, and finally the text from the invoked format. That way, the result of one `write` invocation will never be split across page boundaries (unless it is so large that it won't even fit on a page by itself).

The top-of-page format is defined just like any other format. The default name of a top-of-page format for a particular filehandle is the name of the filehandle followed by `_TOP` (in uppercase only).

Perl defines the variable `$%` to be the number of times the top-of-page format has been called for a particular filehandle, so you can use this variable in your top-of-page format to number the pages properly. For example, adding the following format definition to the previous program fragment prevents labels from being broken across page boundaries and also numbers consecutive pages:

```
format ADDRESSLABEL_TOP =
My Addresses -- Page @<
                      $%
```

The default page length is 60 lines. You can change this by setting a special variable, described shortly.

Perl doesn't notice whether you also `print` to the same filehandle, so that might throw the number of lines on the current page off a bit. You can either rewrite your code to use formats to send everything or fudge the "number of lines on the current page" variable after you do your `print`. In a moment, we'll see how to change this value.

Changing Defaults for Formats

We have often referred to the "default" for this or that. Well, Perl provides a way to override the defaults for just about every step. Let's talk about these.

Using select( ) to Change the Filehandle

Back when we talked about `print`, in Chapter 6, *Basic I/O*, I mentioned that `print` and `print STDOUT` were identical, because `STDOUT` was the default for `print`. Not quite. The real default for `print` (and `write`, and a few other operations that we'll get to in a moment) is an odd notion called the *currently selected filehandle*.

The currently selected filehandle starts out as `STDOUT`, which makes it easy to print things on the standard output. However, you can change the currently selected filehandle with the `select` function. This function takes a single filehandle (or a scalar variable containing the name of a filehandle) as an argument. Once the currently selected filehandle is changed, it affects all future operations that depend on the currently selected filehandle. For example:

```
print "hello world\n";       # like print STDOUT "hello world\n";
select (LOGFILE);            # select a new filehandle
print "howdy, world\n";      # like print LOGFILE "howdy, world\n";
print "more for the log\n";  # more for LOGFILE
select (STDOUT);             # re-select STDOUT
print "back to stdout\n";    # this goes to standard output
```

Note that the `select` operation is sticky; once you've selected a new handle, it stays in effect until the next `select`.

So, a better definition for `STDOUT` with respect to `print` and `write` is that `STDOUT` is the default currently selected handle, or the *default* handle.

Subroutines may find a need to change the currently selected filehandle. However, it would be shocking to call a subroutine and then find out that all of your carefully crafted text lines were going into some bit bucket because the subroutine changed the currently selected filehandle without restoring it. So what's a well-behaved subroutine to do? If the subroutine knows that the current handle is `STDOUT`, the subroutine can restore the selected handle with code similar to that above. However, what if the caller of the subroutine had already changed the selected filehandle?

Well it turns out that the return value from `select` is a string containing the name of the previously selected handle. You can capture this value to restore the previously selected filehandle later, using code like this:

```
$oldhandle = select LOGFILE;
```

```
print "this goes to LOGFILE\n";
select ($oldhandle); # restore the previous handle
```

Yes, for these examples, it's much easier simply to put LOGFILE explicitly as the filehandle for the print, but there are some operations that require the currently selected filehandle to change, as we will soon see.

Changing the Format Name

The default format name for a particular filehandle is the same as the filehandle. However, you can change this for the currently selected filehandle by setting the new format name to a special variable called $~. You can also examine the value of the variable to see what the current format is for the currently selected filehandle.

For example, to use the ADDRESSLABEL format on STDOUT, it's as easy as:

```
$~ = "ADDRESSLABEL";
```

But what if you want to set the format for the REPORT filehandle to SUMMARY? Just a few steps to do it here:

```
$oldhandle = select REPORT;
$~ = "SUMMARY";
select ($oldhandle);
```

The next time we say

```
write (REPORT);
```

we get text out on the REPORT filehandle but using the SUMMARY format.*

Note that we saved the previous handle into a scalar variable and then restored it later. This is good programming practice. In fact, in production code we probably would have handled the previous one-line example similarly and not assumed that STDOUT was the default handle.

By setting the current format for a particular filehandle, you can interleave many different formats in a single report.

Changing the Top-of-Page Format Name

Just as we can change the name of the format for a particular filehandle by setting the $~ variable, we can change the top-of-page format by setting the $^ variable. This variable holds the name of the top-of-page format for the currently selected

---

* The object-oriented FileHandle module, part of the Perl standard distribution, provides a simpler way to accomplish the same thing.

filehandle and is read/write, meaning that you can examine its value to see the current format name, and you can change it by assigning to it.

Changing the Page Length

If a top-of-page format is defined, the page length becomes important. By default, the page length is 60 lines; that is, when a `write` won't fit by the end of line 60, the top-of-page format is invoked automatically before printing the text.

Sometimes 60 lines isn't right. You can change this by setting the `$=` variable. This variable holds the current page length for the currently selected filehandle. Once again, to change it for a filehandle other than `STDOUT` (the default currently selected filehandle), you'll need to use the `select()` operator. Here's how to change the `LOGFILE` filehandle to have 30-line pages:

```
$old = select LOGFILE; # select LOGFILE and save old handle
$= = 30;
select $old;
```

Changing the page length won't have any effect until the next time the top-of-page format is invoked. If you set it before any text is output to a filehandle through a format, it'll work just fine because the top-of-page format is invoked immediately at the first `write`.

Changing the Position on the Page

If you `print` your own text to a filehandle, it messes up the page-position line count because Perl isn't counting lines for anything but a `write`. If you want to let Perl know that you've output a few extra lines, you can adjust Perl's internal line count by altering the `$-` variable. This variable contains the number of lines left on the current page on the currently selected filehandle. Each `write` decrements the lines remaining by the lines actually output. When this count reaches zero, the top-of-page format is invoked, and the value of `$-` is then copied from `$=` (the page length).

For example, to tell Perl that you've sent an extra line to `STDOUT`, do something like this:

```
write; # invoke STDOUT format on STDOUT
...;
print "An extra line... oops!\n"; # this goes to STDOUT
$- --; # decrement $- to indicate non-write line went to STDOUT
...;
write; # this will still work, taking extra line into account
```

At the beginning of the program, `$-` is set to zero for each filehandle. This ensures that the top-of-page format will be the first thing invoked for each filehandle upon the first `write`.

Exercises

See Appendix A for answers.

1. Write a program to open the */etc/passwd* file by name and print out the user-name, user ID (number), and real name in formatted columns. Use `format` and `write`.

2. Add a top-of-page format to the previous program. (If your password file is relatively short, you might need to set the pagelength to something like 10 lines so that you can get multiple instances of the top of the page.)

3. Add a sequentially increasing page number to the top of the page, so that you get `page 1`, `page 2`, and so on, in the output.

12

Directory Access

Moving Around the Directory Tree

By now, you're probably familiar with the notion of the current directory and using the shell's *cd* command. In systems programming, you'd be invoking the *chdir* system call to change the current directory of a process, and this is the name used by Perl as well.

The `chdir` function in Perl takes a single argument—an expression evaluating to a directory name to which the current directory will be set. As with most other system calls, `chdir` returns true when you've successfully changed to the requested directory and false if you couldn't. Here's an example:

```
chdir("/etc") || die "cannot cd to /etc ($!)";
```

The parentheses are optional, so you can also get away with stuff like this:

```
print "where do you want to go? ";
chomp($where = <STDIN>);
if (chdir $where) {
            # we got there
} else {
            # we didn't get there
}
```

You can't find out where you are without launching a *pwd* command.* We'll learn about launching commands in Chapter 14, *Process Management*.

Every process† has its own current directory. When a new process is launched, it inherits its parent's current directory, but that's the end of the connection. If your

---

* Or using the `getcwd()` function out of the Cwd module.

† Well, in UNIX and most other modern operating systems.

Perl program changes its directory, it won't affect the parent shell (or whatever) that launched the Perl process. Likewise, the processes that the Perl program creates cannot affect that Perl program's current directory. The current directories for these new processes are inherited from the Perl program's current directory.

The `chdir` function without a parameter defaults to taking you to your home directory, much like the shell's *cd* command.

Globbing

The shell (or whatever your command-line interpreter is) takes a solitary asterisk (*) command-line argument and turns it into a list of all of the filenames in the current directory. So, when you say `rm *`, you'll remove all of the files from the current directory. (Don't try this unless you like irritating your system administrator when you request the files to be restored.) Similarly, `[a-m]*.c` as a command-line argument turns into a list of all filenames in the current directory that begin with a letter in the first half of the alphabet and end in *.c*, and `/etc/host*` is a list of all filenames that begin with *host* in the directory */etc*. (If this is new to you, you probably want to read some more about shell scripting somewhere else before proceeding.)

The expansion of arguments like * or `/etc/host*` into the list of matching filenames is called *globbing*. Perl supports globbing through a very simple mechanism: just put the globbing pattern between angle brackets or use the more mnemonically named `glob` function.

```
@a = </etc/host*>;
@a = glob("/etc/host*");
```

In a list context, as demonstrated here, the glob returns a list of all names that match the pattern (as if the shell had expanded the glob arguments) or an empty list if none match. In a scalar context, the next name that matches is returned, or `undef` is returned if there are no more matches; this is very similar to reading from a filehandle. For example, to look at one name at a time:

```
while (defined($nextname = </etc/host*>)) {
    print "one of the files is $nextname\n";
}
```

Here the returned filenames begin with */etc/host*, so if you want just the last part of the name, you'll have to whittle it down yourself, like so:

```
while ($nextname = </etc/host*>) {
    $nextname =~ s#.*/##; # remove part before last slash
    print "one of the files is $nextname\n";
}
```

Multiple patterns are permitted inside the file glob argument; the lists are constructed separately and then concatenated as if they were one big list:

```
@fred_barney_files = <fred* barney*>;
```

In other words, the glob returns the same values that an equivalent *echo* command with the same parameters would return.*

Although file globbing and regular-expression matching function similarly, the meaning of the various special characters is quite different. Don't confuse the two, or you'll be wondering why <\.c$> doesn't find all of the files that end in *.c*!

The argument to **glob** is variable interpolated before expansion. You can use Perl variables to select files based on a string computed at run-time:

```
if (-d "/usr/etc") {
    $where = "/usr/etc";
} else {
    $where = "/etc";
}
@files = <$where/*>;
```

Here we set $where to be one of two different directory names, based on whether or not the directory */usr/etc* exists. We then get a list of files in the selected directory. Note that the $where variable is expanded, which means the wildcard to be globbed is either /etc/* or /usr/etc/*.

There's one exception to this rule: the pattern <$var> (meaning to use the variable $var as the entire glob expression) must be written as <${var}> for reasons we'd rather not get into at this point.†

Directory Handles

If your particular flavor of operating system provides the *readdir* library function or its moral equivalent, Perl provides access to that routine (and its companions) using *directory handles*. A directory handle is a name from yet another namespace, and the cautions and recommendations that apply to filehandles also apply to directory handles (you can't use a reserved word, and uppercase is recommended). The filehandle FRED and the directory handle FRED are unrelated.

The directory handle represents a connection to a particular directory. Rather than reading data (as from a filehandle), you use the directory handle to read a list of

---

* This is actually no surprise when you understand that to perform the glob, Perl merely fires off a C-shell to glob the specified arglist and parses what it gets back.

† The construct <$fred> reads a line from the filehandle named by the contents of the scalar variable $fred. Together with some other features not covered in this book, this construct enables you to use "indirect filehandles" where the name of a handle is passed around and manipulated as if it were data.

filenames within the directory. Directory handles are always opened read-only; you cannot use a directory handle to change the name of a file or to delete a file.

If your library doesn't provide *readdir()* and friends (and you didn't provide a substitute implementation while building Perl), using any of these routines is a fatal error, and your program won't make it past the compilation: it will abort before the first line of code is executed. Perl tries very hard to isolate you from your environment, but it's not a miracle worker.

Opening and Closing a Directory Handle

The `opendir` function works like the C and C++ library call of the same name. You give it the name of a new directory handle and a string value denoting the name of the directory to be opened. The return value from `opendir` is true if the directory can be opened, false otherwise. Here's an example:

```
opendir(ETC,"/etc") || die "Cannot opendir /etc: $!";
```

Normally, at this point, we'd go playing with the directory handle ETC, but it's probably nice to know how to close the directory handle first. This is done with `closedir`, in a similar manner to using `close`, like so:

```
closedir(ETC);
```

Like `close`, `closedir` is often unnecessary, since all directory handles are automatically closed before they're reopened or at the end of the program.

Reading a Directory Handle

Once we have a directory handle open, we can read the list of names with `readdir`, which takes a single parameter: the directory handle. Each invocation of `readdir` in a scalar context returns the next filename (just the *basename*: you'll never get any slashes in the return value) in a seemingly random order.* If there are no more names, `readdir` returns `undef`.† Invoking `readdir` in a list context returns all of the remaining names as a list with one name per element. Here's an example of listing all of the names from the */etc* directory:

```
opendir(ETC,"/etc") || die "no etc?: $!";
while ($name = readdir(ETC)) { # scalar context, one per loop
    print "$name\n"; # prints ., .., passwd, group, and so on
}
closedir(ETC);
```

---

* Specifically, this is the order in which the filenames are kept in the directory—the same unordered order you get back from the *find* command or *ls -f* under UNIX.

† Which means you'll have to use `while (defined ($name = readdir (...))` when working under Perl's -w option.

And here's a way of getting them all in alphabetical order with the assistance of sort:

```
opendir(ETC,"/etc") || die "no etc?: $!";
foreach $name (sort readdir(ETC)) { # list context, sorted
    print "$name\n"; # prints ., .., passwd, group, and so on
}
closedir(ETC);
```

The names include files that begin with a dot. This is unlike globbing with <*>, which does not return names that begin with a dot. On the other hand, it is like the shell's echo*.

Exercises

Answers are in Appendix A.

1. Write a program to change directory to a location specified as input, then list the names of the files in alphabetical order after changing there. (Don't show a list if the directory change did not succeed: merely warn the user.)

2. Modify the program to include all files, not just the ones that don't begin with dot. Try to do this with both a glob and a directory handle.

13

File and Directory Manipulation

This chapter shows you how to manipulate the files themselves, not merely the data contained in them. We'll use the UNIX (and POSIX and Linux) semantics for demonstrating access to files and directories. Not all filesystems access mechanisms, but these are the standard ones for reasonably support-rich filesystem models.

Removing a File

Earlier, you learned how to create a file from within Perl by opening it for output with a filehandle. Now, we'll get dangerous and learn how to remove a file (very appropriate for Chapter 13, don't you think?).

The Perl `unlink` function (named for the POSIX system call) deletes one name for a file (which could possibly have other names). When the last name for a file is deleted, and no processes have it open, the file itself is removed. This is exactly what the UNIX *rm* command does. Because a file typically has just one name (unless you've created hard links), for the most part, you can think of removing a name as removing the file. Given that, here's how to remove a file called *fred* and then remove a file specified during program execution:

```
unlink ("fred"); # say goodbye to fred
print "what file do you want to delete? ";
chomp($name = <STDIN>);
unlink ($name);
```

The `unlink` function can take a list of names to be unlinked as well:

```
unlink ("cowbird","starling"); # kill two birds
unlink <*.o>;                   # just like "rm *.o" in the shell
```

The glob is evaluated in a list context, creating a list of filenames that match the pattern. This is exactly what we need to feed `unlink`.

The return value of `unlink` is the number of files successfully deleted. If there's one argument, and it is deleted, the result is one, otherwise it is zero. If there are three filenames but only two could be deleted, the result is two. You can't tell which two, so if you need to figure out which deletion failed, you must do them one at a time. Here's how to delete all of the object files (ending in `.o`) while reporting an error for any file that cannot be deleted:

```
foreach $file (<*.o>) { # step through a list of .o files
    unlink($file) || warn "having trouble deleting $file: $!";
}
```

If the `unlink` returns 1 (meaning the one file specified was indeed deleted), the true result skips the **warn** function. If the filename cannot be deleted, the 0 result is false, so the **warn** is executed. Once again, this can be read abstractly as "unlink this file or tell me about it."

If the `unlink` function is given no arguments, the `$_` variable is once again used as a default. Thus, we could have written the loop above as:

```
foreach (<*.o>) { # step through a list of .o files
    unlink || warn "having trouble deleting $_: $!";
}
```

Renaming a File

In the UNIX shell, you change the name of a file with the *mv* command. With Perl, the same operation is denoted with `rename($old, $new)`. Here's how to change the file named `fred` into `barney`:

```
rename("fred","barney") || die "Can't rename fred to barney: $!";
```

Like most other functions, **rename** returns a true value if successful, so test this result to see whether the **rename** has indeed worked.

The *mv* command performs a little behind-the-scenes magic to create a full pathname when you say *mv file some-directory*. However, the **rename** function cannot. The equivalent Perl operation is:

```
rename("file","some-directory/file");
```

Note that in Perl we had to say the name of the file within the new directory explicitly. Also, the *mv* command *copies* the file when the file is renamed from mounted device to another (if you have one of the better operating systems). The `rename` function isn't as smart, so you'll get an error, indicating you have to move it around some other way (perhaps by invoking a *mv* command on the same names). The File::Copy module supports a `move` function.

Creating Alternate Names for a File: Linking

As if one name for a file weren't enough, sometimes you want to have two, three, or a dozen names for the same file. This operation of creating alternate names for a file is called *linking*. The two major forms of linking are hard links and symbolic links (also called symlinks or soft links). Not all kinds of filesystems support both of these or even either of them. This section describes filesystems under POSIX.

About Hard and Soft Links

A *hard link* to a file is indistinguishable from the original name for the file; there's no particular link that is more the "real name" for the file than any other.

The operating system keeps track of how many hard links reference the file at any particular time. When a file is first created, it starts with one link. Each new hard link increases the count. Each removed link reduces the count. When the last link to a file disappears, and the file is closed, the file goes away.

Every hard link to a file must reside on the same mounted filesystem (usually a disk or a part of a disk). Because of this, you cannot make a new hard link to a file that is on a different mounted filesystem.

Under most systems, hard links are also restricted for directories. To keep the directory structure as a tree rather than an arbitrary mish-mash, a directory is allowed only one name from the root, a link from the dot file within itself, and a bunch of dot-dot hard links from each of its subdirectories. If you try to create another hard link to a directory, you will get an error (unless you're the superuser, and then you get to spend all night restoring your mangled filesystem).

A symbolic link is a special kind of a file that contains a pathname as data. When this file is opened, the operating system regards its contents as replacement characters for the pathname, causing the kernel to hunt through the directory tree some more, starting with the new name.

For example, if a symlink named *fred* contains the name *barney*, opening *fred* is really an indication to open *barney*. If *barney* is a directory, then *fred/wilma* refers to *barney/wilma* instead.

The contents of a symlink (where a symlink points) do not have to refer to an existing file or directory. When *fred* is made, *barney* doesn't even have to exist: in fact, it may never exist! The contents of a symlink can refer to a path that leads you off the current filesystem, so you can create a symlink to a file on another mounted filesystem.

While following the new name, the kernel may run across another symlink. This new symlink gives even more new parts to the path to be followed. In fact, symlinks can point to other symlinks, with usually at least eight levels of symlinks allowed, although this is rarely used in practice.

A hard link protects the contents of a file from being lost (because it counts as one of the names of the file). A symlink cannot keep the contents from disappearing. A symlink can cross mounted filesystems; a hard link cannot. Only a symlink can be made to a directory.

Creating Hard and Soft Links with Perl

The UNIX *ln* command creates hard links. The command

```
ln fred bigdumbguy
```

creates a hard link from the file *fred* (which must exist) to *bigdumbguy*. In Perl, this is expressed as:

```
link("fred","bigdumbguy") ||
    die "cannot link fred to bigdumbguy";
```

The `link` function takes two parameters, the old filename and a new alias for that file. The function returns true if the link was successful. As with the *mv* command, the UNIX *ln* command performs some behind-the-scenes magic, allowing you to specify the target directory for the new alias without naming the file within the directory. The `link` function (like the `rename` function) is not so smart, and you must specify the full filename explicitly.

For a hard link, the old filename cannot be a directory,* and the new alias must be on the same filesystem. (These restrictions are part of the reason that symbolic links were created.)

On systems that support symbolic links, the *ln* command may be given the *-s* option to create a symbolic link. So, to create a symbolic link from *barney* to *neighbor* (so that a reference to *neighbor* is actually a reference to *barney*), you'd use something like this:

```
ln -s barney neighbor
```

---

* Unless you are root and enjoy running *fsck.*

and in Perl, you'd use the `symlink` function, like so:

```
symlink("barney","neighbor") ||
    die "cannot symlink to neighbor";
```

Note that *barney* need not exist (poor Betty!), either now or in the future. In this case, a reference to *neighbor* will return something vaguely like `No such file or directory`.

When you invoke *ls -l* on the directory containing a symbolic link, you get an indication of both the name of the symbolic link and where the link points. Perl gives you this same information through the `readlink` function, which works surprisingly like the system call of the same name, returning the name pointed at by the specified symbolic link. So, this operation

```
if (defined($x = readlink("neighbor"))) {
    print "neighbor points at '$x'\n";
}
```

should talk about *barney* if all is well. If the selected symbolic link does not exist or can't be read or isn't even a symlink, `readlink` returns `undef` (definitely false), which is why we're testing it here.

On systems without symbolic links, both the `symlink` and `readlink` functions will fail, producing a run-time error. This is because there is no comparable equivalent for symbolic links on systems that don't support them. Perl can hide some system-dependent features from you, but some just leak right through. This is one of them.

Making and Removing Directories

You probably couldn't have made it this far (on a UNIX system, anyway) without knowing about the *mkdir*(1) command, which makes directories that hold other filenames and other directories. Perl's equivalent is the `mkdir` function, which takes a name for a new directory and a mode that will affect the permissions of the created directory. The mode is specified as a number interpreted in internal permissions format. If you're not familiar with internal permissions, see *chmod*(2). If you're in a hurry, just say `0777` for the mode and everything will work.* Here's an example of how to create a directory named `gravelpit`:

```
mkdir("gravelpit",0777) || die "cannot mkdir gravelpit: $!";
```

The UNIX *rmdir*(1) command removes empty directories; you'll find a Perl equivalent with the same name. Here's how to make Fred unemployed:

---

* You aren't making a directory with wide-open permissions. Your process's current umask will also help determine the permissions. On UNIX systems, see the shell's *umask* command or *umask*(2).

```
rmdir("gravelpit") || die "cannot rmdir gravelpit: $!";
```

Although these Perl operators take advantage of the same-named system calls, they'll work even on systems without those system calls (albeit a bit slower). Perl calls the *mkdir* and *rmdir* utilities automatically for you (or whatever they're called on your system). Strike one blow in the name of portability!

Modifying Permissions

The permissions on a file or directory define who (in broad categories) can do what (more or less) to that file or directory. Under UNIX, the typical way to change permissions on a file is with the *chmod*(1) command. (See its manpage if you are unfamiliar with its operation.) Similarly, Perl changes permissions with the chmod function. This operator takes an octal numeric mode and a list of filenames, and attempts to alter the permissions of all the filenames to the indicated mode. To make the files *fred* and *barney* both read/write for everyone, for example, do something like this:

```
chmod(0666,"fred","barney");
```

Here, the value of 0666 happens to be read/write for user, group, and other, giving us the desired permission.

The return value of chmod is the number of files successfully adjusted (even if the adjustment does nothing); so it works like unlink, and you should treat it as such with regard to error checking. Here's how to change the permissions of *fred* and *barney* while checking the errors for each:

```
foreach $file ("fred","barney") {
    unless chmod (0666,$file) {
        warn "hmm... couldn't chmod $file: $!";
    }
}
```

Modifying Ownership

Every file (or directory, or device entry, or whatever) in the filesystem has an owner and group. The owner and group of a file determine to whom the owner and group permissions apply (read, write, and/or execute). The owner and group of a file are determined at the time the file is created, but under certain circumstances, you can change them. (The exact circumstances depend on the particular flavor of UNIX you are running: see the *chown* manpage for details.)

The chown function takes a user ID number (UID), a group ID number (GID), and a list of filenames, and attempts to change the ownership of each of the listed files as specified. A success is indicated by a nonzero return value equal to the number of files successfully changed—just like `chmod` or `unlink`. Note that you are changing both the owner and the group at once. Use -1 instead of an actual user or group ID if you do not want to change the ID. Also note that you must use the numeric UID and GID, not the corresponding symbolic names (even though the *chmod* command accepts the names). For example, if `fred` is UID 1234 and `fred`'s default group `stoners` is GID 35, then the following command makes the files *slate* and *granite* belong to `fred` and his default group:

```
chown(1234, 35, "slate", "granite"); # same as:
                           #   chown fred slate granite
                           #   chgrp stoners slate granite
```

In Chapter 16, *System Database Access*, you'll learn how to convert `fred` to 1234 and `stoners` to 35.

Modifying Timestamps

Associated with each file is a set of three timestamps. These timestamps were discussed briefly when we talked about getting information about a file: the last access time, the last modification time, and the last inode-change time. The first two timestamps can be set to arbitrary values by the `utime` function (which corresponds directly to the same-named UNIX system call). Setting these two values automatically sets the third value to the current time, so there's no point in having a way to set the third value.

The values are measured in internal time, namely an integer number of seconds past midnight GMT, January 1, 1970—a figure that had reached 800-million-something when this book was being written. (Internally, it's represented as a 32-bit unsigned number, and if we haven't all upgraded to 64-bit machines (or beyond), will overflow sometime well into the next century. We have much more to worry about in the year 2000.*)

The `utime` function works like `chmod` and `unlink`. It takes a list of filenames and returns the number of files affected. Here's how to make the *fred* and *barney* files look as though they were modified sometime in the recent past:

```
$atime = $mtime = 700_000_000; # a while ago
utime($atime,$mtime,"fred","barney");
```

There's no "reasonableness" value for the timestamps: you can make a file look arbitrarily old or as though it were modified at some time in the distant future (useful if you are writing science fiction stories). For example, using the `time`

---

* Perl's `localtime` and `gmtime` functions work just like C's: they return the year with 1,900 subtracted. In 2003, `localtime` will give the year as 103.

function (which returns the current time as a UNIX timestamp), here's how to make the file *max_headroom* look like it was updated 20 minutes into the future:

```
$when = time() + 20*60; # 20 minutes from now
utime($when,$when,"max_headroom");
```

Exercises

See Appendix A for answers.

1. Write a program that works like *rm*, deleting the files given as command-line arguments when the program is invoked. (You don't need to handle any options of *rm*.)

    Be careful to test this program in a mostly empty directory so you don't accidentally delete useful stuff! Remember that the command-line arguments are available in the @ARGV array when the program starts.

2. Write a program that works like *mv*, renaming the first command-line argument to the second command-line argument. (You don't need to handle any options of *mv*, or more than two arguments.) You may wish to consider how to handle the rename when the destination is a directory.

3. Write a program that works like *ln*, creating a hard link from the first command-line argument to the second. (You don't need to handle any options of *ln*, or more than two arguments.)

4. If you have symlinks, modify the program from the previous exercise to handle an optional -s switch.

5. If you have symlinks, write a program that looks for all symlinked files in the current directory and prints out their name and symlinked value similar to the way *ls -l* does it (name -> value). Create some symlinks in the current directory and test it out.

14

Process Management

In this chapter:
- *Using system and exec*
- *Using Backquotes*
- *Using Processes as Filehandles*
- *Using fork*
- *Summary of Process Operations*
- *Sending and Receiving Signals*
- *Exercises*

Using system and exec

When you give the shell a command line to execute, the shell usually creates a new process to execute the command. This new process becomes a child of the shell, executing independently, yet coordinating with the shell.

Similarly, a Perl program can launch new processes, and like most other operations, has more than one way to do so.

The simplest way to launch a new process is to use the **system** function. In its simplest form, this function hands a single string to a brand new */bin/sh* shell to be executed as a command. When the command is finished, the **system** function returns the exit value of the command (typically 0 if everything went OK). Here's an example of a Perl program executing a *date* command using a shell:[*]

```
system("date");
```

We're ignoring the return value here, but it's not likely that the *date* command is going to fail anyway.

Where does the command's output go? In fact, where does the input come from, if it's a command that wants input? These are good questions, and the answers to these questions are most of what distinguishes the various forms of process-creation.

For the **system** function, the three standard files (standard input, standard output, and standard error) are inherited from the Perl process. So for the *date*

---

[*] This doesn't actually use the shell: Perl performs the operations of the shell if the command line is simple enough, and this one is.

command in the previous example, the output goes wherever the `print STDOUT` output goes—probably the invoker's display screen. Because you are firing off a shell, you can change the location of the standard output using the normal */bin/sh* I/O redirections. For example, to put the output of the *date* command into a file named *right_now*, something like this will work just fine:

```
system("date >right_now") && die "cannot create right_now";
```

This time, we not only send the output of the *date* command into a file with a redirection to the shell, but also check the return status. If the return status is true (nonzero), something went wrong with the shell command, and the `die` function will do its deed. This is backwards from normal Perl operator convention: a nonzero return value from the `system` operator generally indicates that something went wrong.

The argument to `system` can be anything you would feed */bin/sh*, so multiple commands can be included, separated by semicolons or newlines. Processes that end in & are launched and not waited for, just as if you had typed a line that ends in an & to the shell.

Here's an example of generating a *date* and *who* command to the shell, sending the output to a filename specified by a Perl variable. This all takes place in the background so that we don't have to wait for it before continuing with the Perl script:

```
$where = "who_out.".++$i; # get a new filename
system "(date; who) >$where &";
```

The return value from `system` in this case is the exit value of the shell, and would thus indicate whether the background process had launched successfully, but not whether the *date* and *who* commands executed successfully. The double-quoted string is variable interpolated, so `$where` is replaced with its value (by Perl, not by the shell). If you wanted to reference a shell variable named `$where`, you'd have to backslash the dollar sign or use a single-quoted string.

A child process inherits many things from its parent besides the standard filehandles. These include the current umask, current directory, and of course, the user ID.

Additionally, all environment variables are inherited by the child. These variables are typically altered by the *csh setenv* command or the corresponding assignment and *export* by the */bin/sh* shell. Environment variables are used by many utilities, including the shells, to alter or control the way that utility operates.

Perl gives you a way to examine and alter current environment variables through a special hash called `%ENV` (uppercase). Each key of this hash corresponds to the name of an environment variable, with the corresponding value being, well, the corresponding value. Examining this hash shows you the environment handed to Perl by the parent shell; altering the hash affects the environment used by Perl and by its child processes, but not parents.

For example, here's a simple program that acts like *printenv*:

```
foreach $key (sort keys %ENV) {
    print "$key=$ENV{$key}\n";
}
```

Note the equal sign here is not an assignment, but simply a text character that the `print` is using to say stuff like `TERM=xterm` or `USER=merlyn`.

Here's a program snippet that alters the value of `PATH` to make sure that the *grep* command run by `system` is looked for only in the normal places:

```
$oldPATH = $ENV{"PATH"};                # save previous path
$ENV{"PATH"} = "/bin:/usr/bin:/usr/ucb"; # force known path
system("grep fred bedrock >output");    # run command
$ENV{"PATH"} = $oldPATH;                # restore previous path
```

That's a lot of typing. It'd be faster just to set a local value for this hash element.

Despite its other shortcomings, the `local` operator can do one thing that `my` cannot: it can give just one element of an array or a hash a temporary value.

```
{
    local $ENV{"PATH"} = "/bin:/usr/bin:/usr/ucb";
    system "grep fred bedrock >output";
}
```

The `system` function can also take a list of arguments rather than a single argument. In that case, rather than handing the list of arguments off to a shell, Perl treats the first argument as the command to run (located according to the `PATH` if necessary) and the remaining arguments as arguments to the command without normal shell interpretation. In other words, you don't need to quote whitespace or worry about arguments that contain angle brackets because those are all merely characters to hand to the program. So, the following two commands are equivalent:

```
system "grep 'fred flintstone' buffaloes";   # using shell
system "grep","fred flintstone","buffaloes"; # avoiding shell
```

Giving `system` a list rather than giving it a simple string saves one shell process as well, so do this when you can. (Actually, when the one-argument form of `system` is simple enough, Perl itself optimizes away the shell invocation entirely, calling the resulting program directly as if you had used the multiple-argument invocation.)

Here's another example of equivalent forms:

```
@cfiles = ("fred.c","barney.c");             # what to compile
```

```
@options = ("-DHARD","-DGRANITE");       # options
system "cc -o slate @options @cfiles";   # using shell
system "cc","-o","slate",@options,@cfiles; # avoiding shell
```

Using Backquotes

Another way to launch a process is to put a */bin/sh* shell command line between backquotes. Like the shell, this fires off a command and waits for its completion, capturing the standard output as it goes along:

```
$now - "the time is now ".`date`; # gets text and date output
```

The value of $now winds up with the text **the time is now** along with the result of the *date*(1) command (including the trailing newline), so it looks something like this:

```
the time is now Fri Aug 13 23:59:59 PDT 1993
```

If the backquoted command is used in a list context rather than a scalar context, you get a list of strings, each one being a line (terminated in a newline*) from the command's output. For the *date* example, we'd have just one element because it generated only one line of text. The output of *who* looks like this:

```
merlyn     tty42    Dec  7 19:41
fred       tty1A    Aug 31 07:02
barney     tty1F    Sep  1 09:22
```

Here's how to grab this output in a list context:

```
foreach $_ (`who`) { # once per text line from who
    ($who,$where,$when) = /(\S+)\s+(\S+)\s+(.*)/;
    print "$who on $where at $when\n";
}
```

Each pass through the loop works on a separate line of the output of *who*, because the backquoted command is evaluated within a list context.

The standard input and standard error of the command within backquotes are inherited from the Perl process.† This means that you normally get just the standard output of the commands within the backquotes as the value of the backquoted-string. One common thing to do is to merge the standard error into the standard output so that the backquoted command picks up both, using the 2>&1 construct of the shell:

```
die "rm spoke!" if `rm fred 2>&1`;
```

---

* Or whatever you've set $/ to.

† Actually, it's a bit more complicated that this. See the question in Section 8 of the Perl FAQ on "How can I capture STDERR from an external command?" If you're running Perl version 5.004, the FAQ is distributed as a normal manpage—*perlfaq8*(1) in this case.

Here, the Perl process is terminated if *rm* says anything, either to standard output or standard error, because the result will no longer be an empty string (an empty string would be false).

Using Processes as Filehandles

Yet another way to launch a process is to create a process that looks like a filehandle (similar to the *popen*(3) C library routine if you're familiar with that). We can create a process-filehandle that either captures the output from or provides input to the process.* Here's an example of creating a filehandle out of a *who*(1) process. Because the process is generating output that we want to read, we make a filchandle that is open for reading, like so:

```
open(WHOPROC, "who|"); # open who for reading
```

Note the vertical bar on the right side of who. That bar tells Perl that this **open** is not about a filename, but rather a command to be started. Because the bar is on the right of the command, the filehandle is opened for reading, meaning that the standard output of *who* is going to be captured. (The standard input and standard error remain shared with the Perl process.) To the rest of the program, the WHOPROC handle is merely a filehandle that is open for reading, meaning that all normal file I/O operators apply. Here's a way to read data from the *who* command into an array:

```
@whosaid = <WHOPROC>;
```

Similarly, to open a command that expects input, we can open a process-filehandle for writing by putting the vertical bar on the left of the command, like so:

```
open(LPR,"|lpr -Pslatewriter");
print LPR @rockreport;
close(LPR);
```

In this case, after opening LPR, we write some data to it and then close it. Opening a process with a process-filehandle allows the command to execute in parallel with the Perl program. Saying **close** on the filehandle forces the Perl program to wait until the process exits. If you don't close the filehandle, the process can continue to run even beyond the execution of the Perl program.

Opening a process for writing causes the command's standard input to come from the filehandle. The process shares the standard output and standard error with Perl. As before, you may use */bin/sh*-style I/O redirection, so here's one way to simply discard the error messages from the *lpr* command in that last example:

---

* But not both at once. See Chapter 6 of *Programming Perl* or *perlipc*(1) for examples of bidirectional communication.

```
open(LPR,"|lpr -Pslatewriter >/dev/null 2>&1");
```

The `>/dev/null` causes standard output to be discarded by being redirected to the null device. The `2>&1` causes standard error to be sent to where the standard output is sent, resulting in errors being discarded as well.

You could even combine all this, generating a report of everyone except Fred in the list of logged-on entries, like so:

```
open (WHO,"who|");
open (LPR,"|lpr -Pslatewriter");
while (<WHO>) {
    unless (/fred/) { # don't show fred
        print LPR $_;
    }
}
close WHO;
close LPR;
```

As this code fragment reads from the WHO handle one line at a time, it prints all of the lines that don't contain the string `fred` to the LPR handle. So the only output on the printer is the lines that don't contain `fred`.

You don't have to open just one command at a time. You can open an entire pipeline. For example, the following line starts up an *ls*(1) process, which pipes its output into a *tail*(1) process, which finally sends its output along to the WHOPR filehandle:

```
open(WHOPR, "ls | tail -r |");
```

Using fork

Still another way of creating an additional process is to clone the current Perl process using a UNIX primitive called `fork`. The `fork` function simply does what the *fork*(2) system call does: it creates a clone of the current process. This clone (called the child, with the original called the parent) shares the same executable code, variables, and even open files. To distinguish the two processes, the return value from `fork` is zero for the child, and nonzero for the parent (or `undef` if the system call fails). The nonzero value received by the parent happens to be the child's process ID. You can check for the return value and act accordingly:

```
if (!defined($child_pid = fork())) {
    die "cannot fork: $!";
} elsif ($child_pid) {
    # I'm the parent
} else {
    # I'm the child
}
```

To best use this clone, we need to learn about a few more things that parallel their UNIX namesakes closely: the `wait`, `exit`, and `exec` functions.

The simplest of these is the `exec` function. It's just like the `system` function, except that instead of firing off a new process to execute the shell command, Perl replaces the current process with the shell. (In UNIX parlance, Perl `exec`'s the shell.) After a successful `exec`, the Perl program is gone, having been replaced by the requested program. For example,

```
exec "date";
```

replaces the current Perl program with the *date* command, causing the output of the *date* to go to the standard output of the Perl program. When the *date* command finishes, there's nothing more to do because the Perl program is long gone.

Another way of looking at this is that the `system` function is like a `fork` followed by an `exec`, as follows:

```
# METHOD 1... using system:
system("date");

# METHOD 2... using fork/exec:
unless (fork) {
    # fork returned zero, so I'm the child, and I exec:
    exec("date"); # child process becomes the date command
}
```

Using `fork` and `exec` this way isn't quite right though, because the *date* command and the parent process are both chugging along at the same time, possibly intermingling their output and generally mucking things up. What we need is a way to tell the parent to wait until the child process completes. That's exactly what the `wait` function does; it waits until the child (any child, to be precise) has completed. The `waitpid` function is more discriminating: it waits for a specific child process to complete rather just any kid:

```
if (!defined($kidpid = fork())) {
    # fork returned undef, so failed
    die "cannot fork: $!";
} elsif ($kidpid == 0) {
            # fork returned 0, so this branch is the child
    exec("date");
            # if the exec fails, fall through to the next statement
    die "can't exec date: $!";
} else {
            # fork returned neither 0 nor undef,
            # so this branch is the parent
    waitpid($kidpid, 0);
}
```

If this all seems rather fuzzy to you, you should probably study up on the *fork*(2) and *exec*(2) system calls in a traditional UNIX text, because Perl is pretty much just passing the function calls right down to the UNIX system calls.

The `exit` function causes an immediate exit from the current Perl process. You'd use this to abort a Perl program from somewhere in the middle, or with `fork` to execute some Perl code in a process and then quit. Here's a case of removing some files in */tmp* in the background using a forked Perl process:

```
unless (defined ($pid = fork)) {
    die "cannot fork: $!";
}
unless ($pid) {
    unlink </tmp/badrock.*>;        # blast those files
    exit;                           # the child stops here
}

                                    # Parent continues here
waitpid($pid, 0);                   # must clean up after dead kid
```

Without the `exit`, the child process would continue executing Perl code (at the line marked `Parent continues here`), and that's definitely not what we want.

The `exit` function takes an optional parameter, which serves as the numeric exit value that can be noticed by the parent process. The default is to exit with a zero value, indicating that everything went OK.

Summary of Process Operations

Table 14-1 summarizes the operations that you have for launching a process.

Table 14-1. Summary of Subprocess Operations

Operation	Standard Input	Standard Output	Standard Error	Waited for?
`system()`	Inherited from program	Inherited from program	Inherited from program	Yes
Backquoted string	Inherited from program	Captured as string value	Inherited from program	Yes
`open()` command as filehandle for output	Connected to filehandle	Inherited from program	Inherited from program	Only at time of `close()`
`open()` command as filehandle for input	Inherited from program	Connected to filehandle	Inherited from program	Only at time of `close()`
`fork, exec, wait, waitpid`	User selected	User selected	User selected	User selected

The simplest way to create a process is with the `system` function. Standard input, output, and error are unaffected (they're inherited from the Perl process). A backquoted string creates a process, capturing the standard output of the process as a string value for the Perl program. Standard input and standard error are unaffected. Both these methods require that the process finish before any more code is executed.

A simple way to get an asynchronous process (one that allows the Perl program to continue before the process is complete) is to open a command as a filehandle, creating a pipe for the command's standard input or standard output. A command opened as a filehandle for reading inherits the standard input and standard error from the Perl program; a command opened as a filehandle for writing inherits the standard output and standard error from the Perl program.

The most flexible way of starting a process is to have your program invoke the `fork`, `exec`, and `wait` or `waitpid` functions, which map directly to their UNIX system call namesakes. Using these functions, you can select whether you are waiting or not, and configure the standard input, output, and error any way you choose.*

Sending and Receiving Signals

One method of interprocess communication is to send and receive signals. A signal is a one-bit message (meaning "this signal happened") sent to a process from another process or from the kernel. Signals are numbered, usually from one to some small number like 15 or 31. Some signals have predefined meanings and are sent automatically to a process under certain conditions (such as memory faults or floating-point exceptions); others are strictly user-generated from other processes. Those processes must have permission to send such a signal. Only if you are the superuser or if the sending process has the same user ID as the receiving process is the signal permitted.

The response to a signal is called the signal's *action*. Predefined signals have certain useful default actions, such as aborting the process or suspending it. Other signals are completely ignored by default. Nearly all signals can have their default action overridden, to either be ignored or else *caught* (invoking a user-specified section of code automatically).

So far, this is all standard stuff; here's where it gets Perl-specific. When a Perl process catches a signal, a subroutine of your choosing gets invoked asynchronously and automatically, momentarily interrupting whatever was executing.

---

* Although it might also help to know about `open(STDERR,">&STDOUT")` forms for fine tuning the filehandles. See the `open` entry in Chapter 3 of *Programming Perl*, or in *perlfunc*(1).

When the subroutine exits, whatever was executing resumes as if nothing had happened (except for the actions performed by the subroutine, if any).

Typically, the signal-catching subroutine will do one of two things: abort the program after executing some cleanup code, or set some flag (such as a global variable) that the program routinely checks.*

You need to know the signal names to register a signal handler with Perl. By registering a signal handler, Perl will call the selected subroutine when the signal is received.

Signal names are defined in the *signal*(2) manpage, and usually also in the C include file */usr/include/sys/signal.h*. Names generally start with `SIG`, such as `SIGINT`, `SIGQUIT`, and `SIGKILL`. To declare the subroutine `my_sigint_catcher()` as the signal handler to deal with the `SIGINT`, we set a value into the magic `%SIG` hash. In this hash, we set the value of the key `INT` (that's `SIGINT` without the `SIG`) to the name of the subroutine that will catch the `SIGINT` signal, like so:

```
$SIG{'INT'} = 'my_sigint_catcher';
```

But we also need a definition for that subroutine. Here's a simple one:

```
sub my_sigint_catcher {
    $saw_sigint = 1; # set a flag
}
```

This signal catcher sets a global variable and then returns immediately. Returning from this subroutine causes execution to resume wherever it was interrupted. Typically, you'd first zero the **$saw_sigint** flag, set this subroutine up as a `SIGINT` catcher, and then do your long-running routine, like so:

```
$saw_sigint = 0;                    # clear the flag
$SIG{'INT'} = 'my_sigint_catcher'; # register the catcher
foreach (@huge_array) {
                                    # do something
                                    # do more things
                                    # do still more things
    if ($saw_sigint) {             # interrupt wanted?
                                    # some sort of cleanup here
        last;
    }
}
$SIG{'INT'} = 'DEFAULT'; # restore the default action
```

---

* In fact, doing anything more complicated than this is likely to mess things up; most of Perl's inner workings do not like to be executed in the main program and from the subroutine at the same time. Neither do your system libraries.

The trick here is that the value of the flag is checked at useful points during the evaluation and is used to exit the loop prematurely, here also handling some cleanup actions. Note the last statement in the preceding code: setting the action to DEFAULT restores the default action on a particular signal (another SIGINT will abort the program immediately). Another useful special value like this is IGNORE, meaning to ignore the signal (if the default action is not to ignore the signal, like SIGINT). You can make a signal action IGNORE if no cleanup actions are required, and you don't want to terminate operations early.

One of the ways that the SIGINT signal is generated is by having the user press the selected interrupt character (like CTRL-C) on the terminal. But a process can also generate the SIGINT signal directly using the kill function. This function takes a signal number or name, and sends that signal to the list of processes (identified by process ID) following the signal. So sending a signal from a program requires determining the process IDs of the recipient processes. (Process IDs are returned from some of the functions, such as fork and—when opening a program as a filehandle—open). Suppose you want to send a signal 2 (also known as SIGINT) to the processes 234 and 237. It's as simple as this:

```
kill(2,234,237); # send SIGINT to 234 and 237
kill ('INT', 234, 237); #same
```

For more about signal handling, see Chapter 6 of *Programming Perl* or the *perlipc*(1) manpage.

Exercises

See Appendix A for answers.

1. Write a program to parse the output of the *date* command to get the current day of the week. If the day of the week is a weekday, print get to work, otherwise print go play.

2. Write a program that gets all of the real names of the users from the */etc/passwd* file, then transforms the output of the *who* command, replacing the login name (the first column) with the real name. (Hint: create a hash where the key is the login name and the value is the real name.) Try this both with the *who* command in backquotes and opened as a pipe. Which was easier?

3. Modify the previous program so that the output automatically goes to the printer. (If you can't access a printer, perhaps you can send yourself mail.)

4. Suppose the mkdir function were broken. Write a subroutine that doesn't use mkdir, but invokes /bin/mkdir with system instead. (Be sure that it works with directories that have a space in the name.)

5. Extend the routine from the previous exercise to employ chmod to set the permissions.

Other Data Transformation

Finding a Substring

Finding a substring depends on where you have lost it. If you happen to have lost it within a bigger string, you're in luck, because `index` can help you out. Here's how it looks:

```
$x = index($string, $substring);
```

Perl locates the first occurrence of *substring* within *string*, returning an integer location of the first character. The index value returned is zero-based; if the *substring* is found at the beginning of the *string*, you get a 0. If it's one character later, you get a 1, and so on. If the *substring* can't be found in *string*, you get -1.

Take a look at these:

```
$where   = index("hello","e");              # $where gets 1
$person  = "barney";
$where   = index("fred barney",$person);    # $where gets 5
@rockers = ("fred","barney");
$where   = index(join(" ",@rockers),$person); # same thing
```

Notice that both the string being searched and the string being searched for can be a literal string, a scalar variable containing a string, or even an expression that has a string value. Here are some more examples:

```
$which = index("a very long string","long"); # $which gets 7
$which = index("a very long string","lame"); # $which gets -1
```

If the string contains the substring at more than one location, the `index` function returns the leftmost location. To find later locations, you can give `index` a third parameter. This parameter is the minimum value that will be returned by `index`, allowing you to look for the next occurrence of the substring that follows a selected position. It looks like this:

```
$x = index($bigstring, $littlestring, $skip);
```

Here are some examples of how this third parameter works:

```
$where = index("hello world","l");    # returns 2 (first l)
$where = index("hello world","l",0); # same thing
$where = index("hello world","l",1); # still same
$where = index("hello world","l",3); # now returns 3
                        # (3 is the first place greater than or equal to 3)
$where = index("hello world","o",5); # returns 7 (second o)
$where = index("hello world","o",8); # returns -1 (none after 8)
```

Going the other way, you can scan from the right to get the rightmost occurrence using **rindex**. The return value is still the number of characters between the left end of the string and the start of the substring, as before, but you'll get the rightmost occurrence instead of the leftmost occurrence if there are more than one. The **rindex** function also takes a third parameter like **index** does, so that you can get an occurrence that is less than or equal to a selected position. Here are some examples of what you get:

```
$w = rindex("hello world","he");  # $w gets 0
$w = rindex("hello world","l");   # $w gets 9 (rightmost l)
$w = rindex("hello world","o");   # $w gets 7
$w = rindex("hello world","o ");  # now $w gets 4
$w = rindex("hello world","xx");  # $w gets -1 (not found)
$w = rindex("hello world","o",6); # $w gets 4 (first before 6)
$w = rindex("hello world","o",3); # $w gets -1 (not found before 3)
```

Extracting and Replacing a Substring

Pulling out a piece of a string can be done with careful application of regular expressions, but if the piece is always at a known character position, this is inefficient. Instead, you should use **substr**. This function takes three arguments: a string value, a start position (measured like it was measured for **index**), and a length, like so:

```
$s = substr($string, $start, $length);
```

The start position works like **index**: the first character is zero, the second character is one, and so on. The length is the number of characters to grab at that point: a length of zero means no characters, one means get the first character, two means two characters, and so on. (It stops at the end of the string, so if you ask for too many, it's no problem.) It looks like this:

```
$hello = "hello, world!";
$grab  = substr($hello, 3, 2);   # $grab gets "lo"
$grab  = substr($hello, 7, 100); # 7 to end, or "world!"
```

You could even create a "ten to the power of" operator for small integer powers, as in:

```
$big = substr("10000000000",0,$power+1); # 10 ** $power
```

If the count of characters is zero, an empty string is returned. If either the starting position or ending position is less than zero, the position is counted that many characters from the end of the string. So -1 for a start position and 1 (or more) for the length gives you the last character. Similarly, -2 for a start position starts with the second-to-last character like this:

```
$stuff = substr("a very long string",-3,3); # last three chars
$stuff = substr("a very long string",-3,1); # the letter "i"
```

If the starting position is before the beginning of the string (like a huge negative number bigger than the length of the string), the beginning of the string is the start position (as if you had used 0 for a starting position). If the start position is a huge positive number, the empty string is always returned. In other words, it probably does what you expect it to do, as long as you expect it to always return something other than an error.

Omitting the length argument is the same as if you had included a huge number for that argument—grabbing everything from the selected position to the end of the string.*

If the first argument to `substr` is a scalar variable (in other words, it could appear on the left side of an assignment operator), then the `substr` itself can appear on the left side of an assignment operator. This may look strange if you come from a C background, but if you've ever played with some dialects of BASIC, it's quite normal.

What gets changed as the result of such an assignment is the part of the string that would have been returned had the `substr` been used on the right-hand side of the expression instead. In other words, `substr($var,3,2)` returns the fourth and fifth characters (starting at 3, for a count of 2), so assigning to that changes those two characters for `$var` like so:

```
$hw = "hello world!";
substr($hw, 0, 5) = "howdy"; # $hw is now "howdy world!"
```

The length of the replacement text (what gets assigned into the `substr`) doesn't have to be the same as the text it is replacing, as it was in this example. The string will automatically grow or shrink as necessary to accommodate the text. Here's an example where the string gets shorter:

---

* Very old Perl versions did not allow the third argument to be omitted, leading to the use of a huge number for that argument by pioneer Perl programmers. You may come across this in your Perl archeological expeditions.

```
substr($hw, 0, 5) = "hi"; # $hw is now "hi world!"
```

and here's one that makes it longer:

```
substr($hw, -6, 5) = "nationwide news"; # replaces "world"
```

The shrinking and growing are fairly efficient, so don't worry about using them arbitrarily, although it is faster to replace a string with a string of equal length.

Formatting Data with sprintf( )

The `printf` function is sometimes handy when used to take a list of values and produce an output line that displays the values in controllable ways. The `sprintf` function is identical to `printf` for its arguments, but returns whatever would have been output by `printf` as a single string. (Think of it as "string `printf`.") For example, to create a string consisting of the letter X followed by a five-digit zero-padded value of $y, it's as easy as this:

```
$result = sprintf("X%05d",$y);
```

See the `sprintf` entry in Chapter 3 of *Programming Perl*, and the *printf*(3) manpage (if you have it) for a description of the arguments required by `sprintf`.

Advanced Sorting

Earlier, you learned that you could take a list and sort it in ascending ASCII order (like you do strings) using the built-in `sort` function. What if you don't want an ascending ASCII sort, but something else instead, like a numeric sort? Well, Perl gives you the tools you need to do the job. In fact, you'll see that the Perl `sort` is completely general and able to perform any well-defined sort order.

To define a sort of a different color, you need to define a comparison routine that describes how two elements compare. Why is this necessary? Well, if you think about it, sorting is putting a bunch of things in order by comparing them all. Since you can't compare them all at once, you need to compare two at a time, eventually using what you find out about each pair's order to put the whole kit'n'caboodle in line.

The comparison routine is defined as an ordinary subroutine. This routine will be called repeatedly, each time passing two elements of the list to be sorted. The routine must determine whether the first value is less-than, equal-to, or greater-than the second value, and return a coded value (described in a moment). This process is repeated until the list is sorted.

To save a little execution speed, the two values are not passed in an array, but rather are handed to the subroutine as the values of the global variables $a and

$b. (Don't worry: the original values of $a and $b are safely protected.) The routine should return any negative number if $a is less than $b, zero if $a is equal to $b, and any positive number if $a is greater than $b. Now remember, the less than is according to your meaning of less than; it could be a numeric comparison, according to the third character of the string, or even according to the values of a hash using the passed-in values as keys. It's really pretty flexible.

Here's an example of a comparison routine that sorts in numeric order:

```
sub by_number {
    if ($a < $b) {
        return -1;
    } elsif ($a == $b) {
        return 0;
    } elsif ($a > $b) {
        return 1;
    }
}
```

Notice the name **by_number**. There's nothing special about the name of this subroutine, but you'll see why we like names that start with **by_** in a minute.

Let's look through this routine. If the value of $a is less than (numerically in this case) the value of $b, we return a –1 value. If the values are numerically equal, we get back a zero, and otherwise a 1. So, according to our specification for a sort comparison routine, this should work.

How do we use it? Let's try sorting the following list:

```
@somelist = (1,2,4,8,16,32,64,128,256);
```

If we use the ordinary **sort** without any adornment on the list, we get the numbers sorted as if they were strings, and in their ASCII order, like so:

```
@wronglist - sort @somelist;
# @wronglist is now (1,128,16,2,256,32,4,64,8)
```

Certainly not very numeric. Well, let's give **sort** our newly defined comparison routine. The name of the comparison routine goes immediately following the **sort** keyword, like so:

```
@rightlist = sort by_number @wronglist;
# @rightlist is now (1,2,4,8,16,32,64,128,256)
```

This does the trick. Note that you can read the **sort** with its companion sort routine in a human-like fashion: "sort by number." That's why I named the subroutine with a **by_** prefix.

This kind of three-way value of –1, 0, and +1 on the basis of a numeric comparison occurs often enough in sort routines that Perl has a special operator to do this in one fell swoop. It's often called the *spaceship* operator, and looks like <=>.

Using the spaceship operator, the preceding sort subroutine can be replaced with
this:

```
sub by_number {
    $a <=> $b;
}
```

Note the spaceship between the two variables. Yes, it is indeed a three-character-
long operator. The spaceship returns the same values as the `if/elsif` chain
from the previous definition of this routine. Now this is pretty short, but you can
shortcut the sort invocation even further, by replacing the name of the sort
routine with the entire sort routine in line, like so:

```
@rightlist = sort { $a <=> $b } @wronglist;
```

There are some who argue that this decreases readability. They are wrong. Others
argue that it removes the need to go somewhere else for the definition. Perl
doesn't care. Our personal rule is that if it doesn't fit on one line or we have to
use it more than once, it goes into a subroutine.

The spaceship operator for numeric comparison has a comparable string operator
called `cmp`. The `cmp` operator returns one of three values, depending on the relative string comparisons of the two arguments. So, here's another way to write the
default sort order:[*]

```
@result = sort { $a cmp $b } @somelist;
```

You probably won't ever write this exact subroutine (mimicking the built-in
default sort), unless you're writing a book about Perl. However, the `cmp` operator
does have its uses in the construction of cascaded ordering schemes. For
example, you might need to put the elements in numeric order unless they're
numerically equal, in which case they should go in ASCII string order. (By
default, the **by_number** routine above just sticks nonnumeric strings in some
random order because there's no numeric ordering when comparing two values
of zero.) Here's a way to say "numeric, unless they're numerically equal, then
string":

```
sub by_mostly_numeric {
    ($a <=> $b) || ($a cmp $b);
}
```

How does this work? Well, if the result of the spaceship is -1 or 1, the rest of the
expression is skipped, and the -1 or 1 is returned. If the spaceship evaluates to
zero, however, the `cmp` operator gets its turn at bat, returning an appropriate
ordering value considering the values as strings.

---

[*] Not exactly. The built-in sort discards `undef` elements, but this one doesn't.

The values being compared are not necessarily the values being passed in. For example, say you have a hash where the keys are the login names and the values are the real names of each user. Suppose you want to print a chart where the login names and real names are sorted in the order of the real names. How would you do that?

Actually, it's fairly easy. Let's assume the values are in the array `%names`. The login names are thus the list of `keys(%names)`. What we want to end up with is a list of the login names sorted by the corresponding value, so for any particular key `$a`, we need to look at `$names{$a}` and sort based on that. If you think of it that way, it almost writes itself, as in:

```
@sortedkeys = sort by_names keys(%names);

sub by_names {
    return $names{$a} cmp $names{$b};
}

foreach (@sortedkeys) {
    print "$_ has a real name of $names{$_}\n";
}
```

To this we should also add a fallback comparison. Suppose the real names of two users are identical. Because of the whimsical nature of the `sort` routine, we might get one value ahead of another the first time through and the values in the reversed order the next time. This is bad if the report might be fed into a comparison program for reporting, so try very hard to avoid such things. With the `cmp` operator, it's easy:

```
sub by_names {
    ($names{$a} cmp $names{$b}) || ($a cmp $b);
}
```

Here, if the real names are the same, we sort based on the login name instead. Since the login name is guaranteed to be unique (after all, they are the keys of this hash, and no two keys are the same), then we can ensure a unique and repeatable order. Good defensive programming during the day is better than a late-night call from a system administrator wondering why the security alarms are going off.

Transliteration

When you want to take a string and replace every instance of some character with some new character, or delete every instance of some character, you can already do that with carefully selected `s///` commands. But suppose you had to change all of the a's into b's, and all of the b's into a's? You can't do that with two `s///` commands because the second one would undo all of the changes the first one made.

From the UNIX shell, however, such a data transformation is simple: just use the standard *tr*(1) command:

```
tr ab ba <indata >outdata
```

(If you don't know anything about the *tr* command, please look at the *tr*(1) manpage; it's a useful tool for your bag of tricks.) Similarly, Perl provides a `tr` operator that works in much the same way:

```
tr/ab/ba/;
```

The `tr` operator takes two arguments: an *old string* and a *new string*. These arguments work like the two arguments to `s///`; in other words, there's some delimiter that appears immediately after the `tr` keyword that separates and terminates the two arguments (in this case, a slash, but nearly any character will do).

The arguments to the `tr` operator are similar to the arguments to the *tr*(1) command. The `tr` operator modifies the contents of the `$_` variable (just like `s///`), looking for characters of the old string within the `$_` variable. All such characters found are replaced with the corresponding characters in the new string. Here are some examples:

```
$_ = "fred and barney";
tr/fb/bf/;        # $_ is now "bred and farney"
tr/abcde/ABCDE/;  # $_ is now "BrED AnD fArnEy"
tr/a-z/A-Z/;      # $_ is now "BRED AND FARNEY"
```

Notice how a range of characters can be indicated by two characters separated by a dash. If you need a literal dash in either string, precede it with a backslash.

If the new string is shorter than the old string, the last character of the new string is repeated enough times to make the strings equal length, like so:

```
$_ = "fred and barney";
tr/a-z/x/; # $_ is now "xxxx xxx xxxxxx"
```

To prevent this behavior, append a `d` to the end of the `tr///` operator, meaning *delete*. In this case, the last character is not replicated. Any character that matches in the old string without a corresponding character in the new string is simply removed from the string.

```
$_ = "fred and barney";
tr/a-z/ABCDE/d; # $_ is now "ED AD BAE"
```

Notice how any letter after `e` disappears because there's no corresponding letter in the new list, and that spaces are unaffected because they don't appear in the old list. This is similar in operation to the `-d` option of the *tr* command.

If the new list is empty and there's no d option, the new list is the same as the old list. This may seem silly, as in why replace an I for an I and a 2 for a 2, but it actually does something useful. The return value of the tr/// operator is the number of characters matched by the old string, and by changing characters into themselves, you can get the count of that kind of character within the string.* For example:

```
$_ = "fred and barney";
$count = tr/a-z//;       # $_ unchanged, but $count is 13
$count2 = tr/a-z/A-Z/;   # $_ is uppercased, and $count2 is 13
```

If you append a c (like appending the d), it means to complement the old string with respect to all 256 characters. Any character you list in the old string is removed from the set of all possible characters; the remaining characters, taken in sequence from lowest to highest, form the resulting old string. So, a way to count or change the nonletters in our string could be:

```
$_ = "fred and barney";
$count = tr/a-z//c; # $_ unchanged, but $count is 2
tr/a-z/_/c;         # $_ is now "fred_and_barney" (non-letters => _)
tr/a-z//cd;         # $_ is now "fredandbarney" (delete non-letters)
```

Notice that the options can be combined, as shown in that last example, where we first complement the set (the list of letters become the list of all nonletters) and then use the d option to delete any character in that set.

The final option for tr/// is s, which squeezes multiple consecutive copies of the same resulting translated letter into one copy. As an example, look at this:

```
$_ = "aaabbbcccdefghi";
tr/defghi/abcddd/s; # $_ is now "aaabbbcccabcd"
```

Note that the def became abc, and ghi (which would have become ddd without the s option) becomes a single d. Also note that the consecutive letters at the first part of the string are not squeezed because they didn't result from a translation. Here are some more examples:

```
$_ = "fred and barney, wilma and betty";
tr/a-z/X/s;  # $_ is now "X X X, X X X"
$_ = "fred and barney, wilma and betty";
tr/a-z/_/cs; # $_ is now "fred_and_barney_wilma_and_betty"
```

In the first example, each word (consecutive letters) was squeezed down to a single letter X. In the second example, all chunks of consecutive nonletters became a single underscore.

---

* This works only for single characters. To count strings, use the /g flag to a pattern match:
```
while (/pattern/g) {
    $count++;
}
```

Like `s///`, the `tr` operator can be targeted at another string besides `$_` using the
`=~` operator:

```
$names = "fred and barney";
$names =~ tr/aeiou/X/; # $names now "frXd Xnd bXrnXy"
```

Exercises

See Appendix A for answers.

1. Write a program to read a list of filenames, breaking each name into its head
   and tail components. (Everything up to the last slash is the head, and everything after the last slash is the tail. If there's no slash, it's *all* in the tail.) Try
   this with things like */fred*, *barney*, and *fred/barney*. Do the results make sense?

2. Write a program to read in a list of numbers on separate lines, and sort them
   numerically, printing out the resulting list in a right-justified column. (Hint:
   the format to print a right-justified column is something like `%20g`.)

3. Write a program to print the real names and login names of the users in the
   /etc/passwd file, sorted by the last name of each user. Does your solution
   work if two people have the same last name?

4. Create a file that consists of sentences, one per line. Write a program that
   makes the first character of each sentence uppercase and the rest of the
   sentence lowercase. (Does it work even when the first character is not a
   letter? How would you do this if the sentences were not already one per line?)

16

System Database Access

Getting Password and Group Information

The information that the UNIX system keeps about your username and user ID is fairly public. In fact, nearly everything but your unencrypted password is available for perusal by any program that cares to scan the */etc/passwd* file. This file has a particular format, defined in *passwd*(5), which looks something like this:

```
name:passwd:uid:gid:gcos:dir:shell
```

The fields are defined as follows:

name
    The login name of the user

passwd
    The encrypted password, or something simple if a shadow password file is being used

uid
    The user ID number (0 for **root**, nonzero for normal users)

gid
    The default login group (group 0 may be privileged, but not necessarily)

gcos
    The GCOS field, which typically contains the user's full name followed by a comma and some other information

dir
    The home directory (where you go when you type *cd* without any arguments and where most of your "dot-files" are kept)

`shell`

> Your login shell, typically */bin/sh* or */bin/csh* (or maybe even */usr/bin/perl*, if you're crazy)

A typical portion of the password file looks like this:

```
fred:*:123:15:Fred Flintstone,,,:/home/fred:/bin/csh
barney:*:125:15:Barney Rubble,,,:/home/barney:/bin/csh
```

Now, Perl has enough tools to parse this kind of line easily (using `split`, for example), without drawing on special purpose routines. But the UNIX programing library does have a set of special routines: *getpwent*(3), *getpwuid*(3), *getpwnam*(3), and so on. These routines are available in Perl using the same names and similar arguments and return values.

For example, the *getpwnam* routine becomes the Perl `getpwnam` function. The single argument is a username (like `fred` or `barney`), and the return value is the */etc/passwd* line split apart into a list with the following values:

```
($name, $passwd, $uid, $gid, $quota, $comment,
 $gcos, $dir, $shell)
```

Note that there are few more values here than in the password file. For every UNIX system we've seen, the `$quota` field is always empty, and the `$comment` and the `$gcos` field often both contain the entire GCOS field. So, for good old `fred`, you get

```
("fred", "*", 123, 15, "", "Fred Flintstone,,,",
 "Fred Flintstone,,,", "/home/fred"," /bin/csh")
```

by invoking either of the following two calls:

```
getpwuid(123)
getpwnam("fred")
```

Note that `getpwuid` takes a UID number, while `getpwnam` takes the login name as its argument.

The `getpwnam` and `getpwuid` functions also have a return value when called in a scalar sense. They each return the thing you've asked them to get. For example:

```
$idnum = getpwuid("daemon");
$login = getpwnam(25);
```

You'll probably want to pick this apart, using some of the list operations that we've seen before. One way is to grab a part of the list using a list slice, such as getting just the home directory for Fred using:

```
($fred_home) = (getpwnam ("fred"))[7]; # put Fred's home
```

How would you scan through the entire password file? Well, you could do something like this:

```
for($id = 0; $id <= 10_000; $id++)     {
    @stuff = getpwuid $id;
} ### not recommended!
```

But this is probably the wrong way to go. Just because there's more than one way
to do it doesn't mean that all ways are equally cool.

You can think of the `getpwuid` and `getpwnam` functions as *random access*;
they grab a specific entry by key, so you have to have a key to start with. Another
way of accessing the password file is *sequential access*—grabbing each entry one
at a time.

The sequential access routines for the password file are the `setpwent`, `getp-
went`, and `endpwent` functions. Together, these three functions perform a
sequential pass over all values in the password file. The `setpwent` function
initializes the scan at the beginning. After initialization, each call to `getpwent`
returns the next entry from the password file. When there is no more data to
process, `getpwent` returns an empty list. Finally, calling `endpwent` frees the
resources used by the scanner; this is performed automatically upon exiting the
program as well.

This description begs for an example, so here's one now:

```
setpwent();                                  # initialize the scan
while (@list = getpwent()) {                 # fetch the next entry
    ($login,$home) = @list[0,7];             # grab login name and home
    print "Home directory for $login is $home\n"; # say so
}
endpwent();                                  # all done
```

This example shows the home directory of everyone in the password file.
Suppose you wanted them alphabetically by home directory? We learned about
`sort` in the previous chapter, so let's use it:

```
setpwent();                       # initialize the scan
while (@list = getpwent()) {      # fetch the next entry
    ($login,$home) = @list[0,7];  # grab login name and home
    $home{$login} = $home;        # save it away
}
endpwent();                       # all done
@keys = sort { $home{$a} cmp $home{$b} } keys %home;
foreach $login (@keys) {          # step through the sorted names
    print "home of $login is $home{$login}\n";
}
```

This fragment, while a little longer, illustrates an important thing about scanning
sequentially through the password file; you can save away the pertinent portions
of the data in data structures of your choice. The first part of the example scans
through the entire password file, creating a hash where the key is the login name
and the value is the corresponding home directory for that login name. The `sort`

line takes the keys of the hash and sorts them according to string value. The final loop steps through the sorted keys, printing each value in turn.

Generally, you should use the random access routines (`getpwuid` and `getpwnam`) when you are looking up just a few values. For more than a few values, or even an exhaustive search, it's generally easier to do a sequential access pass (using `setpwent`, `getpwent`, and `endpwent`) and extract the particular values you'll be looking for into a hash.[*]

The */etc/group* file is accessed in a similar way. Sequential access is provided with the `setgrent`, `getgrent`, and `endgrent` calls. The `getgrent` call returns values of the form:

```
($name, $passwd, $gid, $members)
```

These four values correspond roughly to the four fields of the */etc/group* file, so see the descriptions in the manpages about this file format for details. The corresponding random access functions are `getgrgid` (by group ID) and `getgrnam` (by group name).

Packing and Unpacking Binary Data

The password and group information is nicely represented in textual form. Other system databases are more naturally represented in other forms. For example, the IP address of an interface is internally managed as a four-byte number. While it is frequently decoded into a textual representation consisting of four small integers separated by periods, this encoding and decoding is wasted effort if a human is not interpreting the data in the meantime.

Because of this, the network routines in Perl that expect or return an IP address use a four-byte string that contains one character for each sequential byte in memory. While constructing and interpreting such a byte string is fairly straightforward using `chr` and `ord` (not presented here), Perl provides a short cut that is equally applicable to more difficult structures.

The `pack` function works a bit like `sprintf`, taking a format control string and a list of values, and creating a single string from those values. The `pack` format string is geared towards creating a binary data structure, however. For example, here's how to take four small integers and pack them as successive unsigned bytes in a composite string:

```
$buf = pack("CCCC", 140, 186, 65, 25);
```

---

[*] If you're on a site with a large NIS map, you probably do not want to preprocess the password file this way for performance reasons.

Here, the `pack` format string is four C's. Each C represents a separate value taken from the following list (similar to what a `%` field does in `sprintf`). The C format (according to the Perl manpages, the reference card, *Programming Perl*, the HTML files, or even *Perl: The Motion Picture*) refers to a single byte computed from an unsigned character value (a small integer). The resulting string in `$buf` is a four-character string—each character being one byte from the four values `140`, `186`, `65`, and `25`.

Similarly, the format `l` generates a signed long value. On many machines, this is a four-byte number, although this format is machine-dependent. On a four-byte "long" machine, the statement

```
$buf = pack("l",0x41424344);
```

generates a four-character string that looks like either `ABCD` or `DCBA`, depending on whether the machine is little-endian or big-endian (or something entirely different if the machine doesn't speak ASCII). This happens because we are packing one value into four characters (the length of a long integer), and the one value just happens to be composed of the bytes representing the ASCII values for the first four letters of the alphabet. Similarly,

```
$buf = pack("ll", 0x41424344, 0x45464748);
```

creates an eight-byte string consisting of `ABCDEFGH` or `DCBAHGFE`, once again depending on whether the machine is little- or big-endian.

The exact list of the various `pack` formats is given in the reference documentation (*perlfunc*(1), or *Programming Perl*). You'll see a few here as examples, but we're not going to list them all.

What if you were given the eight-byte string `ABCDEFGH` and were told that it was really the memory image (one character is one byte) of two long (four-byte) signed values? How would you interpret it? Well, you'd need to do the inverse of `pack`, called `unpack`. This function takes a format control string (usually identical to the one you'd give `pack`) and a data string, and returns a list of values that make up the memory image defined in the data string. For example, let's take that string apart:

```
($val1,$val2) = unpack("ll","ABCDEFGH");
```

This gives us back something like `0x41424344` for `$val1`, or possibly `0x44434241` instead (depending on big-endian-ness). In fact, by the values that come back, we can determine if we are on a little- or big-endian machine.

Whitespace in the format control string is ignored, and can be used for readability. A number in the format control string generally repeats the previous specification that many times. For example, `CCCC` can also be written `C4` or `C2C2` with no change in meaning. (A few of the specifications use a trailing number as a part of the specification, and thus cannot be multiplied like that.)

A format character can also be followed by a *, which repeats the format character enough times to swallow up the rest of the list or the rest of the binary image string (depending on whether you are packing or unpacking). So, here's another way to pack four unsigned characters into a string:

```
$buf = pack("C*", 140, 186, 65, 25);
```

The four values here are swallowed up by the one format specification. If you had wanted two short integers followed by "as many unsigned chars as possible," you can say something like this:

```
$buf = pack("s2 C*", 3141, 5926, 5, 3, 5, 8, 9, 7, 9, 3, 2);
```

Here, we take the first two values as shorts (generating four or eight characters, probably) and the remaining nine values as unsigned characters (generating nine characters, almost certainly).

Going in the other direction, **unpack** with an asterisk specification can generate a list of elements of unpredetermined length. For example, unpacking with C* creates one list element (a number) for each string character. So, the statement

```
@values = unpack("C*", "hello, world!\n");
```

yields a list of 14 elements, one for each of the characters of the string.

Getting Network Information

Perl supports network programming in a way that is very familiar to those who have written network code in C programs. In fact, most of the Perl functions that provide network access have the same names and similar parameters as their C counterparts. We can't teach a complete course on network programming in this chapter, but let's look at one of the task fragments to see how it's done in Perl.

One of the things you need to find out is the address that goes with a name, or vice versa. In C, you use the *gethostbyname*(3) routine to convert a network name to a network address. You then use this address to create a connection from your program to another program somewhere else.

The Perl function to translate a hostname to an address has the same name and similar parameters as the C routine, and looks like this:

```
($name, $aliases, $addrtype, $length, @addrs) =
    gethostbyname($name); # generic form of gethostbyname
```

The parameter to this function is a hostname, e.g., **slate.bedrock.com**. The return value is a list of four or more parameters, depending on how many addresses are associated with the name. If the hostname is not valid, the function returns an empty list.

If `gethostbyname` is called in a scalar context, only the (first) address is returned.

When `gethostbyname` completes successfully, `$name` is the *canonical name*, which differs from the input name if the input name is an alias. `$aliases` are a list of space-separated names by which the host is also known. `$addrtype` gives a coded value to indicate the form of the addresses. In this case, for `slate.bedrock.com`, we can presume that the value indicates an IP address, usually represented as four numbers under 256, separated by dots. `$length` gives the number of addresses, which is actually redundant information since you can look at the length of `@addrs` anyway.

But the useful part of the return value is `@addrs`. Each element of the list is a separate IP address, stored in an internal format, handled in Perl as a four-character string.* While this four-character string is exactly what other Perl networking functions are looking for, suppose we wanted to print out the result for the user to see. In this case, we need to convert the return value into a human-readable format with the assistance of the **unpack** function and a little additional massaging. Here's code that prints one of `slate.bedrock.com`'s IP addresses:

```
($addr) = (gethostbyname("slate.bedrock.com"))[4];
print "Slate's address is ",
    join(".",unpack("C4", $addr)), "\n";
```

`unpack` takes the four-byte string and returns four numbers. These just happen to be in the right order for `join` to glue in a dot between each pair of numbers to make the human-readable form. See Appendix C, *Networking Clients*, for information about building simple networking clients.

Exercise

See Appendix A for the answer.

1. Write a program to create a mapping of userIDs and real names from the password entries, then uses that map to show a list of real names that belong to each group in the group file. (Does your list include users who have a default group in the password entry but no explicit mention of that same group in the group entry? If not, how would you accomplish that?)

---

* Well, at least until IPv6.

17

User Database Manipulation

DBM Databases and DBM Hashes

Most UNIX systems have a standard library called DBM. This library provides a simple database management facility that allows programs to store a collection of key-value pairs into a pair of disk files. These files retain the values in the database between invocations of the programs using the database, and these programs can add new values, update existing values, or delete old values.

The DBM library is fairly simple, but being readily available, some system programs have used it for their fairly modest needs. For example, *sendmail* (and its variants and derivatives) stores the *aliases* database (the mapping of mail addresses to recipients) as a DBM database. The most popular Usenet news software uses a DBM database to track current and recently seen articles. The Sun NIS (*née* YP) database masters are also kept in DBM format.

Perl provides access to this same DBM mechanism through a rather clever means: a hash may be associated with a DBM database through a process similar to opening a file. This hash (called a *DBM array*) is then used to access and modify the DBM database. Creating a new element in the array modifies the DBM database immediately. Deleting an element deletes the value from the DBM database. And so on.*

The size, number, and kind of keys and values in a DBM database are restricted, and depending on which version of DBM library you're using, a DBM array may share these same restrictions. See the *AnyDBM_File* manpage for details. In

---

* This is actually just a special use of the general `tie` mechanism. If you want something more flexible, check out the *AnyDBM_File*(3), *DB_File*(3), and *perltie*(1) manpages.

general, if you keep both the keys and the values down to 1000 arbitrary binary characters or less, you'll probably be OK.

Opening and Closing DBM Hashes

To associate a DBM database with a DBM array, use the **dbmopen** function, which looks like this:

```
dbmopen(%ARRAYNAME, "dbmfilename", $mode);
```

The **%ARRAYNAME** parameter is a Perl hash. (If this hash already has values, the values are discarded.) This hash becomes connected to the DBM database called *dbmfilename*, usually stored on disk as a pair of files called *dbmfilename.dir* and *dbmfilename.pag*.

The *$mode* parameter is a number that controls the permission bits of the pair of files if the files need to be created. The number is typically specified in octal: the frequently used value of 0644 gives read-only permission to everyone but the owner, who gets read-write permission. If the files already exist, this parameter has no effect. For example:

```
dbmopen(%FRED, "mydatabase", 0644); # open %FRED onto mydatabase
```

This invocation associates the hash **%FRED** with the disk files *mydatabase.dir* and *mydatabase.pag* in the current directory. If the files don't already exist, they are created with a mode of 0644 modified by the current umask.

The return value from the **dbmopen** is true if the database could be opened or created, and false otherwise, just like an **open** invocation. If you don't want the files created, use a *$mode* value of **undef**. For example:

```
dbmopen(%A,"/etc/xx",undef) || die "cannot open DBM /etc/xx";
```

In this case, if the files */etc/xx.dir* and */etc/xx.pag* cannot be opened, the **dbmopen** call returns false, rather than attempting to create the files.

The DBM array stays open throughout the program. When the program terminates, the association is terminated. You can also break the association in a manner similar to closing a filehandle, by using the **dbmclose** function:

```
dbmclose(%A);
```

Like **close**, **dbmclose** returns false if something goes wrong.

Using a DBM Hash

Once the database is opened, accesses to the DBM hash are mapped into references to the database. Changing or adding a value in the hash causes the corresponding entries to be immediately written into the disk files. For example, once %FRED is opened from the earlier example, we can add, delete, or access elements of the database, like this:

```
$FRED{"fred"} = "bedrock";  # create (or update) an element
delete $FRED{"barney"};     # remove an element of the database
foreach $key (keys %FRED) { # step through all values
    print "$key has value of $FRED{$key}\n";
}
```

That last loop has to scan through the entire disk file twice: once to access the keys, and a second time to look up the values from the keys. If you are scanning through a DBM hash, it's generally more disk-efficient to use the each operator, which makes only one pass:

```
while (($key, $value) = each(%FRED)) {
    print "$key has value of $value\n";
}
```

If you are accessing system DBM databases, such as the ones created by *sendmail* or NIS, you must be aware that dubiously written C programs sometimes tack on a trailing NUL (\0) character to the end of their strings. The DBM library routines do not need this NUL (they handle binary data using a byte count, not a NUL-delimited string), and so the NUL is stored as part of the data. You must therefore append a NUL character to the end of your keys and discard the NUL from the end of the returned values to have the data make sense. For example, to look up merlyn in the aliases database, try something like this:

```
dbmopen(%ALI, "/etc/aliases", undef) || die "no aliases?";
$value = $ALI{"merlyn\0"};                   # note appended NUL
chop($value);                                # remove appended NUL
print "Randal's mail is headed for: $value\n"; # show result
```

Your version of UNIX may stick the aliases database over in */usr/lib* rather than */etc*. You'll have to poke around to find out. Newer versions of *sendmail* are free of the NUL bug.

Fixed-Length Random Access Databases

Another form of persistent data is the fixed-length, record-oriented disk file. In this scheme, the data consists of a number of records of identical length. The numbering of the records is either not important or determined by some indexing scheme.

For example, we might have a series of records in which the data has 40 characters of first name, a one-character middle initial, 40 characters of last name, and then a two-byte integer for the age. Each record is then 83 bytes long. If we were reading all of the data in the database, we'd read chunks of 83 bytes until we got to the end. If we wanted to go to the fifth record, we'd skip ahead four times 83 bytes (332 bytes) and read the fifth record directly.

Perl supports programs that use such a disk file. A few things are necessary in addition to what you already know:

1. Opening a disk file for both reading and writing

2. Moving around in this file to an arbitrary position

3. Fetching data by a length rather than up to the next newline

4. Writing data down in fixed-length blocks

The **open** function takes an additional plus sign before its I/O direction specification to indicate that the file is really being opened for both reading and writing. For example:

```
open(A,"+<b");   # open file b read/write (error if file absent)
open(C,"+>d");   # create file d, with read/write access
open(E,"+>>f");  # open or create file f with read/write access
```

Notice that all we've done was to prepend a plus sign to the I/O direction.

Once we've got the file open, we need to move around in it. We do this with the **seek** function, which takes the same three parameters as the *fseek*(3) library routine. The first parameter is a filehandle; the second parameter gives an offset, which is interpreted in conjunction with the third parameter. Usually, you'll want the third parameter to be zero so that the second parameter selects a new absolute position for next read from or write to the file. For example, to go to the fifth record on the filehandle **NAMES** (as described above), you can do this:

```
seek(NAMES,4*83,0);
```

Once the file pointer has been repositioned, the next input or output will start there. For output, use the **print** function, but be sure that the data you are writing is the right length. To obtain the right length, we can call upon the **pack** function:

```
print NAMES pack("A40 A A40 s", $first, $middle, $last, $age);
```

That **pack** specifier gives 40 characters for **$first**, a single character for **$middle**, 40 more characters for **$last**, and a short (two bytes) for the **$age**. This should be 83 bytes long, and will be written at the current file position.

Last, we need to fetch a particular record. Although the **<NAMES>** construct returns all of the data from the current position to the next newline, that's not correct; the data is supposed to go for 83 bytes, and there probably isn't a newline right there. Instead, we use the **read** function, which looks and works a lot like its UNIX system call counterpart:

```
$count = read(NAMES, $buf, 83);
```

The first parameter for **read** is the filehandle. The second parameter is a scalar variable that holds the data that will be read. The third parameter gives the number of bytes to read. The return value from **read** is the number of bytes actually read; typically the same number as the number of bytes asked for unless the filehandle is not opened or you are too close to the end of the file.

Once you have the 83-character data, just break it into its component parts with the **unpack** function:

```
($first, $middle, $last, $age) = unpack("A40 A A40 s", $buf);
```

Note that the **pack** and **unpack** format strings are the same. Most programs store this string in a variable early in the program, and even compute the length of the records using **pack** instead of sprinkling the constant 83 everywhere:

```
$names = "A40 A A40 s";
$names_length = length(pack($names)); # probably 83
```

Variable-Length (Text) Databases

Many UNIX system databases (and quite a few user-created databases) are a series of human-readable text lines, with one record per line. For example, the password file consists of one line per user on the system, and the hosts file contains one line per hostname.

Most often, these databases are updated with simple text editors. Updating such a database consists of reading it all into a temporary area (either memory or another disk file), making the necessary changes, and then either writing the result back to the original file or creating a new file with the same name after deleting or renaming the old version. You can think of this as a *copy pass*: the data is copied from the original database to a new version of the database, making changes during the copy.

Perl supports a copy-pass-style edit on line-oriented databases using *inplace editing*. Inplace editing is a modification of the way the diamond operator (<>) reads data from the list of files specified on the command line. Most often, this editing mode is accessed by setting the *-i* command-line argument, but we can also trigger the inplace editing mode from within a program, as shown in the examples that follow.

To trigger the inplace editing mode, set a value into the $^I scalar variable. The value of this variable is important and will be discussed in a moment.

When the `<>` construct is used and `$^I` has a value other than **undef**, the steps marked `##INPLACE##` in the following code are added to the list of implicit actions the diamond operator takes:

```
$ARGV = shift @ARGV;
open(ARGV,"<$ARGV");
rename($ARGV,"$ARGV$^I");   ## INPLACE ##
unlink($ARGV);             ## INPLACE ##
open(ARGVOUT,">$ARGV");    ## INPLACE ##
select(ARGVOUT);          ## INPLACE ##
```

The effect is that reads from the diamond operator come from the old file, and writes to the default filehandle go to a new copy of the file. The old file remains in a backup file, which is the filename with a suffix equal to the value of the `$^I` variable. (There's also a bit of magic to copy the permission bits from the old file to the new file.) These steps are repeated each time a new file is taken from the `@ARGV` array.

Typical values for `$^I` are things like `.bak` or `~`, to create backup files much like the editor creates. A strange and useful value for `$^I` is the empty string, `""`, which causes the old file to be neatly eliminated after the edit is complete. Unfortunately, if the system or program crashes during the execution of your program, you lose all of your old data, so this is recommended only for brave, foolish, or trusting souls.

Here's a way to change everyone's login shell to */bin/sh* by editing the password file:

```
@ARGV = ("/etc/passwd");  # prime the diamond operator
$^I = ".bak";             # write /etc/passwd.bak for safety
while (<>) {              # main loop, once for each line of /etc/passwd
    s#:[^:]*$#:/bin/sh#;  # change the shell to /bin/sh
    print;               # send output to ARGVOUT: the new /etc/passwd
}
```

As you can see, this program is pretty simple. In fact, the same program can be generated entirely with a few command-line arguments, as in:

```
perl -p -i.bak -e 's#:[^:]*$#:/bin/sh#' /etc/passwd
```

The `-p` switch brackets your program with a **while** loop that includes a **print** statement. The `-i` switch sets a value into the `$^I` variable. The `-e` switch defines the following argument as a piece of Perl code for the loop body, and the final argument gives an initial value to `@ARGV`.

Command-line arguments are discussed in greater detail in *Programming Perl* and the *perlrun* manpage.

Exercises

See Appendix A for answers.

1. Create a program to open the *sendmail* alias database and print out all the entries.

2. Create two programs: one that reads the data from <>, splits it into words, and updates a DBM file noting the number of occurrences of each word; and another program to open the DBM file and display the results sorted by descending count. Run the first program on a few files and see if the second program picks up the proper counts.

18

Converting Other Languages to Perl

Converting awk Programs to Perl

One of the many cool things about Perl is that it is (at least) a semantic superset of *awk*. In practical terms, this means if you can do something in *awk*, you can also do it somehow in Perl. However, Perl isn't *syntactically* compatible with *awk*. For example, *awk*'s NR (input record number) variable is represented as $. in Perl.

If you have an existing *awk* program, and wish it to run with Perl, you can perform a mechanical translation using the *a2p* utility provided with the Perl distribution. This utility converts the *awk* syntax into the Perl syntax, and for the vast majority of *awk* programs, provides a directly runnable Perl script.

To use the *a2p* utility, put your *awk* program into a separate file and invoke *a2p* with the name of the file as its argument, or redirect the standard input of *a2p* to the file. The resulting standard output will be a valid Perl program. For example:

```
$ cat myawkprog
BEGIN { sum = 0 }
/llama/ { sum += $2 }
END { print "The llama count is " sum }
$ a2p <myawkprog >myperlprog
$ perl myperlprog somefile
The llama count is 15
$
```

You can also feed the standard output of *a2p* directly into Perl, because the Perl interpreter accepts a program on standard input if so instructed:

```
$ a2p <myawkprog | perl - somefile
The llama count is 15
$
```

An *awk* script converted to Perl will generally perform the identical function, often with an increase in speed, and certainly without any of *awk*'s built-in limits on line lengths or parameter counts or whatever. A few converted Perl programs may actually run slower; the equivalent action in Perl for a given *awk* operation may not necessarily be the most efficient Perl code if one was programming from scratch.

You may choose to hand-optimize the converted Perl code, or add new functionality to the Perl version of the program. This is fairly easy, because the Perl code is rather readable (considering that the translation is automatic, this is quite an accomplishment).

A few translations are not mechanical. For example, the less-than comparison for both numbers and strings in *awk* is expressed with the < operator. In Perl, you have lt for strings and < for numbers. *awk* generally makes a reasonable guess about the number-ness or string-ness of two values being compared, and the *a2p* utility makes a similar guess. However, it's possible that there isn't enough known about two values to determine whether a number or a string comparison is warranted, so *a2p* outputs the most likely operator and marks the possibly erroneous line with #?? (a Perl comment) and an explanation. Be sure to scan the output for such comments after conversion to verify the proper guesses. For more details about the operation of *a2p*, consult its manpage. If *a2p* is not found in the same directory that you get Perl from, complain loudly to your Perl installer.

Converting sed Programs to Perl

Well, this may begin to sound like a repeat, but guess what? Perl is a semantic superset of *sed* as well as *awk*.

And with the distribution comes a *sed*-to-Perl translator called *s2p*. As with *a2p*, *s2p* takes a *sed* script on standard input and writes a Perl program on standard output. Unlike *a2p*, the converted program rarely misbehaves, so you can pretty much count on it working, barring any bugs in *s2p* or Perl.

Converted *sed* programs may work faster or slower than the original, but are generally much faster (thanks to the highly optimized regular expression routines of Perl).

The converted *sed* script can operate either with or without a -n option, having the same meaning as the corresponding switch for *sed*. To do this, the converted script must feed itself into the C preprocessor, and this slows down the startup a little bit. If you know that you will always invoke the converted *sed* script with or without a -n option (such as when you are converting a *sed* script used in a larger shell program with known arguments), you can inform *s2p* (via the -n and -p switches), and it will optimize the script for that switch setting.

As an example of how versatile and powerful Perl is, the *s2p* translator is written in Perl. If you want to see how Larry codes in Perl (even though it's very ancient code relatively unchanged since Perl Version 2), take a look at the translator. Be sure you are sitting down.

Converting Shell Programs to Perl

Heh. Thought there'd be a shell-to-Perl translator, eh?

Nope. Many have asked for such a beast, but the real problem is that most of what a shell script does is not done by the shell. Most shell scripts spend practically all of their time calling separate programs to extract pieces of strings, compare numbers, concatenate files, remove directories, and so forth and so on. Converting such a script to Perl would either require understanding the operation of each of the called utilities, or leave Perl calling each of the utilities, which gains nothing.

So, the best you can do is stare at a shell script, figure out what it does, and start from scratch with Perl. Of course, you can do a quick-and-dirty transliteration, by putting major portions of the original script inside system() calls or backquotes. You might be able to replace some of the operations with native Perl: for example, replace system(rm fred) with unlink(fred), or a shell for loop with a Perl for loop. But generally you'll find it's a bit like converting a COBOL program into C (with about the same reduction in the number of characters and increase in illegibility).

Exercise

See Appendix A for the answer.

1. Convert the following shell script into a Perl program:

```
cat /etc/passwd |
awk -F: '{print $1, $6}' |
while read user home
do
  newsrc="$home/.newsrc"
  if [ -r $newsrc ]
  then
    if grep -s '^comp\.lang\.perl\.announce:' $newsrc
    then
      echo -n "$user is a good person, ";
      echo "and reads comp.lang.perl.announce!"
    fi
  fi
done
```

19

CGI Programming

Unless you've been holed up in a log cabin without electricity for the last few years, you've heard of the World Wide Web. Web addresses (better known as URLs) pop up everywhere from billboards to movie credits, from magazines and newspapers to government reports.

Many of the more interesting web pages include some sort of entry form. You supply input to this form and click on a button or picture. This fires up a program at the web server that examines your input and generates new output. Sometimes this program (commonly known as a *CGI* program) is just an interface to an existing database, massaging your input into something the database understands and massaging the database's output into something a web browser can understand (usually HTML).

CGI programs do more than process form input. They are also invoked when you click on a graphic image, and may in fact be used to provide whatever output that your browser sees. Instead of being dull and boring, CGI-enabled web pages can be marvelously alive with dynamic content. Dynamic information is what makes the Web an interesting and interactive place, and not just a way to read a book from your terminal.

Despite what all those bouncing balls and jumping adverts might lead you to believe, the Web contains a lot of text. Since we're dealing with text, files, network communications, and a little bit of binary data now and then, Perl is perfect for web programming.

In this chapter we'll not only explore the basics of CGI programming, but we'll also steal a little introductory knowledge about references, library modules, and object-oriented programming with Perl as we go along. Then, at the end, we'll make a quick survey of Perl's usefulness for other sorts of web programming.

As a standalone tutorial, this chapter (and most any other document shorter than a couple of hundred pages) will not be adequate to teach the more complex topics touched on here, such as object programming and the use of references. But as a means to gain a preliminary taste of what's ahead of you, the examples presented here, together with their explanations, may whet your appetite and give you some practical orientation as you slog through the appropriate textbooks. And if you're the learn-by-doing type, you'll actually start writing useful programs based on the models you find here.

We assume you already possess a basic familiarity with HTML.

The CGI.pm Module

Starting with the 5.004 release, the standard Perl distribution includes the all-singing, all-dancing CGI.pm module.*

Written by Lincoln Stein, author of the acclaimed book *How to Setup and Maintain Your Web Site*, this module makes writing CGI programs in Perl a breeze. Like Perl itself, CGI.pm is platform independent, so you can use it on systems running everything from UNIX and Linux to VMS; it even runs on systems like Windows and the MacOS.

Assuming CGI.pm is already installed on your system, you can read its complete documentation in whatever fashion you're used to reading the Perl manpages, such as with the *man*(1) or *perldoc*(1) commands or as HTML. If all else fails, just read the *CGI.pm* file: the documentation for the module is embedded in the module itself, written in simple *pod* format.†

---

* If you have an earlier release of Perl (but at least Version 5.001) and haven't gotten around to upgrading yet, just grab CGI.pm from CPAN.

† Pod stands for "plain old documentation," the simplistic mark-up used for all Perl documentation. See the *perlpod*(1) manpage for how it works, plus *pod2man*(1), *pod2html*(1), or *pod2text*(1) for some of the pod translators.

While developing CGI programs, keep a copy of the CGI.pm manpage handy. Not only does it describe the module's functions, it's also loaded with examples and tips.

Your CGI Program in Context

Figure 19-1 shows the relationships between a web browser, web server, and CGI program. When you click on a link while using your browser, there is a URL associated with the link. This URL specifies a web server and a resource accessible through that server. So the browser communicates with the server, requesting the given resource. If, say, the resource is an HTML fill-out form, the web server responds by downloading the form to the browser, which then displays the form for you to fill out.

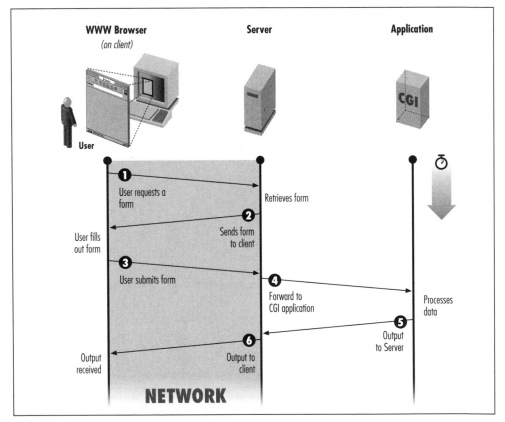

Figure 19-1. Form interaction with CGI

Each text-input field on the form has a name (given in the form's HTML code) and an associated value, which is whatever you type into the field. The form itself is associated (via the HTML `<FORM>` tag) with a CGI program that processes the form input. When you fill out the form and click on "Submit", the browser accesses the URL of the CGI program. But first it tacks onto the end of the URL what is called a *query string* consisting of one or more `name=value` pairs; each name is the name of a text input field, and each value is the corresponding input you provided. So the URL to which the browser submits your form input looks something like this (where the query string is everything after the question mark):

```
http://www.SOMEWHERE.org/cgi-bin/some_cgi_prog?flavor=vanilla&size=double
```

In this case there are two `name=value` pairs. Such pairs are separated by an ampersand (&), a detail you won't have to worry about when you use the CGI.pm module. The part of the URL that reads */cgi-bin/some_cgi_prog/* receives further explanation later; at the moment, it only matters that this provides a path to the CGI program that will process the HTML form input.

When the web server (*www.SOMEWHERE.org* in this case) receives the URL from your browser, it invokes the CGI program, passing the `name=value` pairs to the program as arguments. The program then does whatever it does, and (usually) returns HTML code to the server, which in turn downloads it to the browser for display to you.

The conversation between the browser and the server, and also between the server and the CGI program, follows the protocol known as HTTP. You needn't worry much about this when writing your CGI program, because CGI.pm takes care of the protocol requirements for you.

The way in which the CGI program expects to receive its arguments (and other information) from the browser via the server is governed by the Common Gateway Interface specification. Again, you don't need to worry too much about this; as you will see, CGI.pm automatically unpacks the arguments for you.

Finally, you should know that CGI programs can work with any HTML document, not just forms. For example, you could write the HTML code

```
Click <a href="http://www.SOMEWHERE.org/cgi-bin/fortune.cgi">here</a> to
receive your fortune.
```

and *fortune.cgi* could be a program that simply invokes the *fortune* program (on UNIX systems). In this case, there wouldn't be any argument supplied to the CGI program with the URL. Or the HTML document could give two links for the user to click on—one to receive a fortune, and one to receive the current date. Both links could point to the same program, in one case with the argument `fortune` following the question mark in the URL, and in the other case with the argument `date`. The HTML links would look like this:

```
<a href="http://www.SOMEWHERE.org/cgi-bin/fortune_or_date?fortune">
<a href="http://www.SOMEWHERE.org/cgi-bin/fortune_or_date?date">
```

The CGI program (*fortune_or_date* in this case) would then see which of the two possible arguments it received and execute either the *fortune* or *date* program accordingly.

So you see that arguments do not have to be of the **name=date** variety characteristic of fill-out forms. You can write a CGI program to do most anything you please, and you can pass it most any arguments you please.

In this chapter we will primarily illustrate HTML fill-out forms. And we will assume that you understand basic HTML code already.*

Simplest CGI Program

Here's the source code for your first CGI program; it's so simple, it doesn't even need to use the CGI.pm module:

```
#!/usr/bin/perl -w
# howdy--the easiest of CGI programs
print <<END_of_Multiline_Text;
Content-type: text/html

<HTML>
    <HEAD>
    <TITLE>Hello World</TITLE>
    </HEAD>
    <BODY>
    <H1>Greetings, Terrans!</H1>
    </BODY>
</HTML>

END_of_Multiline_Text
```

Every time this program is called, it displays exactly the same thing. That's not particularly interesting, of course, but we'll spice it up later.

This little program contains just one statement: a call to the **print** function. That somewhat funny looking argument is a *here document*. It starts with two less-than signs and a word that we'll call the *end token*. Although this may look like I/O redirection to a shell programmer, it's really just a convenient way to quote a multiline string. The string begins on the next line and continues up to a line containing the end token, which must stand by itself at the start of the line. Here documents are especially handy for generating HTML.

The first part in that long string is arguably the most important: the **Content-Type** line identifies the type of output you're generating. It's immediately followed by a blank line, which must not contain any spaces or tabs. Most begin-

---

* For the full story about HTML, see the O'Reilly book, *HTML: The Definitive Guide, Second Edition.*

ners' first CGI programs fail because they forget that blank line, which separates the header (somewhat like a mail header) from an optional body following it.* After the blank line comes the HTML, which is sent on to be formatted and displayed on the user's browser.

First make sure your program runs correctly from the command line. This is a necessary but not a sufficient step to making sure your program will run as a server script. A lot of other things can go wrong; see the section on "Trouble-shooting CGI Programs" later in this chapter.

Once it runs properly from the command line, you need to get the program installed on the server machine. Acceptable locations are server-dependent, although */usr/etc/httpd/cgi-bin/* and its subdirectories are often used for CGI scripts. Talk to your friendly system administrator or webmaster to make sure.

Once your program is installed in a CGI directory, you can execute it by giving its pathname to your browser as part of a URL. For example, if your program is called *howdy*, the URL might be *http://www.SOMEWHERE.org/cgi-bin/howdy*.

Servers typically define aliases for long pathnames. The server at *www.SOME-WHERE.org* might well translate *cgi-bin/howdy* in this URL to something like *usr/etc/httpd/cgi-bin/howdy*. Your system administrator or webmaster can tell you what alias to use when accessing your program.

Passing Parameters via CGI

You don't need a form to pass a parameter to (most) CGI programs. To test this, change the URL to *http://www.SOMEWHERE.org/cgi-bin/ice_cream?flavor=mint*

When you point your browser at this URL, the browser not only requests the web server to invoke the *ice_cream* program, but it also passes the string `flavor=mint` to the program. Now it's up to the program to read the argument string and pick it apart. Doing this properly is not as easy as you might think. Many programs try to wing it and parse the request on their own, but most hand-rolled algorithms only work some of the time. Given how hard it is to get it right in all cases, you probably shouldn't try to write your own code, especially when perfectly fine modules already handle the tricky parsing business for you.

Enter the CGI.pm module, which always parses the incoming CGI request correctly. To pull this module into your program, merely say

```
use CGI;
```

somewhere near the top of your program.†

---

* This header is required by the HTTP protocol we mentioned above.

† All Perl modules end in the suffix ".pm"; in fact, the use statement assumes this suffix. You can learn how to build your own modules in Chapter 5 of *Programming Perl* or the *perlmod*(1) manpage.

The `use` statement is like an `#include` statement in C programming in that it pulls in code from another file at compile-time. But it also allows optional arguments specifying which functions and variables you'd like to access from that module. Put those in a list following the module name in the `use` statement. You can then access the named functions and variables as if they were your own.

In this case, all we need to use from CGI.pm is the `param()` function.*

If given no arguments, `param()` returns a list of all the fields that were in the HTML form this CGI script is responding to. (In the current example that's the `flavor` field. In general, it's the list of all the names in `name=value` strings received from the submitted form.) If given an argument naming a field, `param()` returns the value (or values) associated with that field. Therefore, `param("flavor")` returns `"mint"`, because we passed in `?flavor=mint` at the end of the URL.

Even though we have only one item in our import list for `use`, we'll employ the `qw()` notation. This way it will be easier to expand the list later.

```
#!/usr/bin/perl -w
# cgi-bin/ice_cream: program to answer ice cream
# favorite flavor form (version 1)
use CGI qw(param);

print <<END_of_Start;
Content-type: text/html

<HTML>
    <HEAD>
    <TITLE>Hello World</TITLE>
    </HEAD>
    <BODY>
    <H1>Greetings, Terrans!</H1>
END_of_Start

my $favorite = param("flavor");
print "<P>Your favorite flavor is $favorite.";
print <<All_Done;
    </BODY>
</HTML>
All_Done
```

Less Typing

That's still a lot of typing. It turns out that CGI.pm includes a whole slew of convenience functions for simplifying this. Each of these routines returns a string for

---

* Some modules automatically export all their functions, but because CGI.pm is really an object module masquerading as a traditional module, we have to ask for its functions explicitly.

you to output. For example, `header()` returns a string containing the `Content-type` line with a following blank line, `start_html`(*string*) returns *string* as an HTML title, `h1`(*string*) returns `string` as a first-level HTML heading, and `p`(*string*) returns *string* as a new HTML paragraph.

We could list all these functions in the import list given with `use`, but that will eventually grow too unwieldy. However, CGI.pm, like many modules, provides you with *import tags*—labels that stand for groups of functions to import. You simply place the desired tags (each of which begins with a colon) at the beginning of your import list. The tags available with CGI.pm include these:

`:cgi`
> Import all argument-handling methods, such as `param()`.

`:form`
> Import all fill-out form generating methods, such as `textfield()`.

`:html2`
> Import all methods that generate HTML 2.0 standard elements.

`:html3`
> Import all methods that generate HTML 3.0 elements (such as `<table>`, `<super>`, and `<sub>`).

`:netscape`
> Import all methods that generate Netscape-specific HTML extensions.

`:shortcuts`
> Import all HTML-generating shortcuts (that is, "html2" + "html3" + "netscape").

`:standard`
> Import "standard" features: "html2", "form", and "cgi".

`:all`
> Import all the available methods. For the full list, see the CGI.pm module, where the variable `%TAGS` is defined.

We'll just use `:standard`. (For more about importing functions and variables from modules, see the Exporter module in Chapter 7 of *Programming Perl*, or the *Exporter*(3) manpage.)

Here's our program using all the shortcuts CGI.pm provides:

```
#!/usr/bin/perl -w
# cgi-bin/ice_cream: program to answer ice cream
# favorite flavor form (version 2)
use CGI qw(:standard);
print header(), start_html("Hello World"), h1("Greetings, Terrans!");
my $favorite = param("flavor");
print p("Your favorite flavor is $favorite.");
print end_html();
```

See how much easier that is? You don't have to worry about form decoding, headers, or HTML if you don't want to.

Form Generation

Perhaps you're tired of typing your program's parameter to your browser. Just make a fill-out form instead, which is what most folks are used to. The parts of the form that accept user input are typically called *widgets*, a much handier term than "graphical input devices." Form widgets include single- and multiline text-fields, pop-up menus, scrolling lists, and various kinds of buttons and checkboxes.

Create the following HTML page, which includes a form with one text-field widget and a submit button. When the user clicks on the submit button,* the *ice_ cream* script specified in the ACTION tag is called.

```
<!-- ice_cream.html -->
<HTML>
    <HEAD>
    <TITLE>Hello Ice Cream</TITLE>
    </HEAD>
    <BODY>
    <H1>Hello Ice Cream</H1>
    <FORM ACTION="http://www.SOMEWHERE.org/cgi-bin/ice_cream">
    What's your flavor? <INPUT NAME="favorite" VALUE="mint">
    <P>
    <INPUT TYPE="submit">
    </FORM>
    </BODY>
</HTML>
```

Remember that a CGI program can generate any HTML output you want, which will then be passed to any browser that fetches the program's URL. A CGI program can, therefore, produce the HTML page with the form on it, just as a CGI program can respond to the user's form input. Moreover, the *same* program can perform both tasks, one after the other. All you need to do is divide the program into two parts, which do different things depending on whether or not the program was invoked with arguments. If no arguments were received, then the program sends the empty form to the browser; otherwise, the arguments contain a user's input to the previously sent form, and the program returns a response to the browser based on that input.

Keeping everything in a single CGI file this way eases maintenance. The cost is a little more processing time when loading the original page. Here's how it works:

---

* Some browsers allow you to leave out the submit button when the form has only a single input text field. When the user types a return in this field, it is treated as a submit request. But it's best to use portable HTML here.

```
#!/usr/bin/perl -w
# cgi-bin/ice_cream: program to answer *and generate* ice cream
# favorite flavor form (version 3)
use CGI qw(:standard);
my $favorite = param("flavor");
print header, start_html("Hello Ice Cream"), h1("Hello Ice Cream");
if ($favorite) {
    print p("Your favorite flavor is $favorite.");
} else {
    print hr, start_form; # hr() emits html horizontal rule: <HR>
    print p("Please select a flavor: ", textfield("flavor","mint"));
    print end_form, hr;
}
```

If, while using your browser, you click on a link that points to this program (and if the link does not specify ?whatever at the end of the URL), you'll see a screen like that in Figure 19-2. The text field is initially filled out with the default value, but the user's typed input, if any, will replace the default

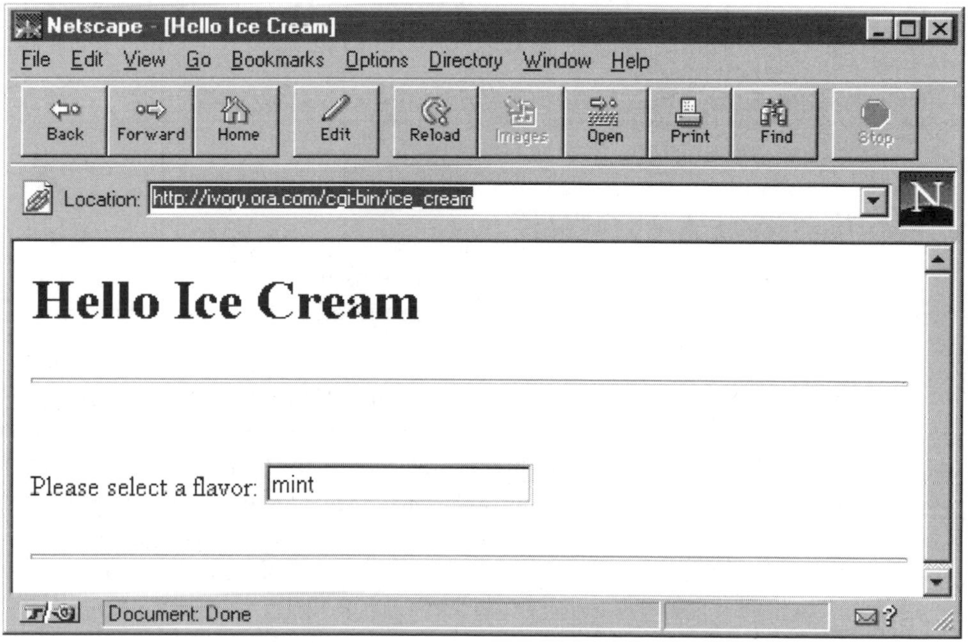

Figure 19-2. A basic fill-out form

Now fill in the flavor field, hit Return, and Figure 19-3 shows what you'll see.

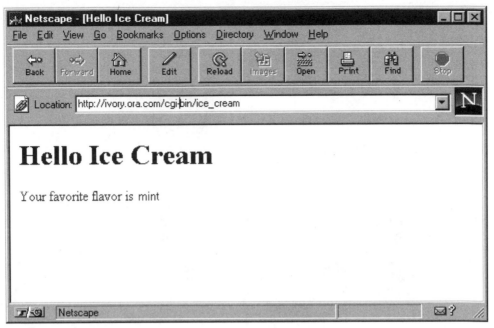

Figure 19-3. Result of submitting the form shown in Figure 19-2

Other Form Elements

Now that you know how to create simple text fields in your form and respond to them, you're probably wondering how to make the other kinds of widgets you've seen, like buttons, checkboxes, and menus.

Here's a more elaborate version of our program. We've thrown in some new widgets: popup menus, a submit button (named "order"), and a button to reset the entire form, erasing all user input. Popup menus are pretty much just what they say they are, but the arguments given to `popup_menu` may perplex you until you've read the following section on "References." The `textfield()` function creates a text-input field with the indicated name. We'll give more details about this function when describing the guestbook program later in this chapter.

```
#!/usr/bin/perl -w
# cgi-bin/ice_cream: program to answer and generate ice cream
# order form (version 4)
use strict; # enforce variable declarations and quoting
use CGI qw(:standard);

print header, start_html("Ice Cream Stand"), h1("Ice Cream Stand");
if (param()) { # the form has already been filled out
    my $who = param("name");
    my $flavor = param("flavor");
```

```
    my $scoops = param("scoops");
    my $taxrate = 1.0743;
    my $cost = sprintf("%.2f", $taxrate * (1.00 + $scoops * 0.25));
    print p("Ok, $who, have $scoops scoops of $flavor for \$$cost.");
} else { # first time through, so present clean form
    print hr(); # draw a horizontal rule before the form
    print start_form();
    print p("What's your name? ", textfield("name"));
    # FOR EXPLANATION OF FOLLOWING TWO LINES, SEE NEXT SECTION
    print p("What flavor: ", popup_menu("flavor",
                                        ['mint','cherry','mocha']));
    print p("How many scoops? ", popup_menu("scoops", [ 1..3 ]));
    print p(submit("order"), reset("clear"));
    print end_form(), hr();
}
print end_html;
```

Figure 19-4 shows the initial screen it generates.

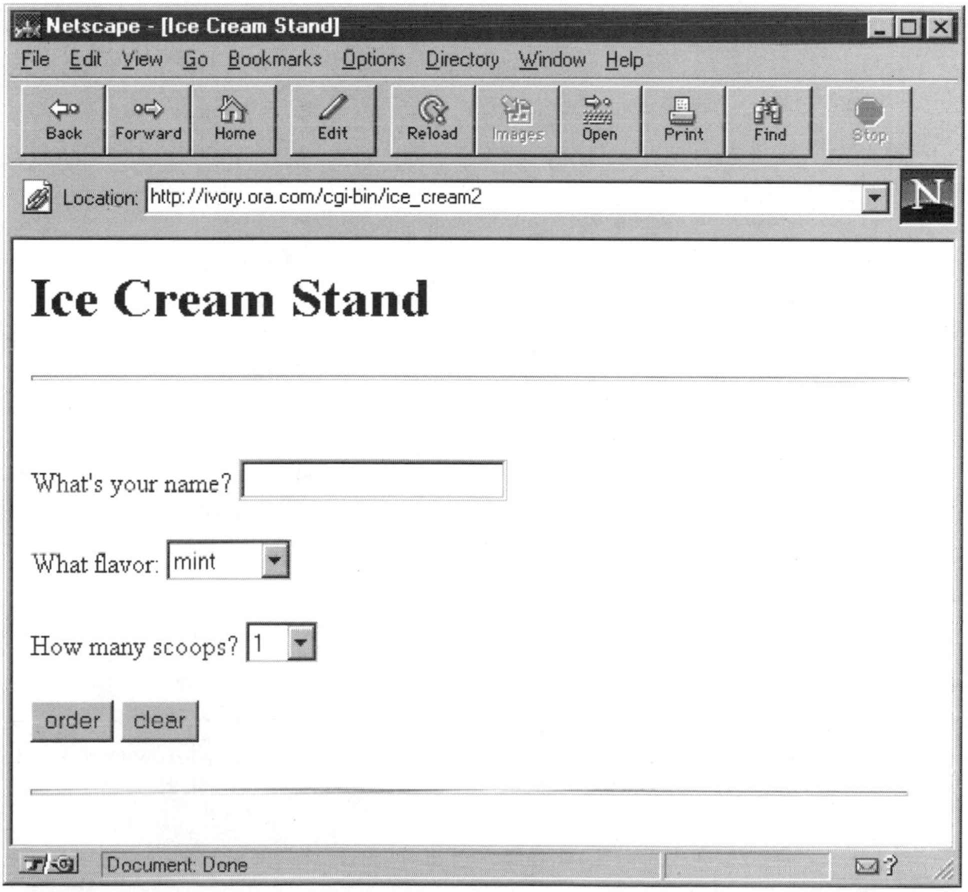

Figure 19-4. A slightly more elaborate fill-out form

As you'll recall, the `param()` function, when called without arguments, returns the names of all form-input fields that were filled out. That way you can tell whether or not the URL was called from a filled-out form. If you have parameters, then the user filled in some of the fields of an existing form, so respond to them. Otherwise generate a new form, expecting to have this very same program called a second time.

References

You may have noticed that the *popup_menu()* functions in the previous example both have a strange kind of argument. Just what are ['mint','cherry','mocha'] and [1..3] doing there? The brackets create something you haven't seen before: a reference to an anonymous array. That's because the `popup_menu()` function expects an array reference for an argument. Another way to create an array reference is to use a backslash in front of a named array, as in `\@choices`. So this

```
@choices = ('mint','cherry','mocha');
print p("What flavor: ", popup_menu("flavor", \@choices));
```

works just as well as this:

```
print p("What flavor: ", popup_menu("flavor",
['mint','cherry','mocha']));
```

References behave somewhat as pointers do in other languages, but with less danger of error. They're values that refer to other values (or variables). Perl references are very strongly typed (and uncastable), and they can never cause core dumps. Even better, the memory storage pointed to by references is automatically reclaimed when it's no longer used. References play a central role in object-oriented programming. They're also used in traditional programming, forming the basis for data structures more complex than simple one-dimensional arrays and hashes. Perl supports references to both named and anonymous scalars, arrays, hashes, and functions.

Just as you can create references to named arrays with `\@array` and to anonymous arrays with [`list`], you can also create references to named hashes using `\%hash` and to anonymous ones like this:*

```
{ key1, value1, key2, value2, ... }
```

You can learn more about references in Chapter 4 of *Programming Perl*, or the *perlref*(1) manpage.

---

* Yes, braces now have quite a few meanings in Perl. The context in which you use them determines what they're doing.

Fancier Calling Sequences

We'll round out the discussion of form widgets by creating a really fancy widget— one that allows the user to select any number of its items. The `scrolling_` `list()` function of CGI.pm can take an arbitrary number of argument pairs, each of which consists of a named parameter (beginning with –) and a value for the parameter.

To add a scrolling list to a form, here's all you need to do:

```
print scrolling_list(
    -NAME => "flavors",
    -VALUES => [ qw(mint chocolate cherry vanilla peach) ],
    -LABELS => {
        mint => "Mighty Mint",
        chocolate => "Cherished Chocolate",
        cherry => "Cheery Cherry",
        vanilla => "Very Vanilla",
        peach => "Perfectly Peachy",
    },
    -SIZE => 3,
    -MULTIPLE => 1, # 1 for true, 0 for false
);
```

The parameter values have meanings as follows:

–NAME

The name of the widget. You can use the value of this later to retrieve user data from the form with `param()`.

–LABELS

A reference to an anonymous hash. The values of the hash provide the labels (list items) seen by the form user. When a particular label is selected by the user, the corresponding hash key is what gets returned to the CGI program. That is, if the user selects the item given as `Perfectly Peachy`, the CGI program will receive the argument, `peach`.

–VALUES

A reference to an anonymous array. The array consists of the keys of the hash referenced by **–LABELS**.

–SIZE

A number determining how many list items will be visible to the user at one time.

–MULTIPLE

A true or false value (in Perl's sense of true and false) indicating whether the form user will be allowed to choose more than one list item.

When you've set −MULTIPLE to true, you'll want to assign param()'s return list to an array:

```
@choices = param("flavors");
```

Here's another way to create the same scrolling list, passing a reference to an existing hash instead of creating one on the fly:

```
%flavors = (
    mint => "Mighty Mint",
    chocolate => "Cherished Chocolate",
    cherry => "Cheery Cherry",
    vanilla => "Very Vanilla",
    peach => "Perfectly Peachy",
);
print scrolling_list(
    -NAME => "flavors",
    -LABELS => \%flavors,
    -VALUES => [ keys %flavors ],
    -SIZE => 3,
    -MULTIPLE => 1, # 1 for true, 0 for false
);
```

This time we send in values computed from the keys of the %flavors hash, which is itself passed in by reference using the backslash operator. Notice how the −VALUES parameter is still wrapped in square brackets? It wouldn't work to just pass in the result of keys as a list, because the calling convention for the scrolling_list() function requires an array reference there, which the brackets happily provide. Think of the brackets as a convenient way to treat multiple values as a single value.

Creating a Guestbook Program

If you have followed the examples above, you can now get some simple CGI programs going. But what about harder ones? A common request is to create a CGI program to manage a guestbook, so that visitors to your web site can record their own messages.*

Actually, the form for this kind of thing is quite easy, easier in fact than some of our ice cream forms. Other matters get trickier. But don't worry, we'll explain it all as we go.

You probably want guestbook messages to survive a user's visit to your site, so you need a file to store them in. The CGI program (probably) runs under a different user, not as you; therefore, it won't normally have permission to update a file of yours. So, first, create a file with wide-open permissions. If you're on a

---

* As we will note later on, this application might also be called a *webchat* program.

UNIX system, then you can do this (from your shell) to initialize a file for the guestbook program to use:

```
touch /usr/tmp/chatfile
chmod 0666 /usr/tmp/chatfile
```

Okay, but how will you accommodate several folks using the guestbook program simultaneously? The operating system doesn't block simultaneous access to files, so if you're not careful, you could get a jumbled file as everyone writes to it at the same time. To avoid this, we'll use Perl's `flock` function to request exclusive access to the file we're going to update. It will look something like this:

```
use Fcntl qw(:flock); # imports LOCK_EX, LOCK_SH, LOCK_NB
....
flock(CHANDLE, LOCK_EX) || bail("cannot flock $CHATNAME: $!");
```

The LOCK_EX argument to `flock` is what buys us exclusive file access.*

`flock` presents a simple but uniform locking mechanism even though its underlying implementation varies wildly between systems. It reliably "blocks," not returning until it gets the lock. Note that file locks are purely advisory: they only work when all processes accessing a file honor the locks in the same way. If three processes honor them, but another doesn't, all bets are off.

Object-Oriented Programming in Perl

Finally, and most important, it's time to teach you how to use objects and classes. Although building your own object module is beyond the scope of this book, you don't have to know about that in order to use existing, object-oriented library modules. For in-depth information about using and creating object modules, see Chapter 5 of *Programming Perl* and the *perltoot*(1) manpage.

We won't go into the theory behind objects here, but you can just treat them as packages (which they are!) of wonderful and marvelous things that you invoke indirectly. Objects provide subroutines that do anything you need to do with the object.

For instance, suppose the CGI.pm module returns an object called `$query` that represents the user's input. If you want to get a parameter from the query, invoke the `param()` subroutine like this:

```
$query->param("answer");
```

This says, "Run the `param()` subroutine on the `$query` object, with `"answer"` as an argument." It's just like invoking any other subroutine, except that you

---

* With Perl versions prior to the 5.004 release, you must comment out the use Fcntl and just use 2 as the argument to *flock*.

employ the name of the object followed by the `->` syntax. Subroutines associated with objects, by the way, are called *methods*.

If you want to retrieve the return value of the `param()` subroutine, just use the usual assignment statement and store the value in a regular old variable named `$he_said`:

```
$he_said = $query->param("answer");
```

Objects look like scalars; you store them in scalar variables (like `$query` in our example), and you can make arrays or hashes of objects. But you don't treat them as you would strings or numbers. They're actually a particular kind of reference,* but you don't even treat them as you would ordinary references. Instead, you treat them like a special, user-defined type of data.

The type of a particular object is known as its *class*. The class name is normally just the module name—without the .pm suffix—and often the words "class" and "module" are used interchangeably. So we can speak of the CGI module and also the CGI class. Objects of a particular class are created and managed by the module implementing that class.

You access classes by loading in a module, which looks just like any other module except that object-oriented ones don't usually export anything. You can think of the class as a factory that cranks out brand-new objects. To get the class to produce one of these new objects, you invoke special methods called *constructors*. Here's an example:

```
$query = CGI->new(); # call method new() in class "CGI"
```

What you have there is the invocation of a *class method*. A class method looks just like an *object method* (which is what we were talking about a moment ago), except instead of using an object to call the method, you use the name of the class as though it were itself an object. An object method is saying "call the function by this name that is related to this object"; a class method is saying "call the function by this name that is related to this class."

Sometimes you'll see that same thing written this way:

```
$query = new CGI; # same thing
```

The second form is identical in behavior to the first. It's got less punctuation, so is sometimes preferred. But it's less convenient to use as part of a larger expression, so we'll use the first form exclusively in this book.

From the standpoint of the designer of object modules, an object is a reference to a user-defined data structure, often an anonymous hash. Inside this structure is

---

* A *blessed* reference, to be precise.

stored all manner of interesting information. But the well-behaved user of an object is expected to get at this information (to inspect or change it), not by treating the object as a reference and going straight for the data it points to, but by employing only the available object and class methods. Changing the object's data by other means amounts to hanky-panky that is bound to get you talked about. To learn what those methods are and how they work, just read the object module's documentation, usually included as embedded pods.

Objects in CGI.pm

The CGI module is unusual in that it can be treated either as a traditional module with exported functions or as an object module. Some kinds of programs are more easily written using the object interface to CGI.pm rather than the procedural one. A guestbook program is one of these. We access the input that the user supplied to the form via a CGI object, and we can, if we want, use this same object to generate new HTML code for sending back to the user.

First, however, we need to create the object explicitly. For CGI.pm, as for so many other classes, the method that generates objects is the class method named `new()`.*

This method constructs and returns a new CGI object corresponding to a filled-out form. The object contains all the user's form input. Without arguments, `new()` builds the object by reading the data passed by the remote browser. With a filehandle as an argument, it reads the handle instead, expecting to find form input saved from previous communication with a browser.

We'll show you the program and explain its details in a moment. Let's assume that the program is named *guestbook* and is in the *cgi-bin* directory. While this program does not look like one of the two-part scripts shown earlier (where one part outputs an HTML form, and the other part reads and responds to form input from a user), you will see that it nevertheless does handle both functions. So there is no need for a separate HTML document containing a guestbook form. The user might first trigger our program simply by clicking on a link like this:

```
Please sign our
<A HREF="http://www.SOMEWHERE.org/cgi-bin/guestbook">guestbook</A>.
```

---

* Unlike C++, Perl doesn't consider `new` a keyword; you're perfectly free to have constructor methods called `gimme_another()` or `fred()`. But most classes end up naming their constructors `new()` anyway.

The program then downloads an HTML form to the browser and, for good measure, also downloads any previous guest messages (up to a stated limit) for the user to review. The user then fills out the form, submits it, and the program reads what is submitted. This is added to the list of previous messages (saved in a file), which is then output to the browser again, along with a fresh form. The user can continue reading the current set of messages and submitting new messages via the supplied forms as long as he wishes.

Here's the program. You might want to scan it quickly before we step you through it.

```perl
#!/usr/bin/perl -w

use 5.004;
use strict;               # enforce declarations and quoting
use CGI qw(:standard);    # import shortcuts
use Fcntl qw(:flock);     # imports LOCK_EX, LOCK_SH, LOCK_NB

sub bail {                # function to handle errors gracefully
    my $error = "@_";
    print h1("Unexpected Error"), p($error), end_html;
    die $error;
}

my (
    $CHATNAME,  # name of guestbook file
    $MAXSAVE,   # how many to keep
    $TITLE,     # page title and header
    $cur,       # new entry in the guestbook
    @entries,   # all cur entries
    $entry      # one particular entry
);

$TITLE = "Simple Guestbook";
$CHATNAME = "/usr/tmp/chatfile"; # wherever makes sense on your system
$MAXSAVE = 10;

print header, start_html($TITLE), h1($TITLE);

$cur = CGI->new();                          # current request
if ($cur->param("message")) {               # good, we got a message
    $cur->param("date", scalar localtime);  # set to the current time
 @entries = ($cur);                         # save message to array
 }

# open the file for read-write (preserving old contents)
open(CHANDLE, "+< $CHATNAME") || bail("cannot open $CHATNAME: $!");

# get exclusive lock on the guestbook (LOCK_EX == exclusive lock)
flock(CHANDLE, LOCK_EX) || bail("cannot flock $CHATNAME: $!");

# grab up to $MAXSAVE old entries, newest first
```

```
while (!eof(CHANDLE) && @entries < $MAXSAVE) {
    $entry = CGI->new(\*CHANDLE); # pass the filehandle by reference
    push @entries, $entry;
}
seek(CHANDLE, 0, 0) || bail("cannot rewind $CHATNAME: $!");
foreach $entry (@entries) {
    $entry->save(\*CHANDLE); # pass the filehandle by reference
}
truncate(CHANDLE, tell(CHANDLE)) ||
                            bail("cannot truncate $CHATNAME: $!");
close(CHANDLE) || bail("cannot close $CHATNAME: $!");

print hr, start_form;          # hr() emits html horizontal rule: <HR>
print p("Name:", $cur->textfield(
    -NAME => "name"));
print p("Message:", $cur->textfield(
    -NAME => "message",
    -OVERRIDE => 1,            # clears previous message
    -SIZE => 50));
print p(submit("send"), reset("clear"));
print end_form, hr;

print h2("Prior Messages");
foreach $entry (@entries) {
    printf("%s [%s]: %s",
    $entry->param("date"),
    $entry->param("name"),
    $entry->param("message"));
    print br();
}
print end_html;
```

Figure 19-5 shows an example screen dump after running the guestbook program.

Note that the program begins with:

```
use 5.004;
```

If you want to run it with an earlier version of Perl 5, you'll need to comment out the line reading:

```
use Fcntl qw (:flock);
```

and change LOCK_EX in the first flock invocation to be 2.

Since every execution of the program results in the return of an HTML form to the particular browser that sought us out, the program begins by getting a start on the HTML code:

```
print header, start_html($TITLE), h1($TITLE);
```

It then creates a new CGI object:

```
$cur = CGI->new();                        # current request
if ($cur->param("message")) {             # good, we got a message
```

```
╔═════════════════════════════════════════════════════════════════════╗
║ ▓▓ Netscape - [Simple Guestbook]                              _ □ ✕  ║
╟─────────────────────────────────────────────────────────────────────╢
║  File  Edit  View  Go  Bookmarks  Options  Directory  Window  Help   ║
╟─────────────────────────────────────────────────────────────────────╢
║  ⇦o    o⇨    ⌂     ⌀     ⓒ    ▤     ⇨o    ▤     ▥     ●              ║
║  Back  Forward Home  Edit  Reload  Images  Open  Print  Find  Stop    ║
╟─────────────────────────────────────────────────────────────────────╢
║  🖉 Location: http://ivory.ora.com/cgi-bin/guestbook            ▼  Ⓝ  ║
╟─────────────────────────────────────────────────────────────────────╢
║                                                                       ║
║   Simple Guestbook                                                    ║
║                                                                       ║
║   ─────────────────────────────────────────────────────────────      ║
║                                                                       ║
║                                                                       ║
║   Name: [                         ]                                   ║
║                                                                       ║
║   Message: [                                          ]               ║
║                                                                       ║
║   [ send ]  [ clear ]                                                 ║
║                                                                       ║
║   ─────────────────────────────────────────────────────────────      ║
║                                                                       ║
║                                                                       ║
║   Prior Messages                                                      ║
║                                                                       ║
║   Mon Jun 2 14:17:45 1997 [Princess Leia Organa]: Help me Obi Wan,    ║
║   you're my only hope.                                                ║
║                                                                       ║
╟─────────────────────────────────────────────────────────────────────╢
║  ⬚⬚  Document: Done                                          ✉?      ║
╚═════════════════════════════════════════════════════════════════════╝
```

Figure 19-5. A simple guestbook form

```
    $cur->param("date", scalar localtime); # set to the current time
    @entries = ($cur);                      # save message to array
}
```

If we are being called via submission of a form, then the `$cur` object now
contains information about the input text given to the form. The form we supply
(see below) has two input fields: a *name field* for the name of the user, and a
message field for the message. In addition, the code shown above puts a date
stamp on the form data after it is received. Feeding the `param()` method two
arguments is a way to set the parameter named in the first argument to the value
given in the second argument.

If we are not being called via submission of a form, but rather because the user has clicked on "Please sign our guestbook," then the query object we create here will be empty. The `if` test will yield a false value, and no entry will be added to the `@entries` array.

In either case, we proceed to check for any entries previously saved in our save-file. We will read those into the `@entries` array. (Recall that we have just now made the current form input, if any, the first member of this array.) But, first, we have to open the savefile:

```
open(CHANDLE, "+< $CHATNAME") || bail("cannot open $CHATNAME: $!");
```

This opens the file in nondestructive read-write mode. Alternatively, we could use `sysopen()`. This way a single call opens an old file (if it exists) without clobbering it, or else creates a new one:

```
# need to import two "constants" from Fcntl module for sysopen
use Fcntl qw( O_RDWR O_CREAT );
sysopen(CHANDLE, $CHATNAME, O_RDWR|O_CREAT, 0666)
    || bail "can't open $CHATNAME: $!";
```

Then we lock the file, as described earlier, and proceed to read up to a total of `$MAXSAVE` entries into `@entries`:

```
flock(CHANDLE, LOCK_EX) || bail("cannot flock $CHATNAME: $!");
while (!eof(CHANDLE) && @entries < $MAXSAVE) {
    $entry = CGI->new(\*CHANDLE); # pass the filehandle by reference
    push @entries, $entry;
}
```

`eof` is a Perl built-in function that tells whether we have hit the end of the file. By repeatedly passing to the `new()` method a reference to the savefile's filehandle[*] we retrieve the old entries—one entry per call. Then we update the file so that it now includes the new entry we (may) have just received:

```
seek(CHANDLE, 0, 0) || bail("cannot rewind $CHATNAME: $!");
foreach $entry (@entries) {
    $entry->save(\*CHANDLE); # pass the filehandle by reference
}
truncate(CHANDLE, tell(CHANDLE)) || bail("cannot truncate $CHATNAME:
$!");
close(CHANDLE) || bail("cannot close $CHATNAME: $!");
```

`seek`, `truncate`, and `tell` are all built-in Perl functions whose descriptions you will find in any Perl reference work. Here `seek` repositions the file pointer to the beginning of the file, `truncate` truncates the indicated file to the specified length, and `tell` returns the current offset of the file pointer from the beginning

---

[*] Actually, it's a glob reference, not a filehandle reference, but that's close enough.

of the file. The effect of these lines is to save only the most recent `$MAXSAVE` entries, beginning with the one just now received, in the savefile.

The `save()` method handles the actual writing of the entries. The method can be invoked here as `$entry->save` because `$entry` is a CGI object, created with `CGI->new()` as previously discussed.

The format of a savefile entry looks like this, where the entry is terminated by "=" standing alone on a line:

```
NAME1=VALUE1
NAME2=VALUE2
NAME3=VALUE3
=
```

Now it's time to return a fresh form to the browser and its user. (This will, of course, be the first form he is seeing if he has just clicked on "Please sign our guestbook.") First, some preliminaries:

```
print hr, start_form; # hr() emits html horizontal rule: <HR>
```

As already mentioned, CGI.pm allows us to use either straight function calls or method calls via a CGI object. Here, for basic HTML code, we've reverted to the simple function calls. But for generation of form input fields, we continue to employ object methods:

```
print p("Name:", $cur->textfield(
    -NAME => "name"));
print p("Message:", $cur->textfield(
    -NAME => "message",
    -OVERRIDE => 1, # clears previous message
    -SIZE => 50));
print p(submit("send"), reset("clear"));
print end_form, hr;
```

The `textfield()` method returns a text-input field for a form. The first of the two invocations here generates HTML code for a text-input field with the HTML attribute, `NAME="name"`, while the second one creates a field with the attribute, `NAME="message"`.

Widgets created by CGI.pm are by default sticky: they retain their values between calls. (But only during a single "session" with a form, beginning when the user clicks on "Please sign our guestbook.") This means that the `NAME="name"` field generated by the first `textfield()` above will have the value of the user's name if he has already filled out and submitted the form at least once during this session. So the input field we are now creating will actually have these HTML attributes:

```
NAME="name" VALUE="Sam Smith"
```

The second invocation of `textfield()` is a different matter. We don't want the message field to contain the value of the old message. So the `-OVERRIDE => 1` argument pair says, in effect, "throw out the previous value of this text field and restore the default value." The `-SIZE => 50` argument pair of `textfield()` gives the size of the displayed input field in characters. Other optional argument pairs beside those shown: `-DEFAULT => 'initial value'` and `-MAXLENGTH => n`, where n is the maximum number of input characters the field will accept.

Finally, we output for the user's delectation the current set of saved messages, including, of course, any he has just submitted:

```
print h2("Prior Messages");
foreach $entry (@entries) {
    printf("%s [%s]: %s",
    $entry->param("date"),
    $entry->param("name"),
    $entry->param("message"));
    print br();
}
print end_html;
```

As you will doubtless realize, the `h2` function outputs a second-level HTML heading. For the rest, we simply iterate through the current list of saved entries (the same list we earlier wrote to the savefile), printing out date, name, and message from each one.

Users can sit there with the guestbook form, continually typing messages and hitting the submit button. This simulates an electronic bulletin-board system, letting them see each others' new messages each time they send off their own. When they do this, they call the same CGI program repeatedly, which means that the previous widget values are automatically retained between invocations. This is particularly convenient when creating multistage forms, such as those used in so-called "shopping cart" applications.

Troubleshooting CGI Programs

CGI programs launched from a web server run under a fundamentally different environment than they do when invoked from the command line. While you should always verify that your CGI program runs properly from the command line,[*] this isn't enough to guarantee that your program will work when called from the web server.

You should get the CGI programming FAQ and a good book on CGI programming to help you in this. Some of these are listed at the end of this chapter.

---

[*] See the CGI.pm documentation for tips on command-line debugging.

Here's a brief list of the frequent problems that arise in CGI programming. Almost all of them trigger those annoyingly unhelpful `500 Server Error` messages that you will soon come to know and hate.

- If, when sending HTML to a browser, you forget the blank line between the HTTP header (that is, the `Content-type` line) and the body, it won't work. Remember to output a proper `Content-Type` line (and possibly other HTTP headers) plus a totally blank line before you do anything else.

- The server needs read and execute access to the script, so its permissions should usually be mode 0555 or, better, 0755. (This is UNIX-specific.)

- The directory where the script resides must itself be executable, so give it permissions of 0111 or, better, 0755. (This is UNIX-specific.)

- The script must be installed in the proper directory for your server configuration. For example, on some systems, it may be */usr/etc/httpd/cgi-bin/*.

- You may need to have your script's filename end in a particular suffix, like *.cgi* or *.pl*. We advise against this setup, preferring to enable CGI execution on a per-directory basis instead, but some configurations may require it. Automatically assuming that anything ending in *.cgi* is executable is perilous if any directories are writable by FTP clients, or when mirroring someone else's directory structure. In both cases, executable programs may suddenly appear on your server without the webmaster's knowledge or consent. It also means that any files whose names end in *.cgi* or *.pl* can never again be fetched via a normal URL, an effect that ranges between undesirable and disastrous.

  Remember that the *.pl* suffix means it's a Perl library, not a Perl executable. Confusing these two will only make you unhappy in the long run. If you absolutely *must* have a unique suffix on a script to enable Perl execution (because your operating system just isn't clever enough to use something like the `#!/usr/bin/perl` notation), we suggest a suffix of *.plx* instead. But you still incur the other problems we just mentioned.

- Your server configuration requires CGI execution specially enabled for the directory you put your CGI script in. Make sure both GET and POST are allowed. (Your webmaster will know what that means.)

- The web server doesn't execute your script under your user ID. Make sure the files and directories accessed by the script are open to whatever user the web server runs scripts as, for example, `nobody`, `wwwuser`, or `httpd`. You may need to precreate such files and directories and give them wide-open write permissions. Under UNIX, this is done with `chmod a+w`. Always be alert to the risks when you grant such access to files.

- Always run your script under Perl's −w flag to get warnings. These go to the web-server error log, which contains any errors and warnings generated by your script. Learn the path to that logfile from your webmaster and check it for problems. See also the standard CGI::Carp module for how to handle errors better.

- Make sure that the versions and paths to Perl and any libraries you use (like CGI.pm) are what you're expecting them to be on the machine the web server is running on.

- Enable autoflush on the STDOUT filehandle at the top of your script by setting the $| variable to a true value, like 1. If you've the used the FileHandle module or any of the IO modules (like IO::File, IO::Socket, and so on), then you can use the more mnemonically named `autoflush()` method on the filehandle instead:

  ```
  use FileHandle;
  STDOUT->autoflush(1);
  ```

- Check the return value of every system call your program makes, and take appropriate action if the call fails.

Perl and the Web: Beyond CGI Programming

Perl is used for much more than CGI programming. Other uses include logfile analysis, cookie and password management, clickable images, and image manipulation.* And that's still just the tip of the iceberg.

Custom Publishing Systems

Commercial web publishing systems may make easy things easy, especially for nonprogrammers, but they just aren't infinitely flexible the way a real programming language is. Without source code, you're locked into someone else's design decisions: if something doesn't work quite the way you want it to, you can't fix it. No matter how many whiz-bang programs become available for the consumer to purchase, a programmer will always be needed for those special jobs that don't quite fit the mold. And of course someone has to write the publishing software in the first place.

Perl is great for creating custom publishing systems tailored to your unique needs. It's easy to convert raw data into zillions of HTML pages en masse. Sites all over the Web use Perl to generate and maintain their entire web site. *The Perl Journal* (*www.tpj.com*) uses Perl to generate all its pages. The Perl Language Home Page

---

* See the GD.pm module on CPAN for a Perl interface to Thomas Boutell's gd graphics library.

(*www.perl.com*) has nearly 10,000 web pages all automatically maintained and updated by various Perl programs.

Embedded Perl

The fastest, cheapest (it's hard to get any cheaper than free), and most popular web server on the Net, Apache, can run with Perl embedded inside it using the mod_perl module from CPAN. With mod_perl, Perl becomes the extension language for your web server. You can write little Perl snippets to handle authorization requests, error handling, logging, and anything else you can think of. These don't require a new process because Perl is now built-in to the web server. Even more appealing for many is that under Apache you don't have to fire off a whole new process each time a CGI request comes in. Instead, a new thread executes a precompiled Perl program. This speeds up your CGI programs significantly; typically it's the `fork/exec` overhead that slows you down, not the size of the program itself.

Another strategy for speeding up CGI execution is through the standard CGI::Fast module. Unlike the embedded Perl interpreter described above, this approach doesn't require the Apache web server. See the CGI::Fast module's manpage for more details about this.

If you're running a web server under WindowsNT, you should definitely check out the ActiveWare site, *www.activeware.com*. Not only do they have prebuilt binaries of Perl for Windows platforms,[*] they also provide PerlScript and PerlIS. PerlScript is an ActiveX scripting engine that lets you embed Perl code in your web pages as you would with JavaScript or VBScript. PerlIS is an ISAPI DLL that runs Perl scripts directly from IIS and other ISAPI compliant web servers, providing significant performance benefits.

Web Automation with LWP

Have you ever wanted to check a web document for dead links, find its title, or figure out which of its links have been updated since last Thursday? Or wanted to download the images contained within a document or mirror an entire directory full of documents? What happens if you have to go through a proxy server or server redirects?

Now, you *could* do these things by hand using your browser. But because graphical interfaces are woefully inadequate for programmatic automation, this would

---

[*] As of release 5.004, the standard distribution of Perl builds under Windows, assuming you have a C compiler, that is.

be a slow and tedious process requiring more patience and less laziness* than most of us tend to possess.

The LWP ("Library for WWW access in Perl") modules from CPAN do all this for you and more. For example, fetching a document from the Web in a script is so easy using these modules that you can write it as a one-liner. For example, to get the */perl/index.html* document from *www.perl.com*, just type this into your shell or command interpreter:

```
perl -MLWP::Simple -e "getprint 'http://www.perl.com/perl/index.html'"
```

Apart from the LWP::Simple module, most of the modules included in the LWP suite are strongly object-oriented. For example, here's a tiny program that takes URLs as arguments and produces their titles:

```perl
#!/usr/bin/perl
use LWP;
$browser = LWP::UserAgent->new(); # create virtual browser
$browser->agent("Mothra/126-Paladium"); # give it a name
foreach $url (@ARGV) { # expect URLs as args
    # make a GET request on the URL via fake browser
    $webdoc = $browser->request(HTTP::Request->new(GET => $url));
    if ($webdoc->is_success) { # found it
    print STDOUT "$url: ", $webdoc->title, "\n";
    } else { # something went wrong
    print STDERR "$0: Couldn't fetch $url\n";
    }
}
```

As you see, familiarity with Perl's objects is important. But just as with the CGI.pm module, the LWP modules hide most of the complexity.

This script works as follows: first create a user agent object, something like an automated, virtual browser. This object is used to make requests to remote servers. Give our virtual browser a silly name just to make people's logfiles more interesting. Then pull in the remote document by making an HTTP GET request to the remote server. If the result is successful, print out the URL and its title; otherwise, complain a bit.

Here's a program that prints out a sorted list of unique links and images contained in URLs passed as command-line arguments:

```perl
#!/usr/bin/perl -w
use strict;
use LWP 5.000;
use URI::URL;
use HTML::LinkExtor;
```

---

* Remember that according to Larry Wall, the three principal virtues of a programmer are Laziness, Impatience, and Hubris.

```
my($url, $browser, %saw);
$browser = LWP::UserAgent->new(); # make fake browser
foreach $url ( @ARGV ) {
    # fetch the document via fake browser
    my $webdoc = $browser->request(HTTP::Request->new(GET => $url));
    next unless $webdoc->is_success;
    next unless $webdoc->content_type eq 'text/html';
                                            # can't parse gifs

    my $base = $webdoc->base;

    # now extract all links of type <A ...> and <IMG ...>
    foreach (HTML::LinkExtor->new->parse($webdoc->content)->eof->
                                        links) {
        my($tag, %links) = @$_;
        next unless $tag eq "a" or $tag eq "img";
        my $link;
        foreach $link (values %links) {
            $saw{ url($link,$base)->abs->as_string }++;
        }
    }
}
print join("\n", sort keys %saw), "\n";
```

This looks pretty complicated, but most of the complexity lies in understanding how the various objects and their methods work. We aren't going to explain all these here, because this book is long enough already. Fortunately, LWP comes with extensive documentation and examples.

Further Reading

There's quite a bit more to modules, references, objects, and web programming than we can possibly hope to cover in this one small chapter. A whole book could be written on CGI programming. In fact, dozens have been. For your continued research into these matters, check out the following reference list:

- CGI.pm docs
- The LWP library from CPAN
- O'Reilly & Associates' *CGI Programming on the World Wide Web* by Shishir Gundavaram
- O'Reilly & Associates' *Web Client Programming with Perl* by Clinton Wong
- O'Reilly & Associates' *HTML: The Definitive Guide, Second Edition* by Chuck Musciano and Bill Kennedy
- Addison-Wesley's *How to Setup and Maintain a Web Site* by Lincoln Stein, M.D., Ph.D.
- Addison-Wesley's *CGI Programming in C and Perl*, by Thomas Boutell

- Nick Kew's CGI FAQ

- Manpages: *perltoot, perlref, perlmod, perlobj*

Exercises

1. Write a form that provides two input fields that are added together when the user submits it.

2. Write a CGI script that detects the browser type making the request and says something in response. (Hint: look at the HTTP_USER_AGENT environment variable.)

A

Exercise Answers

This appendix gives the answers for the exercises found at the end of each chapter.

Chapter 2, Scalar Data

1. Here's one way to do it:

```
$pi = 3.141592654;
$result = 2 * $pi * 12.5;
print "radius 12.5 is circumference $result\n";
```

First, we give a constant value (π) to the scalar variable $pi. Next, we compute the circumference using this value of $pi in an expression. Finally, we print the result using a string containing a reference to the result.

2. Here's one way to do it:

```
print "What is the radius: ";
chomp($radius = <STDIN>);
$pi = 3.141592654;
$result = 2 * $pi * $radius;
print "radius $radius is circumference $result\n";
```

This is similar to the previous exercise, but here we've asked the person running the program for a value, using a `print` statement for a prompt, and then the <STDIN> operator to read a line from the terminal.

If we had left off the chomp, we'd get a newline in the middle of the displayed string at the end. It's important to get that newline off the string as soon as we can.

3. Here's one way to do it:

```
print "First number: "; chomp($a = <STDIN>);
print "Second number: "; chomp($b = <STDIN>);
```

```
$c = $a * $b; print "Answer is $c.\n";
```

The first line does three things: prompts you with a message, reads a line from standard input, and then gets rid of the inevitable newline at the end of the string. Note that since we are using the value of $a strictly as a number, we can omit the chomp here, because 45\n is 45 when used numerically. However, such careless programming would likely come back to haunt us later on (for example, if we were to include $a in a message).

The second line does the same thing for the second number and places it into the scalar variable $b.

The third line multiplies the two numbers together and prints the result. Note the newline at the end of the string here, contrasted with its absence in the first two lines. The first two messages are prompts, for which user input was desired on the same line. This last message is a complete statement; if we had left the newline out of the string, the shell prompt would appear immediately after the message. Not very cool.

4. Here's one way to do it:

```
print "String: "; $a = <STDIN>;
print "Number of times: "; chomp($b = <STDIN>);
$c = $a x $b; print "The result is:\n$c";
```

Like the previous exercise, the first two lines ask for, and accept, values for the two variables. Unlike the previous exercise, we don't chomp the newline from the end of the string, because we need it! The third line takes the two entered values and performs a string repetition on them, then displays the answer. Note that the interpolation of $c is not followed by a newline, because we believe that $c will always end in a newline anyway.

Chapter 3, Arrays and List Data

1. One way to do this is:

```
print "Enter the list of strings:\n";
@list = <STDIN>;
@reverselist = reverse @list;
print @reverselist;
```

The first line prompts for the strings. The second reads the strings into an array variable. The third line computes the list in the reverse order, storing it into another variable, and the final line displays the result.

We can actually combine the last three lines, resulting in:

```
print "Enter the list of strings:\n";
print reverse <STDIN>;
```

This works because the `print` operator is expecting a list, and `reverse` returns a list—so they're happy. And `reverse` wants a list of values to reverse, and `<STDIN>` in a list context returns a list of the lines, so they're happy too!

2. One way to do this is:

```
print "Enter the line number: "; chomp($a = <STDIN>);
print "Enter the lines, end with ^D:\n"; @b = <STDIN>;
print "Answer: $b[$a-1]";
```

The first line prompts for a number, reads it from standard input, and removes that pesky newline. The second line asks for a list of strings, then uses the `<STDIN>` operator in a list context to read all of the lines until end-of-file into an array variable. The final statement prints the answer, using an array reference to select the proper line. Note that we don't have to add a newline to the end of this string, because the line selected from the `@b` array still has its newline ending.

If you are trying this from a terminal configured in the most common way, you'll need to type CTRL-D at the terminal to indicate an end-of-file.

3. One way to do this is.

```
srand;
print "List of strings: "; @b = <STDIN>;
print "Answer: $b[rand(@b)]";
```

The first line initializes the random number generator. The second line reads a bunch of strings. The third line selects a random element from that bunch of strings and prints it.

Chapter 4, Control Structures

1. Here's one way to do it:

```
print "What temperature is it? ";
chomp($temperature = <STDIN>);
if ($temperature > 72) {
    print "Too hot!\n";
} else {
    print "Too cold!\n";
}
```

The first line prompts you for the temperature. The second line accepts the temperature for input. The `if` statement on the final 5 lines selects one of two messages to print, depending on the value of `$temperature`.

2. Here's one way to do it:

```
print "What temperature is it? ";
chomp($temperature = <STDIN>);
if ($temperature > 75) {
```

```
    print "Too hot!\n";
} elsif ($temperature < 68) {
    print "Too cold!\n";
} else {
    print "Just right!\n";
}
```

Here, we've modified the program to include a three-way choice. First, the temperature is compared to 75, then to 68. Note that only one of the three choices will be executed each time through the program.

3. Here's one way to do it:

```
print "Enter a number (999 to quit): ";
chomp($n = <STDIN>);
while ($n != 999) {
    $sum += $n;
    print "Enter another number (999 to quit): ";
    chomp($n = <STDIN>);
}
print "the sum is $sum\n";
```

The first line prompts for the first number. The second line reads the number from the terminal. The `while` loop continues to execute as long as the number is not 999.

The `+=` operator accumulates the numbers into the `$sum` variable. Note that the initial value of `$sum` is `undef`, which makes a nice value for an accumulator, because the first value added in will be effectively added to 0 (remember that `undef` used as a number is zero).

Within the loop, we must prompt for and receive another number, so that the test at the top of the loop is against a newly entered number.

When the loop is exited, the program prints the accumulated results.

Note that if you enter `999` right away, the value of `$sum` is not zero, but an empty string—the value of `undef` when used as a string. If you want to ensure that the program prints zero in this case, you should initialize the value of `$sum` in the beginning of the program with `$sum = 0`.

4. Here's one way to do it:

```
print "Enter some strings, end with ^D:\n";
@strings = <STDIN>;
while (@strings) {
    print pop @strings;
}
```

First, this program asks for the strings. These strings are saved in the array variable `@strings`, one per element.

The control expression of the `while` loop is `@strings`. The control expression is looking for a single value (*true* or *false*), and is therefore computing the expression in a scalar context. The name of an array (such as `@strings`) when used in a scalar context is the number of elements currently in the array. As long as the array is not empty, this number is nonzero and therefore true. This is a very common Perl idiom for "do this while the array is nonempty."

The body of the loop prints a value, obtained by pop'ing off the rightmost element of the array. Thus, because that element has been popped, each time through the loop the array is one element shorter.

You may have considered using subscripts for this problem. As we say, there's more than one way to do it. However, you'll rarely see subscripts in true Perl Hackers' programs because there's almost always a better way.

5. Here's a way to do it without a list:

```
for ($number = 0; $number <= 32; $number++) {
    $square = $number * $number;
    printf "%5g %8g\n", $number, $square;
}
```

And here's how to do it *with* a list:

```
foreach $number (0..32) {
    $square = $number * $number;
    printf "%5g %8g\n", $number, $square;
}
```

These solutions both involve loops, using the `for` and `foreach` statements. The body of the loops are identical, because for both solutions, the value of `$number` proceeds from 0 to 32 on each iteration.

The first solution uses a traditional C-like `for` statement. The three expressions respectively: set `$number` to 0, test to see if `$number` is less than or equal to 32, and increment `$number` on each iteration.

The second solution uses a C-shell-like `foreach` statement. A list of 33 elements (0 to 32) is created, using the list contructor. The variable `$number` is then set to each element in turn.

Chapter 5, Hashes

1. Here is one way to do it:

```
%map = qw(red apple green leaves blue ocean);
print "A string please: "; chomp($some_string = <STDIN>);
print "The value for $some_string is $map{$some_string}\n";
```

The first line creates the hash, giving it the desired key-value pairs. The second line fetches a string, removing the pesky newline. The third line prints the entered value and its mapped value.

You can also create the hash through a series of separate assignments, like so:

```
$map{'red'} = 'apple';
$map{'green'} = 'leaves';
$map{'blue'} = 'ocean';
```

2. Here's one way to do it:

```
chomp(@words = <STDIN>);                    # read the words, minus newlines
foreach $word (@words) {
    $count{$word} = $count{$word} + 1; # or $count{$word}++
}
foreach $word (keys %count) {
    print "$word was seen $count{$word} times\n";
}
```

The first line reads the lines into the @words array. Recall that this will cause each line to end up as a separate element of the array, with the newline character still intact.

The next four lines step through the array, setting $word equal to each line in turn. The newline is discarded with chomp, and then the magic comes. Each word is used as a key into a hash. The value of the element selected by the key (the word) is a count of the number of times we've seen that word so far. Initially, there are no elements in the hash, so if the word wild is seen on the first line, we have $count{"wild"}, which is undef. The undef value plus one turns out to be zero plus one, or one. (Recall that undef looks like a zero if used as a number.) The next time through, we'll have one plus one, or two, and so on.

Another common way to write the increment is given in the comments. Fluent Perl programmers tend to be lazy (we call it "concise") and would never go for writing the same hash reference on both sides of the assignment when a simple autoincrement will do.

After the words have been counted, the last few lines step through the hash by looking at each of its keys one at a time. The key and the corresponding value are printed after having been interpolated into the string.

The extra challenge answer looks like this answer, with the sort operator inserted just before the word keys on the third-to-last line. Without the sorting, the resulting output is seemingly random and unpredictable. However, once sorted, the output is predictable and consistent. (Personally, I rarely use the keys operator without also adding a sort immediately in front of it; this ensures that reruns over the same or similar data generate comparable results.)

Chapter 6, Basic I/O

1. Here's one way to do it:

```
print reverse <>;
```

You may be surprised at the brevity of this answer, but it will get the job done. Here's what is happening, from the inside out:

 a. First, the **reverse** function is looking for a list for its arguments. This means that the diamond operator (<>) is being evaluated in a list context. Thus, all of the lines of the files named by command-line arguments (or standard input, if none are named) are read in and massaged into a list with one line per element.

 b. Next, the **reverse** function reverses the list end for end.

 c. Finally, the **print** function takes the resulting list, and displays it.

2. See the Addendum on page 271, after the index, for the answer to this exercise.

3. Here's one way to do it:

```
print "List of strings:\n";
chomp(@strings = <STDIN>);
foreach (@strings) {
    printf "%20s\n", $_;
}
```

The first line prompts for a list of strings.

The next line reads all of the strings into one array and gets rid of the newlines at the end of each line.

The **foreach** loop steps through this array, giving $_ the value of each line.

The **printf** function gets two arguments: the first argument defines the format: "%20s\n" means a 20-character right-justified column, followed by a newline.

4. Here's one way to do it:

```
print "Field width: ";
chomp($width = <STDIN>);
print "List of strings:\n";
chomp(@strings = <STDIN>);
foreach (@strings) {
    printf "%${width}s\n", $_;
}
```

To the previous exercise answer, we've added a prompt and response for the field width.

The other change is that the **printf** format string now contains a variable reference. The value of $width is included into the string before **printf** considers the format. Note that we cannot write this string as

```
printf "%$widths\n", $_; # WRONG
```

because then Perl would be looking for a variable named `$widths`, not a variable named `$width` to which we attach an `s`. Another way to write this is

```
printf "%$width"."s\n", $_; # RIGHT
```

because the termination of the string also terminates the variable name, protecting the following character from being sucked up into the name.

Chapter 7, Regular Expressions

1. Here are some possible answers:

    a. `/a+b*/`

    b. `/\\*\**/` (Remember that the backslash cancels the meaning of the special character following.)

    c. `/($whatever){3}/` (You must have the parentheses, or else the multiplier applies only to the last character of `$whatever`; this also fails if `$whatever` has special characters.)

    d. `/[\000-\377]{5}/` or `/(.|\n){5}/` (You can't use dot alone here, because dot doesn't match newline.)

    e. `/(^|\s)(\S+)(\s+\2)+(\s|$)/` (`\S` is nonwhitespace, and `\2` is a reference to whatever the "word" is; the caret or whitespace alternative ensures that the `\S+` begins at a whitespace boundary.)

2.   a. One way to do this is:

```
while (<STDIN>) {
    if (/a/i && /e/i && /i/i && /o/i && /u/i) {
        print;
    }
}
```

Here, we have an expression consisting of five match operators. These operators are all looking at the contents of the `$_` variable, which is where the control expression of the `while` loop is putting each line. The match operator expression will be true only when all five vowels are found.

Note that as soon as any of the five vowels are not found, the remainder of the expression is skipped, because the `&&` operator doesn't evaluate its right argument if the left argument is false.

    b. Another way to do this is:

```
while (<STDIN>) {
    if (/a.*e.*i.*o.*u/i) {
        print;
    }
}
```

This answer turns out to be easier than the other part of this exercise. Here we have a simple regular expression that looks for the five vowels in sequence, separated by any number of characters.

c. One way to do this is:

```
while (<>) {
    print if
        (/^[^aeiou]*a[^eiou]*e[^aiou]*i[^aeou]*o[^aeiu]*u[^aeio]*$ );
}
```

Ugly, but it works. To construct this, just think "What can go between the beginning of the line, and the first a?," and then "What can go between the first a and the first e?" Eventually, it all works itself out, with a little assistance from you.

3. One way to do this is:

```
while (<STDIN>) {
    chomp;
    ($user, $gcos) = (split /:/)[0,4];
    ($real) = split(/,/, $gcos);
    print "$user is $real\n";
}
```

The outer **while** loop reads one line at a time from the password-format file into the $_ variable, terminating when there are no more lines to be read.

The second line of the **while** loop body breaks the line apart by colons, saving two of the seven values into individual scalar variables with hopefully meaningful names.

The GCOS field (the fifth field) is then split apart by commas, with the resulting list assigned to a single scalar variable enclosed in parentheses. The parentheses are important: they make this assignment an array assignment rather than a scalar assignment. The scalar variable $real gets the first element of the list, and the remaining elements are discarded.

The **print** statement then displays the results.

4. One way to do this is:

```
while (<STDIN>) {
    chomp;
    ($gcos) = (split /:/)[4];
    ($real) = split(/,/, $gcos);
    ($first) = split(/\s+/, $real);
    $seen{$first}++;
}
foreach (keys %seen) {
    if ($seen{$_} > 1) {
        print "$_ was seen $seen{$_} times\n";
    }
}
```

The `while` loop works a lot like the `while` loop from the previous exercise. In addition to splitting the line apart into fields and the GCOS field apart into the real name (and other parts), this loop also splits apart the real name into a first name (and the rest). Once the first name is known, a hash element in `%seen` is incremented, noting that we've seen a particular first name. Note that this loop doesn't do any `print`'ing.

The `foreach` loop steps through all of the keys of `%seen` (the first names from the password file), assigning each one to `$_` in turn. If the value stored in `%seen` at a given key is greater than 1, we've seen the first name more than once. The `if` statement tests for this, and prints a message if so.

5. One way to do this is:

```perl
while (<STDIN>) {
    chomp;
    ($user, $gcos) = (split /:/)[0,4];
    ($real) = split /,/, $gcos;
    ($first) = split /\s+/, $real;
    $names{$first} .= " $user";
}
foreach (keys %names) {
    $this = $names{$_};
    if ($this =~ /. /) {
        print "$_ is used by:$this\n";
    }
}
```

This program is like the previous exercise answer, but instead of merely keeping a count, we append the login name of the user to the `%names` element that has a key of the first name. Thus, for Fred Rogers (login `mrrogers`), `$names{"Fred"}` becomes `" mrrogers"`, and when Fred Flintstone (login `fred`) comes along, we get `$names{"Fred"}` as `" mrrogers fred"`. After the loop is complete, we have a mapping of all of the first names to all of the users that have them.

The `foreach` loop, like the previous exercise answer, then steps through the resulting hash. However, rather than testing a hash element value for a number greater than one, we must see now if there is more than one login name in the value. We do this by saving the value into a scalar variable `$this` and then seeing if the value has a space after any character. If so, the first name is shared, and the resulting message tells which logins share that first name.

Chapter 8, Functions

1. Here's one way to do it:

```perl
sub card {
    my %card_map;
```

```
    @card_map{1..9} = qw(
        one two three four five six seven eight nine
    );

    my($num) = @_;
    if ($card_map{$num}) {
      return $card_map{$num};
    } else {
      return $num;
    }
}
# driver routine:
while (<>) {
    chomp;
    print "card of $_ is ", &card($_), "\n";
}
```

The &card subroutine (so named because it returns a *cardinal* name for a given value) begins by initializing a constant hash called %card_map. This array has values such that $card_map{6} is six, making it fairly easy to do the mapping.

The if statement determines if the value is in range by looking the number up in the hash: if there's a corresponding hash element, the test is true, so that array element is returned. If there's no corresponding element (such as when $num is 11 or -4), the value returned from the hash lookup is undef, so the else-branch of the if statement is executed, returning the original number. You can also replace that entire if statement with the single expression:

```
$card_map{$num} || $num;
```

If the value on the left of the || is true, it's the value for the entire expression, which then gets returned. If it's false (such as when $num is out of range), the right side of the || operator is evaluated, returning $num as the return value.

The driver routine takes successive lines, chomping off their newlines, and hands them one at a time to the &card routine, printing the result.

2. Here's one way to do it:

```
sub card { ...; } # from previous problem
print "Enter first number: ";
chomp($first = <STDIN>);
print "Enter second number: ";
chomp($second = <STDIN>);
$message = card($first) . " plus " .
    card($second) . " equals " .
    card($first+$second) . ".\n";
print "\u$message";
```

The first two `print` statements prompt for two numbers, with the immediately following statements reading the values into `$first` and `$second`.

A string called `$message` is then built up by calling `&card` three times, once for each value and once for the sum.

Once the message is constructed, its first character is uppercased by the case-shifting backslash operator `\u`. The message is then printed.

3. Here's one way to do it:

```
sub card {
    my %card_map;
    @card_map{0..9} = qw(
        zero one two three four five six seven eight nine
    );

    my($num) = @_;
    my($negative);
    if ($num < 0) {
        $negative = "negative ";
        $num = - $num;
    }
    if ($card_map{$num}) {
        return $negative . $card_map{$num};
    } else {
        return $negative . $num;
    }
}
```

Here, we've given the `%card_map` array a name for zero.

The first `if` statement inverts the sign of `$num` and sets `$negative` to the word negative, if the number is found to be less than zero. After this `if` statement, the value of `$num` is always nonnegative, but we will have an appropriate prefix string in `$negative`.

The second `if` statement determines if the (now positive) `$num` is within the hash. If so, the resulting hash value is appended to the prefix within `$negative` and returned. If not, the value within `$negative` is attached to the original number.

That last `if` statement can be replaced with the expression:

```
$negative . ($card_map{$num} || $num);
```

Chapter 9, Miscellaneous Control Structures

1. Here's one way to do it:

```
sub card {} # from previous exercise

while () { ## NEW ##
```

```
    print "Enter first number: ";
    chomp($first = <STDIN>);
    last if $first eq "end"; ## NEW ##

    print "Enter second number: ";
    chomp($second = <STDIN>);
    last if $second eq "end"; ## NEW ##

    $message = &card($first) . " plus " .
        card($second) . " equals " .
        card($first+$second) . ".\n";
    print "\u$message";
} ## NEW ##
```

Note the addition of the `while` loop and the two `last` operators. That's it!

2. See the Addendum on page 271, after the index, for the answer to this exercise.

Chapter 10, Filehandles and File Tests

1. Here's one way to do it:

```
print "What file? ";
chomp($filename = <STDIN>);
open(THATFILE, "$filename") ||
    die "cannot open $filename: $!";
while (<THATFILE>) {
    print "$filename: $_"; # presume $_ ends in \n
}
```

The first two lines prompt for a filename, which is then opened with the filehandle `THATFILE`. The contents of the file are read using the filehandle and printed to `STDOUT`.

2. Here's one way to do it:

```
print "Input file name: ";
chomp($infilename = <STDIN>);
print "Output file name: ";
chomp($outfilename = <STDIN>);
print "Search string: ";
chomp($search = <STDIN>);
print "Replacement string: ";
chomp($replace = <STDIN>);
open(IN,$infilename) ||
    die "cannot open $infilename for reading: $!";
## optional test for overwrite...
die "will not overwrite $outfilename" if -e $outfilename;
open(OUT,">$outfilename") ||
    die "cannot create $outfilename: $!";
while (<IN>) {     # read a line from file IN into $_
    s/$search/$replace/g; # change the lines
    print OUT $_; # print that line to file OUT
}
close(IN);
close(OUT);
```

This program is based on the file-copying program presented earlier in the chapter. New features here include prompting for the strings and the substitute command in the middle of the `while` loop, as well as the test for overwriting a file.

Note that backreferences in the regular expression do work, but referencing memory in the replacement string does not.

3. Here's one way to do it:

```
while (<>) {
    chomp; # eliminate the newline
    print "$_ is readable\n" if -r;
    print "$_ is writable\n" if -w;
    print "$_ is executable\n" if -x;
    print "$_ does not exist\n" unless -e;
}
```

This `while` loop reads a filename each time through. After discarding the newline, the series of statements tests the file for the various permissions.

4. Here's one way to do it:

```
while (<>) {
    chomp;
    $age = -M;
    if ($oldest_age < $age) {
        $oldest_name = $_;
        $oldest_age = $age;
    }
}
print "The oldest file is $oldest_name ",
    "and is $oldest_age days old.\n";
```

First, we loop on each filename being read in. The newline is discarded, and then the age in days gets computed with the **-M** operator. If the age for this file exceeds the oldest file we've seen so far, we remember the filename and its corresponding age. Initially, `$oldest_age` will be 0, so we're counting on there being at least one file that is more than 0 days old.

The final `print` statement generates the report when we're done.

Chapter 11, Formats

1. Here's one way to do it:

```
open(PW,"/etc/passwd") || die "How did you get logged in?";
while (<PW>) {
    ($user,$uid,$gcos) = (split /:/)[0,2,4];
    ($real) = split /,/,$gcos;
    write;
}
```

```
format STDOUT =
@<<<<<<< @>>>>>> @<<<<<<<<<<<<<<<<<<<<<<<<<<<<<<
$user, $uid, $real
.
```

The first line opens the password file. The `while` loop processes the password file line by line. Each line is torn apart (with colon delimiters), loading up the scalar variables. The real name of the user is pulled out of the GCOS field. The final statement of the `while` loop invokes `write` to display all of the data.

The format for the `STDOUT` filehandle defines a simple line with three fields. The values come from the three scalar variables that are given values in the `while` loop.

2. Here's one way to do it:

```
# append to program from the first problem...
format STDOUT_TOP =
Username User ID Real Name
======== ======= =========
.
```

All it takes to get page headers for the previous program is to add a top of-page format. Here, we put column headers on the columns.

To get the columns to line up, we copied the text of format `STDOUT` and used overstrike mode in our text editor to replace @<<< fields with ==== bars. That's the nice thing about the one-character-to-one-character correspondence between a format and the resulting display.

3. Here's one way to do it:

```
# append to program from the first problem...
format STDOUT_TOP =
Page @<<<
$%

Username User ID Real Name
======== ======= =========
.
```

Well, here again, to get stuff at the top of the page, I've added a top-of-page format. This format also contains a reference to `$%`, which gives me a page number automatically.

Chapter 12, Directory Access

1. Here's one way to do it:

```
print "Where to? ";
chomp($newdir = <STDIN>);
chdir($newdir) || die "Cannot chdir to $newdir: $!";
```

```
foreach (<*>) {
    print "$_\n";
}
```

The first two lines prompt for and read the name of the directory.

The third line attempts to change directory to the given name, aborting if this isn't possible.

The `foreach` loop steps through a list. But what's the list? It's the glob in a list context, which expands to a list of all of the filenames that match the pattern (here, `*`).

2. Here's one way to do it, with a directory handle:

```
print "Where to? ";
chomp($newdir = <STDIN>);
chdir($newdir) ||
    die "Cannot chdir to $newdir: $!";
opendir(DOT,".") ||
    die "Cannot opendir . (serious dainbramage): $!";
foreach (sort readdir(DOT)) {
        print "$_\n";
    }
closedir(DOT);
```

Just like the previous program, we prompt and read a new directory. Once we've `chdir`'ed there, we open the directory, creating a directory handle named DOT. In the `foreach` loop, the list returned by `readdir` (in a list context) is sorted, and then stepped through, assigning each element to `$_` in turn.

And here's how to do it with a glob instead:

```
print "Where to? ";
chomp($newdir = <STDIN>);
chdir($newdir) || die "Cannot chdir to $newdir: $!";
foreach (sort <* .*>) {
    print "$_\n";
}
```

Yes, it's basically the other program from the previous exercise, but I've added a `sort` operator in front of the glob and also added `.*` to the glob to pick up the files that begin with dot. We need the `sort` because a file named `!fred` belongs before the dot files, but `barney` belongs after them, and there isn't an easy shell glob that can get them all in the proper sequence.

Chapter 13, File and Directory Manipulation

1. Here's one way to do it:

```
unlink @ARGV;
```

Yup, that's it. The @ARGV array is a list of names to be removed. The unlink operator takes a list of names, so we just marry the two, and we're done.

Of course, this doesn't handle error reporting, or the -f or -i options, or anything like that, but that'd just be gravy. If you did that, good!

2. Here's one way to do it:

```
($old, $new) = @ARGV; # name them
if (-d $new) { # new name is a directory, need to patch it up
    ($basename = $old) =~ s#.*/##s; # get basename of $old
    $new .= "/$basename"; # and append it to new name
}
rename($old,$new) || die "Cannot rename $old to $new: $!";
```

The workhorse in this program is the last line, but the remainder of the program is necessary for the case where the name we are renaming to is a directory.

First, we give understandable names to the two elements of @ARGV. Then, if the $new name is a directory, we need to patch it by adding the basename of the $old name to the end of the new name. This means that renaming */usr/src/fred* to */etc* results in really renaming */usr/src/fred* to */etc/fred*.

Finally, once the basename is patched up, we're home free, with a rename invocation.

3. Here's one way to do it:

```
($old, $new) = @ARGV; # name them
if (-d $new) { # new name is a directory, need to patch it up
    ($basename = $old) =~ s#.*/##s; # get basename of $old
    $new .= "/$basename"; # and append it to new name
}
link($old,$new) || die "Cannot link $old to $new: $!";
```

This program is identical to the previous program except for the very last line, because we're linking, not renaming.

4. Here's one way to do it:

```
if ($ARGV[0] eq "-s") { # wants a symlink
    $symlink++; # remember that
    shift(@ARGV); # and toss the -s flag
}
($old, $new) = @ARGV; # name them
if (-d $new) { # new name is a directory, need to patch it up
    ($basename = $old) =~ s#.*/##s; # get basename of $old
```

```
    $new .= "/$basename"; # and append it to new name
}
if ($symlink) { # wants a symlink
    symlink($old,$new);
} else { # wants a hard link
    link($old,$new);
}
```

The middle of this program is the same as the previous two exercises. What's new is the first few lines and the last few lines.

The first few lines look at the first argument to the program. If this argument is -s, the scalar variable $symlink is incremented, resulting in a value of 1 for the variable. The @ARGV array is then shifted, removing the -s flag. If the -s flag isn't present, there's nothing to be done, and $symlink will remain undef. Shifting the @ARGV array occurs frequently enough that the @ARGV array is the default argument for shift; that is, we could have said:

```
    shift;
```

in place of

```
    shift(@ARGV);
```

The last few lines look at the value of $symlink. It's going to be either 1 or undef, and based on that, we either symlink the files or link them.

5. Here's one way to do it:

```
foreach $f (<*>) {
    print "$f -> $where\n" if defined($where = readlink($f));
}
```

The scalar variable $f is set in turn to each of the filenames in the current directory. For each name, $where gets set to the readlink() of that name. If the name is not a symlink, the readlink operator returns undef, yielding a false value for the if test, and the print is skipped. But when the readlink operator returns a value, the print displays the source and destination symlink values.

Chapter 14, Process Management

1. Here's one way to do it:

```
if (`date` =~ /^S/) {
    print "Go play!\n";
} else {
    print "Get to work!\n";
}
```

It just so happens that the first output character of the *date* command is an S only on the weekend (Sat or Sun), which makes this program trivial. We invoke *date*, then use a regular expression to see if the first character is an S. Based on that, we print one message or the other.

2. Here's one way to do it:

```
open(PW,"/etc/passwd");
while (<PW>) {
    chomp;
    ($user,$gcos) = (split /:/)[0,4];
    ($real) = split(/,/, $gcos);
    $real{$user} = $real;
}
close(PW);

open(WHO,"who|") || die "cannot open who pipe";
while (<WHO>) {
    ($login, $rest) = /^(\S+)\s+(.*)/;
    $login = $real{$login} if $real{$login};
    printf "%-30s %s\n",$login,$rest;
}
```

The first loop creates a hash **%real** that has login names for keys and the corresponding real names as values. This hash is used in the following loop to change the login name into a real name.

The second loop scans through the output resulting from opening the *who* command as a filehandle. Each line of *who*'s output is broken apart using a regular expression match in a list context. The first word of the line (the login name) is replaced with the real name from the hash, but only if it exists. When that's all done, a nice **printf** puts the result onto **STDOUT**.

You can replace the filehandle **open** and the beginning of the loop with just

```
foreach $_ (`who`) {
```

to accomplish the same result. The only difference is that the version with the filehandle can begin operating as soon as *who* starts spitting out characters, while the version with *who* in backquotes must wait for *who* to finish.

3. Here's one way to do it:

```
open(PW,"/etc/passwd");
while (<PW>) {
    chomp;
    ($user,$gcos) = (split /:/)[0,4];
    ($real) = split(/,/, $gcos);
    $real{$user} = $real;
}
close(PW);

open(LPR,"|lpr") || die "cannot open LPR pipe";
open(WHO,"who|") || die "cannot open who pipe";
while (<WHO>) {
# or replace previous two lines with: foreach $_ (`who`) {
    ($login, $rest) = /^(\S+)\s+(.*)/;
```

```
    $login = $real{$login} if $real{$login};
    printf LPR "%-30s %s\n",$login,$rest;
}
```

The difference between this program and the program from the previous exercise is that we've added an LPR filehandle opened onto an *lpr* process, and modified the `printf` statement to send the data there instead of STDOUT.

4. Here's one way to do it:

```
sub mkdir {
    !system "/bin/mkdir", @_;
}
```

Here, the *mkdir* command is given the arguments directly from the arguments to the subroutine. The return value must be logically negated, however, because a nonzero exit status from `system` must translate into a false value for the Perl caller.

5. Here's one way to do it:

```
sub mkdir {
    my($dir, $mode) = @_;
    (!system "/bin/mkdir", $dir) && chmod($mode, $dir);
}
```

First, the arguments to this routine are named as $dir and $mode. Next, we invoke *mkdir* on the directory named by $dir. If that succeeds, the chmod operator gives the proper mode to the directory.

Chapter 15, Other Data Transformation

1. Here's one way to do it:

```
while (<>) {
    chomp;
    $slash = rindex($_,"/");
    if ($slash > -1) {
        $head = substr($_,0,$slash);
        $tail = substr($_,$slash+1);
    } else {
        ($head,$tail) = ("", $_);
    }
    print "head = '$head', tail = '$tail'\n";
}
```

Each line read by the diamond operator is first chomped (tossing the newline). Next we look for the rightmost slash in the line, using `rindex()`. The next two lines break the string apart using `substr()`. If there's no slash, the result of the `rindex` is −1, so we hack around that. The final line within the loop prints the results.

2. Here's one way to do it:

```
chomp(@nums = <STDIN>); # note special use of chomp
@nums = sort { $a <=> $b } @nums;
foreach (@nums) {
    printf "%30g\n", $_;
}
```

The first line grabs all of the numbers into the @nums array. The second line sorts the array numerically, using an inline definition for a sorting order. The foreach loop prints the results.

3. Here's one way to do it:

```
open(PW,"/etc/passwd") || die "How did you get logged in?";
while (<PW>) {
    chomp;
    ($user, $gcos) = (split /:/)[0,4];
    ($real) = split(/,/, $gcos);
    $real{$user} = $real;
    ($last) = (split /\s+/, $real)[-1];
    $last{$user} = "\L$last";
}
close(PW);

foreach (sort by_last keys %last) {
    printf "%30s %8s\n", $real{$_}, $_;
}

sub by_last { ($last{$a} cmp $last{$b}) || ($a cmp $b) }
```

The first loop creates %last hash, consisting of login names for keys and user's last names for the corresponding values, and the %real hash, containing the full real names instead. The last names are all converted to lowercase, so that FLINTSTONE, Flintstone, and flintstone all sort near each other.

The second loop prints %real out, ordered by the values of %last, using the sort definition presented in by_last subroutine.

4. Here's one way to do it:

```
while (<>) {
    substr($_,0,1) =~ tr/a-z/A-Z/;
    substr($_,1) =~ tr/A-Z/a-z/;
    print;
}
```

For each line read by the diamond operator, we use two tr operators, each on a different portion of the string. The first tr operator uppercases the first character of the line, and the second tr operator lowercases the remainder. The result is printed.

Here's another way to do this, using only double-quoted string operators:

```
while (<>) {
    print "\u\L$_";
}
```

Give yourself an extra five points if you thought of that instead.

Chapter 16, System Database Access

1. Here's one way to do that:

```
$: = " ";
while (@pw = getpwent) {
    ($user, $gid, $gcos) = @pw[0,3,6];
    ($real) = split /,/, $gcos;
    $real{$user} = $real;
    $members{$gid} .= " $user";
    ($last) = (split /\s+/, $real)[-1];
    $last{$user} = "\L$last";
}

while (@gr = getgrent) {
    ($gname,$gid,$members) = @gr[0,2,3];
    $members{$gid} .= " $members";
    $gname{$gid} = $gname;
}

for $gid (sort by_gname keys %gname) {
    %all = ();
    for (split(/\s+/, $members{$gid})) {
        $all{$_}++ if length $_;
    }
    @members = ();
    foreach (sort by_last keys %all) {
        push(@members, "$real{$_} ($_)");
    }
    $memberlist = join(", ", @members);
    write;
}

sub by_gname { $gname{$a} cmp $gname{$b}; }
sub by_last { ($last{$a} cmp $last{$b}) || ($a cmp $b); }

format STDOUT =
@<<<<<<<< @<<<<<<<< ^<<<<<<<<<<<<<<<<<<<<<<<<<<<<<<<<<<<<
$gname{$gid}, "($gid)", $memberlist
~~                     ^<<<<<<<<<<<<<<<<<<<<<<<<<<<<<<<<<<<<
$memberlist
.
```

Yes, this one needs some explaining.

Chapter 17, User Database Manipulation

1. Here's one way to do it:

```
dbmopen(%ALIAS, "/etc/aliases", undef) ||
    die "No aliases!: $!";
while (($key,$value) = each(%ALIAS)) {
    chop($key,$value);
    print "$key $value\n";
}
```

The first line opens the aliases DBM. (Your system may keep the aliases DBM in */usr/lib/aliases* instead—try that if this doesn't work.) The `while` loop steps through the DBM array. The first line within the loop chops off the NUL character from the end of the key and the value. The final line of the loop prints out the result.

2. Here's one way to do it:

```
# program 1:
dbmopen(%WORDS,"words",0644);
while (<>) {
    foreach $word (split(/\W+/)) {
        $WORDS{$word}++;
    }
}
dbmclose(%WORDS);
```

The first program (the writer) opens a DBM in the current directory called **words**, creating files named *words.dir* and *words.pag*. The `while` loop grabs each line using the diamond operator. This line is split apart using the `split` operator, with a delimiter of `/\W+/`, meaning nonword characters. Each word is then counted into the DBM array, using the `foreach` statement to step through the words:

```
# program 2:
dbmopen(%WORDS,"words",undef);
foreach $word (sort { $WORDS{$b} <=> $WORDS{$a} } keys %WORDS) {
    print "$word $WORDS{$word}\n";
}
dbmclose(%WORDS);
```

The second program opens a DBM in the current directory called **words**. That complicated looking `foreach` line does most of the dirty work. The value of $word each time through the loop will be the next element of a list. The list is the sorted keys from %WORDS, sorted by their values (the count) in descending order. For each word in the list, we print the word and the number of times the word has occurred.

Chapter 18, Converting Other Languages to Perl

1. Here's one way to do it:

```
for (;;) {
    ($user,$home) = (getpwent)[0,7];
    last unless $user;
    next unless open(N,"$home/.newsrc");
    next unless -M N < 30; ## added value :-)
    while (<N>) {
        if (/^comp\.lang\.perl\.announce:/) {
            print "$user is a good person, ",
            "and reads comp.lang.perl.announce!\n";
            last;
        }
    }
}
```

The outermost loop is a `for` loop that runs forever; this loop gets exited by the `last` operator inside, however. Each time through the loop, a new value for `$user` (a username) and `$home` (their home directory) is fetched using the `getpwent` operator.

If the value of `$user` is empty, the `for` loop exits. The next two lines look for a recent *.newsrc* file in the user's home directory. If the file cannot be opened, or the modification time of the file is too distant, the next iteration of the `for` loop is triggered.

The `while` loop reads a line at a time from the *.newsrc* file. If the line begins with *comp.lang.perl.announce:*, the `print` statement says so, and the `while` loop is exited early.

Chapter 19, CGI Programming

1. Here's one way to do it:

```
use strict;
use CGI qw(:standard);

print header(), start_html("Add Me");
print h1("Add Me");
if(param()) {
    my $n1 = param('field1');
    my $n2 = param('field2');
    my $n3 = $n2 + $n1;
    print p("$n1 + $n2 = <strong>$n3</strong>\n");
} else {
    print hr(), start_form();
    print p("First Number:", textfield("field1"));
    print p("Second Number:", textfield("field2"));
```

```
        print p(submit("add"), reset("clear"));
        print end_form(), hr();
    }
print end_html();
```

If there's no input, simply generate a form with two textfields (using the `textfield` method). If there is input, we add the two fields together and print the result.

2. Here's one way to do it:

```
use strict;
use CGI qw(:standard);

print header(), start_html("Browser Detective");
print h1("Browser Detective"), hr();
my $browser = $ENV{'HTTP_USER_AGENT'};
$_ = $browser;

BROWSER:{
    if (/msie/i) {
            msie($_);
    } elsif (/mozilla/i) {
            netscape($_);
    } elsif (/lynx/i) {
            lynx($_);
    } else {
            default($_);
    }
}

print end_html();
sub msie{
    print p("Internet Explorer: @_.  Good Choice\n");
}

sub netscape {
    print p("Netscape: @_.  Good Choice\n");
}

sub lynx {
    print p("Lynx: @_.  Shudder...");
}

sub default {
    print p("What the heck is a @_?");
}
```

The key here is checking the environment for the HTTP_USER_AGENT variable. Although this isn't implemented by every server, many of them do set it. This is a good way to generate content geared to the features of a particular browser. Note that we're just doing some basic string matching (case insensitive) to see what they're using (nothing too fancy).

B

Libraries and Modules

For simple programs you can easily write your own Perl routines and subroutines. As the tasks to which you apply Perl become more difficult, however, sometimes you'll find yourself thinking, "someone must have done this already." You are probably more right than you imagine.

For most common tasks, other people have already written the code. Moreover, they've placed it either in the standard Perl distribution or in the freely downloadable CPAN archive. To use this existing code (and save yourself some time), you'll have to understand how to make use of a Perl library. This was briefly discussed in Chapter 19, *CGI Programming*.

One advantage in using modules from the standard distribution is that you can then share your program with others without their having to take any special steps. This is because the same standard library is available to Perl programs almost everywhere.

You'll save yourself time in the long run if you get to know the standard library. There's no point in reinventing the wheel. You should be aware, however, that the library contains a wide range of material. While some modules may be extremely helpful, others may be completely irrelevant to your needs. For example, some are useful only if you are creating extensions to Perl.

To read the documentation for a standard module, use the **man** or **perldoc** program (if you have them), or perhaps your web browser on HTML versions of the documentation. If all else fails, just look in the module itself: the documentation is contained within each module in pod format. To locate the module on your system, try executing this Perl program from the command line:

```
# for (most) Unix-like shells
perl -e 'print "@INC\n"'
```

```
# for (some) other command interpreters
perl -e "print join(' ',@INC),\n"
```

You should find the module in one of the directories listed by this command.

Library Terminology

Before we list all the standard modules, let's untangle some terminology:

Package

A package is a simple namespace management device, allowing two different parts of a Perl program to have a (different) variable named $fred. These namespaces are managed with the *package* declaration, described in Chapter 5 of *Programming Perl*.

Library

A library is a set of subroutines for a particular purpose. Often the library declares itself a separate package so that related variables and subroutines can be kept together, and so that they won't interfere with other variables in your program. Generally, an old-style library was placed in a separate file, often with a name ending in ".pl". The library routines were then pulled into the main program via the *require* function. More recently this older approach has been replaced by the use of *modules* (see next paragraph), and the term *library* often refers to the entire system of modules that come with Perl.

Module

A module is a library that conforms to specific conventions, allowing the library routines to be brought into your program with the *use* directive at compile-time. Module filenames end in ".pm", because the *use* directive insists on that. Chapter 5 of *Programming Perl* describes Perl modules in greater detail.

Pragma

A pragma is a module that affects the compilation phase of your program as well as the execution phase. Think of it as containing hints to the compiler. Unlike other modules, pragmas often (but not always) limit the scope of their effects to the innermost enclosing block of your program (that is, the block enclosing the pragma invocation). The names of pragmas are by convention all lowercase.

Standard Modules

The following is a list of all Perl pragmas and modules included with the current Perl distribution (Version 5.004). The classification of the modules is admittedly arbitrary.

Table B-1. General Programming: Miscellaneous

Module	Function
autouse	Defers loading of a module until it's used
constant	Creates compile-time constants
Benchmark	Checks and compares running times of code
Config	Accesses Perl configuration information
Env	Imports environment variables
English	Uses English or *awk* names for punctuation variables
FindBin	Finds path of currently executing program
Getopt::Long	Extended processing of command-line options
Getopt::Std	Processes single-character switches with switch clustering
lib	Manipulates @INC at compile-time
Shell	Runs shell commands transparently within Perl
strict	Restricts unsafe constructs
Symbol	Generates anonymous globs; qualifies variable names
subs	Predeclares subroutine names
vars	Predeclares global variable names

Table B-2. General Programming: Error Handling and Logging

Module	Function
Carp	Generates error messages
diagnostics	Forces verbose warning diagnostics
sigtrap	Enables stack backtrace on unexpected signals
Sys::Syslog	Perl interface to UNIX *syslog*(3) calls

Table B-3. General Programming: File Access and Handling

Module	Function
Cwd	Gets pathname of current working directory
DirHandle	Supplies object methods for directory handles
Fcntl	Loads the C *Fcntl.h* defines
File::Basename	Parses file specifications
File::CheckTree	Runs many tests on a collection of files
File::Copy	Copies files or filehandles

Table B-3. General Programming: File Access and Handling (continued)

Module	Function
File::Find	Traverses a file tree
File::Path	Creates or removes a series of directories
FileCache	Keeps more files open than the system permits
FileHandle	Supplies object methods for filehandles
SelectSaver	Saves and restores selected filehandle

Table B-4. General Programming: Classes for I/O Operations

Module	Function
IO	Top-level interface to IO::* classes
IO::File	Object methods for filehandles
IO::Handle	Object methods for I/O handles
IO::Pipe	Object methods for pipes
IO::Seekable	Seek-based methods for I/O objects
IO::Select	Object interface to select
IO::Socket	Object interface to sockets

Table B-5. General Programming: Text Processing and Screen Interfaces

Module	Function
locale	Uses POSIX locales for built-in operations
Pod::HTML	Converts pod data to HTML
Pod::Text	Converts pod data to formatted ASCII text
Search::Dict	Searches for key in dictionary file
Term::Cap	Termcap interface
Term::Complete	Word completion module
Text::Abbrev	Creates an abbreviation table from a list
Text::ParseWords	Parses text into an array of tokens
Text::Soundex	Implements the Soundex Algorithm described by Knuth
Text::Tabs	Expands and unexpands tabs
Text::Wrap	Wraps text into a paragraph

Table B-6 . Database Interfaces

Module	Function
AnyDBM_File	Provides framework for multiple DBMs
DB_File	Access to Berkeley DB
GDBM_File	Tied access to GDBM library
NDBM_File	Tied access to NDBM files

Table B-6 . Database Interfaces (continued)

Module	Function
ODBM_File	Tied access to ODBM files
SDBM_File	Tied access to SDBM files

Table B-7. Mathematics

Module	Function
Integer	Does arithmetic in integer instead of double
Math::BigFloat	Arbitrary-length, floating-point math package
Math::BigInt	Arbitrary-length integer math package
Math::Complex	Complex numbers package

Table B-8. The World Wide Web

Module	Function
CGI	Web server interface (Common Gateway Interface)
CGI::Apache	Support for Apache's Perl module
CGI::Carp	Log server errors with helpful context
CGI::Fast	Support for FastCGI (persistent server process)
CGI::Push	Support for server push
CGI::Switch	Simple interface for multiple server types

Table B-9. Networking and Interprocess Communication

Module	Function
IPC::Open2	Opens a process for both reading and writing
IPC::Open3	Opens a process for reading, writing, and error handling
Net::Ping	Checks whether a host is online
Socket	Loads the C *socket.h* defines and structure manipulators
Sys::Hostname	Tries every conceivable way to get hostname

Table B-10. Automated Access to the Comprehensive Perl Archive Network

Module	Function
CPAN	Simple interface to CPAN
CPAN::FirstTime	Utility for creating CPAN configuration file
CPAN::Nox	Runs CPAN while avoiding compiled extensions

Table B-11. Time and Locale

Module	Function
Time::Local	Efficiently computes time from local and GMT time
I18N::Collate	Compares 8-bit scalar data according to the current locale

Table B-12. Object Interfaces to Built-in Functions

Module	Function
Class::Struct	Declares struct-like datatypes as Perl classes
File::stat	Object interface to stat function
Net::hostent	Object interface to `gethost*` functions
Net::netent	Object interface to `getnet*` functions
Net::protoent	Object interface to `getproto*` functions
Net::servent	Object interface to `getserv*` functions
Time::gmtime	Object interface to `gmtime` function
Time::localtime	Object interface to `localtime` function
Time::tm	Internal object for Time::{gm,local}time
User::grent	Object interface to `getgr*` functions
User::pwent	Object interface to `getpw*` functions

Table B-13. For Developers: Autoloading and Dynamic Loading

Module	Function
AutoLoader	Loads functions only on demand
AutoSplit	Splits a package for autoloading
Devel::SelfStubber	Generates stubs for a SelfLoading module
DynaLoader	Automatic dynamic loading of Perl modules
SelfLoader	Loads functions only on demand

Table B-14. For Developers: Language Extensions/Platform Development Support

Module	Function
blib	Finds *blib* directory structure during module builds
ExtUtils::Embed	Utilities for embedding Perl in C programs
ExtUtils::Install	Installs files from here to there
ExtUtils::Liblist	Determines libraries to use and how to use them
ExtUtils::MakeMaker	Creates a *Makefile* for a Perl extension
ExtUtils::Manifest	Utilities to write and check a *MANIFEST* file
ExtUtils::Miniperl	Writes the C code for *perlmain.c*
ExtUtils::Mkbootstrap	Makes a bootstrap file for use by DynaLoader
ExtUtils::Mksymlists	Writes linker option files for dynamic extension
ExtUtils::MM_OS2	Methods to override UNIX behavior in ExtUtils::MakeMaker
ExtUtils::MM_Unix	Methods used by ExtUtils::MakeMaker
ExtUtils::MM_VMS	Methods to override UNIX behavior in ExtUtils::MakeMaker
ExtUtils::testlib	Fixes @INC to use just-built extension
Opcode	Disables opcodes when compiling Perl code

Table B-14. For Developers: Language Extensions/Platform Development Support (continued)

Module	Function
ops	Pragma for use with Opcode module
POSIX	Interface to IEEE Std 1003.1
Safe	Creates safe namespaces for evaluating Perl code
Test::Harness	Runs Perl standard test scripts with statistics
vmsish	Enables VMS-specific features

Table B-15. For Developers: Object-Oriented Programming Support

Module	Function
Exporter	Default import method for modules
overload	Overloads Perl's mathematical operations
Tie::RefHash	Base class for tied hashes with references as keys
Tie::Hash	Base class definitions for tied hashes
Tie::Scalar	Base class definitions for tied scalars
Tie::StdHash	Base class definitions for tied hashes
Tie::StdScalar	Base class definitions for tied scalars
Tie::SubstrHash	Fixed-table-size, fixed-key-length hashing
UNIVERSAL	Base class for all classes

CPAN: Beyond the Standard Library

If you don't find an entry in the standard library that fits your needs, it's still quite possible that someone has written code that will be useful to you. There are many superb library modules that are not included in the standard distribution, for various practical, political, and pathetic reasons. To find out what is available, you can look at the Comprehensive Perl Archive Network (CPAN). See the discussion of CPAN in the *Preface*.

Here are the major categories of modules available from CPAN:

- Module listing format
- Perl core modules, Perl language extensions and documentation tools
- Development support
- Operating system interfaces
- Networking, device control (modems), and interprocess communication
- Data types and data type utilities
- Database interfaces
- User interfaces

- Interfaces to or emulations of other programming languages
- Filenames, filesystems, and file locking (see also filehandles)
- String processing, language text processing, parsing, and searching
- Option, argument, parameter, and configuration file processing
- Internationalization and locale
- Authentication, security, and encryption
- World Wide Web, HTML, HTTP, CGI, MIME
- Server and dacmon utilities
- Archiving, compression, and conversion
- Images, pixmap and bitmap manipulation, drawing, and graphing
- Mail and Usenet news
- Control flow utilities (callbacks and exceptions)
- Filehandle, directory handle, and input/output stream utilities
- Microsoft Windows modules
- Miscellancous modules

C

Networking Clients

Few computers (or computer users, for that matter) are content to remain isolated from the rest of the world. Networking, once mostly limited to government research labs and computer science departments at major universities, is now available to virtually everyone, even home computer users with a modem and dial-up SLIP or PPP service. More than ever, networking is now used daily by organizations and individuals from every walk of life. They use networking to exchange email, schedule meetings, manage distributed databases, access company information, grab weather reports, pull down today's news, chat with someone in a different hemisphere, or advertise their company on the Web.

These diverse applications all share one thing in common: they use TCP networking, the fundamental protocol that links the Net together.* And we don't just mean the Internet, either. Firewalls aside, the underlying technology is the same whether you're connecting far across the Internet, between your corporate offices, or from your kitchen down to your basement. This means you only have to learn one technology for all sorts of application areas.

How can you use networking to let an application on one machine talk to a different application, possibly on a totally different machine? With Perl, it's pretty easy, but first you should probably know a little bit about how the TCP networking model works.

Even if you've never touched a computer network before in your whole life, you already know another connection-based system: the telephone system. Don't let fancy words like "client-server programming" put you off. When you see the word "client," think "caller"; when you see the word "server," think "responder."

---

* Actually it's IP (Internet Protocol) that ties the Internet together, but TCP/IP is just a layer on top of IP.

If you ring someone up on the telephone, you are the client. Whoever picks up the phone at the other end is the server.

Programmers with a background in C programming may be familiar with *sockets.* A socket is the interface to the network in the same sense that a filehandle is the interface to files in the filesystem. In fact, for the simple stream-based clients we're going to demonstrate below, you can use a socket handle just as you would a filehandle.*

You can read from the socket, write to it, or both. That's because a socket is a special kind of bidirectional filehandle representing a network connection. Unlike normal files created via `open`, sockets are created using the low-level `socket` function.

Let's squeeze a little more mileage out of our telephone model. When you call into a big company's telephone switchboard, you can ask for a particular department by one name or another (such as "Personnel" or "Human Resources"), or by an exact number (like "extension 213"). Think of each service running on a computer as a department in a large corporation. Sometimes a particular service has several different names, such as both "http" and "www," but only one number, such as 80. That number associated with a particular service name is its *port.* The Perl functions `getservbyname` and `getservbyport` can be used to look up a service name given its port number, or vice versa. Here are some standard TCP services and their port numbers:

Service	Port	Purpose
echo	7	Accepts all input and echoes it back
discard	9	Accepts anything but does nothing with it
daytime	13	Return the current date and time in local format
ftp	21	Server for file transfer requests
telnet	23	Server for interactive telnet sessions
smtp	25	Simple mail transfer protocol; the mailer daemon
time	37	Return number of seconds since 1900 (in binary)
http	80	The World Wide Web server
nntp	119	The news server

Although sockets were originally developed for Berkeley UNIX, the overwhelming popularity of the Internet has induced virtually all operating-systems vendors to include socket support for client-server programming. For this book, directly using the `socket` function is a bit low-level. We recommend that you

---

* Well, almost; you can't seek on a socket.

use the more user-friendly IO::Socket module,* which we'll use in all our sample code. This means we'll also be employing some of Perl's object-oriented constructs. For a brief introduction to these constructs, see Chapter 19, *CGI Programming*. The *perltoot*(1) manpage and Chapter 5 of *Programming Perl* offer a more complete introduction to object-oriented programming in Perl.

We don't have the space in this book to provide a full TCP/IP tutorial, but we can at least present a few simple clients. For servers, which are a bit more complicated, see Chapter 6 of *Programming Perl*, or the *perlipc*(1) manpage.

A Simple Client

For our simplest client, we'll choose a rather boring service, called "daytime." The daytime server sends a connecting client one line of data containing the time of day on that remote server, then closes the connection.

Here's the client:

```
#!/usr/bin/perl -w
use IO::Socket;
$remote = IO::Socket::INET->new(
    Proto => "tcp",
    PeerAddr => "localhost",
    PeerPort => "daytime(13)",
    )
    or die "cannot connect to daytime port at localhost";
while ( <$remote> ) { print }
```

When you run this program, you should get something back that looks like this:

```
Thu May 8 11:57:15 1997
```

Here are what those parameters to the **new** constructor mean:

`Proto`
> The protocol to use. In this case, the socket handle returned will be connected to a TCP socket, because we want a stream-oriented connection, that is, one that acts pretty much like a plain old file. Not all sockets are of this type. For example, the UDP protocol can be used to make a datagram socket, used for message-passing.

`PeerAddr`
> The name or Internet address of the remote host the server is running on. We could have specified a longer name like *www.perl.com*, or an address like

---

* IO::Socket is included as part of the standard Perl distribution as of the 5.004 release. If you're running an earlier version of Perl, just fetch IO::Socket from CPAN, where you'll find modules providing easy interfaces to the following services: DNS,ftp, Ident (RFC 931), NIS and NISPlus, NNTP, ping, POP3, SMTP, SNMP, SSLeay, telnet, and time—just to name a few.

204.148.40.9. For demonstration purposes, we've used the special hostname `localhost`, which should always mean the current machine you're running on. The corresponding Internet address for localhost is *127.0.0.1*, if you'd rather use that.

PeerPort

This is the service name or port number we'd like to connect to. We could have gotten away with using just `daytime` on systems with a well-configured system services file,* but just in case, we've specified the port number (13) in parentheses. Using just the number would also have worked, but numbers as constants make careful programmers nervous.

Notice how the return value from the **new** constructor is used as a filehandle in the **while** loop? That's what's called an indirect filehandle, a scalar variable containing a filehandle. You can use it the same way you would a normal filehandle. For example, you can read one line from it this way:

```
$line = <$handle>;
```

All remaining lines from it this way:

```
@lines = <$handle>;
```

And send a line of data to it this way:

```
print $handle "some data\n";
```

A Webget Client

Here's a simple client that contacts a remote server and fetches a list of documents from it. This is a more interesting client than the previous one because it sends a line of data to the server before fetching that server's response.

```
#!/usr/bin/perl -w
use IO::Socket;
unless (@ARGV > 1) { die "usage: $0 host document ..." }
$host = shift(@ARGV);
foreach $document ( @ARGV ) {
    $remote = IO::Socket::INET->new( Proto => "tcp",
    PeerAddr => $host,
    PeerPort => "http(80)",
    );
    unless ($remote) { die "cannot connect to http daemon on $host" }
    $remote->autoflush(1);
    print $remote "GET $document HTTP/1.0\n\n";
    while ( <$remote> ) { print }
    close $remote;
}
```

---

* The system services file is in */etc/services* under UNIX.

The web server handling the http service is assumed to be at its standard port, number 80. If the server you're trying to connect to is at a different port (say, 8080), you should give `PeerPort => 8080` as the third argument to *new()*. The `autoflush` method is used on the socket because otherwise the system would buffer up the output we sent it. (If you're on a Mac, you'll need to change every `\n` in your code that sends data over the network to be `\015\012` instead.)

Connecting to the server is only the first part of the process: once you have the connection, you have to use the server's language. Each server on the network has its own little command language that it expects as input. The string that we send to the server starting with "GET" is in HTTP syntax. In this case, we simply request each specified document. Yes, we really are making a new connection for each document, even though it's the same host. That's the way it works with HTTP. (Recent versions of web browsers may request that the remote server leave the connection open a little while, but the server doesn't have to honor such a request.)

We'll call our program *webget*. Here's how it might execute:

```
shell_prompt$ webget www.perl.com /guanaco.html
HTTP/1.1 404 File Not Found
Date: Thu, 08 May 1997 18:02:32 GMT
Server: Apache/1.2b6
Connection: close
Content-type: text/html
<HEAD><TITLE>404 File Not Found</TITLE></HEAD>
<BODY><H1>File Not Found</H1>
The requested URL /guanaco.html was not found on this server.<P>
</BODY>
```

OK, so that's not very interesting, because it didn't find that particular document. But a long response wouldn't have fit on this page.

For a more fully-featured version of this program, you should look for the *lwp-request* program included with the LWP modules from CPAN. (LWP is discussed a bit at the end of Chapter 19.)

An Interactive Client

It's pretty easy to make a client that just reads everything from a server, or that sends one command, gets one answer, and quits. But what about setting up something fully interactive, like *telnet*? That way you can type a line, get the answer, type a line, get the answer, and so on. (OK, usually *telnet* operates in character mode, not line mode, but you get the idea.)

This client is more complicated than the two we've done so far, but if you're on a system that supports the powerful `fork` call, the solution isn't that rough. Once

you've made the connection to whatever service you'd like to chat with, call
`fork` to clone your process. Each of these two identical processes has a very
simple job to do: the parent copies everything from the socket to standard output,
while the child simultaneously copies everything from standard input to the
socket. To accomplish the same thing using just one process would be much
harder, because it's easier to code two processes to do one thing than it is to
code one process to do two things.*

Here's the code:

```perl
#!/usr/bin/perl -w
use strict;
use IO::Socket;
my ($host, $port, $kidpid, $handle, $line);
unless (@ARGV == 2) { die "usage: $0 host port" }
($host, $port) = @ARGV;
# create a tcp connection to the specified host and port
$handle = IO::Socket::INET->new(Proto => "tcp",
    PeerAddr => $host,
    PeerPort => $port)
    or die "can't connect to port $port on $host: $!";
$handle->autoflush(1); # so output gets there right away
print STDERR "[Connected to $host:$port]\n";
# split the program into two processes, identical twins
die "can't fork: $!" unless defined($kidpid = fork());
# the if{} block runs only in the parent process
if ($kidpid) {
    # copy the socket to standard output
    while (defined ($line = <$handle>)) {
    print STDOUT $line;
    }
    kill("TERM", $kidpid); # send SIGTERM to child
}
# the else{} block runs only in the child process
else {
    # copy standard input to the socket
    while (defined ($line = <STDIN>)) {
    print $handle $line;
    }
}
```

The `kill` function in the parent's `if` block is there to send a signal to our child
process (current running in the `else` block) as soon as the remote server has
closed its end of the connection.

---

* This keep-it-simple principle is one of the cornerstones of the UNIX philosophy, and good software
engineering as well, which is probably why it's spread to other systems as well.

Further Reading on Networking

There's a lot more to networking than this, but this should get you started. Chapter 6 of *Programming Perl* and the *perlipc*(1) manpage describe interprocess communication in general; the IO::*Socket*(3) manpage describes the object library; and the *Socket*(3) manpage describes the low-level interface to sockets. For the more intrepid programmers, the book *Unix Network Programming* by Richard Stevens (published by Addison-Wesley) covers the entire topic quite well. Be warned, however, that most texts on socket programming are written from the perspective of a C programmer.

D

Topics We Didn't Mention

Yes, it's amazing. A book this long, and there are still some things that it didn't cover. The footnotes contain additional helpful information.

The purpose of this section is not to teach you about the things listed here, but merely to provide a list. You'll need to go to *Programming Perl*, the *perl*(1) or *perlfaq*(1) manpages, the HTML documents in CPAN's *doc* directory, or the Usenet newsgroups to get further information.

Full Interprocess Communications

Yes, Perl can do networking. Beyond the TCP/IP stream sockets discussed in Appendix C, *Networking Clients*, if your system is up to it, Perl also supports UNIX-domain sockets, UDP-based message passing, shared memory, semaphores, named and anonymous pipes, and signal handling. See Chapter 6 of *Programming Perl* or the *perlipc*(1) manpage for standard modules, and the networking section of the CPAN modules directory for third-party modules.

Yes, Perl can do TCP/IP socket networking, UNIX-domain networking, and shared memory and semaphores on systems that support it. See the *perlipc*(1) manpage for further information.

The Debugger

Perl has a wonderful source-level debugger, which *perldebug*(1) will tell you all about.

The Command Line

The Perl interpreter has a plethora of command-line switches. Check out *perlrun*(1) for information.

Other Operators

The comma operator, for one. And there are the bit manipulation operators &, |, ^, and ~, the ternary ? : operator, and the .. and ... flip-flop operators, just to name a few.

And there are some variations on operators, like using the g modifier on match. For this and more, see *perlop*(1).

Many, Many More Functions

Yes, Perl has a lot of functions. I'm not going to list them here, because the fastest way to find out about them is to read through the function section of *Programming Perl* or the *perlfunc*(1) manpage and look at anything you don't recognize that sounds interesting. Here are a few of the more interesting ones.

grep and map

The `grep` function selects elements from its argument list, based upon the result of an expression that's repeatedly evaluated for its truth value, with the `$_` variable successively set to each element in the list:

```
@bigpowers = grep $_ > 6, 1, 2, 4, 8, 16; # gets (8, 16)
@b_names = grep /^b/, qw(fred barney betty wilma);
@textfiles = grep -T, <*>;
```

The `map` function is similar, but instead of selecting or rejecting items, it merely collects the results of the expression (evaluated in a list context):

```
@more = map $_ + 3, 3, 5, 7;      # gets 6, 8, 10
@squares = map $_ * $_, 1..10;    # first 10 squares
@that = map "$_\n", @this;        # like "unchomp"
@triangle = map 1..$_, 1..5;      # 1,1,2,1,2,3,1,2,3,4,1,2,3,4,5
%sizes = map { $_, -s } <*>;      # hash of files and sizes
```

The eval Operator (and s///e)

Yes, you can construct a piece of code at run-time and then `eval` it, just as you can do with the shell. It's actually rather useful, because you can get some compiletime optimizations (like a compiled regular expression) at run-time. You can also

also use it to trap otherwise fatal errors in a section of code: a fatal error inside the `eval` merely exits the `eval` and gives you an error status.

For example, here's a program that reads a line of Perl code from the user and then executes it as if it were part of the Perl program:

```
print "code line: ";
chop($code = <STDIN>);
eval $code; die "eval: $@" if $@;
```

You can put Perl code inside the replacement string of a substitute operator with the `e` flag. This is handy if you want to construct something complicated for the replacement string, such as calling a subroutine that returns the results of a database lookup. Here's a loop that increments the value of the first column of a series of lines:

```
while (<>) {
    s/^(\S+)/$1+1/e; # $1+1 is Perl code, not a string
    print;
}
```

Another use of `eval` is as an exception-handling mechanism:

```
eval {
    some_hairy_routine_that_might_die(@args);
};
if ($@) {
    print "oops... some_hairy died with $@";
}
```

Here, `$@` will be empty as long as the eval block worked OK but will have the text of the die message if not.

Of these three constructs (`eval "string"`, `eval { BLOCK }`, and `s///e`) only the first is really what you would think of as an `eval` from a shell-programming language. The other two are compiled at compile-time, and incur little additional performance penalty.

Many, Many Predefined Variables

You've seen a few predefined variables, like `$_`. Well, there are a lot more. Pretty much every punctuation character has been pressed into service. The *perlvar*(1) manpage will be of help here. Also see the English module in *perlmod*(1).

Symbol Table Manipulation with *FRED

You can make b an alias for a with `*b = *a`. This means that `$a` and `$b` refer to the same variable, as do `@a` and `@b`, and even filehandles and formats a and b. You can also localize `*b` inside a block with `local(*b)`, and that lets you have local filehandles and formats and other things. Pretty fancy stuff, but useful when you need it.

Additional Regular-Expression Features

Regular expressions can contain "extended" syntax (where whitespace is optional, so a regular expression can be split over multiple lines, and can contain regular Perl comments), and can have positive and negative "lookahead." The syntax is a bit ugly, so rather than scare you off here, go look in *Programming Perl*, or see the *perlre*(1) manpage. Friedl's book, *Mastering Regular Expressions* (published by O'Reilly & Associates) explains all of this and much more.

Packages

When multiple people work on a project, or if you're slightly schizophrenic, you can carve up the variable namespace using packages. A package is just a hidden prefix put in front of most variables (except variables created with the my operator). By changing the prefix, you get different variables. Here's a brief example:

```
$a = 123;              # this is really $main::a
$main::a++;            # same variable, now 124
package fred;          # now the prefix is "fred"
$a = 456;              # this is $fred::a
print $a - $main::a;   # prints 456-124
package main;          # back to original default
print $a + $fred::a;   # prints 124+456
```

So, any name with an explicit package name is used as-is, but all other names get packaged into the current default package. Packages are local to the current file or block, and you always start out in package main at the top of a file. For details, the *perlsub*(1) manpage will help here.

Embeddible, Extensible

The "guts" of Perl are defined well enough that it becomes a relatively straightforward task to embed the Perl compiler/interpreter inside another application (such as has already been done with the Apache web server and the *vi* text editor), or to extend Perl by connecting it with arbitrary code written in C (or having a C-like interface). In fact, about a third of the online documentation for Perl is specifically devoted to embedding and extending Perl. The *perlembed*(1), *perlapio*(1), *perlxs*(1), *perlxstut*(1), *perlguts*(1), and *perlcall*(1) manpages cover these topics in depth.

And since Perl is freely reusable, you can write your proprietary spreadsheet application, using an embedded Perl to evaluate the expressions in your spreadsheet cells, and not have to pay one cent in royalties for all that power. Joy.

Security Matters

Perl was designed with security in mind. See Chapter 6 of *Programming Perl* or the *perlsec*(1) manpage about taint checking. This is the kind of security where you trust the writer of the program, but not the person running it, such as is often the case with setuid programs under UNIX, or server-launched programs anywhere. The Safe module, covered in the Safe(3) manpage and Chapter 7 of *Programming Perl*, provides something else entirely: the kind of security necessary when executing (as with `eval`) unchecked code.

Switch or Case Statements

No, Perl doesn't *really* have these, but it's easy to make them using more basic constructs. See Chapter 2 of *Programming Perl* or the *perlsyn*(1) manpage.

Direct I/O: sysopen, sysread, syswrite, sysseek

Sometimes Perl's high-level I/O is a bit too high-level for what you need to do. Chapter 3 of *Programming Perl* and the *perlfunc*(1) manpage cover direct access to the raw system calls for I/O.

The Perl Compiler

Although we speak of Perl as compiling your code before executing it, this compiled form is not native object code. Malcolm Beatie's Perl compiler project can produce standalone byte code or compilable C code out of your Perl script. The 5.005 release of Perl is expected to have native code generation included as part of the standard release. See the material in the *perlfaq3*(1) manpage about this.

Database Support

Yes, Perl can interface directly with your commercial database servers, including Oracle, Sybase, Informix, and ODBC, just to name a few. See the database section in the CPAN modules directory for the relevant extension modules.

Complex Data Structures

Using references, you can build data structures of arbitrary complexity. These are discussed in Chapter 4 of *Programming Perl*, and in the *perllol*(1), *perldsc*(1), and *perlref*(1) manpages. If you prefer an object-oriented data structure, see Chapter 5 of *Programming Perl*, or the *perltoot*(1) and *perlobj*(1) manpages.

Function Pointers

Perl can store and pass pointers to functions via the `\&funcname` notation, and call them indirectly via `&$funcptr($args)`. You can even write functions that create and return new anonymous functions, just as you could in languages like Lisp or Scheme. Such anonymous functions are often called *closures*. See Chapter 2 of *Programming Perl*, and the *perlsub*(1) and *perlfaq7*(1) manpages for details.

And Other Stuff

Perl just keeps getting more powerful and more useful, and it's quite an effort to keep the documentation up to date. (Who knows? By the time this book hits the shelves, there could be a Visual Perl.) But in any case, thanks, Larry!

Index

Addendum:
Additional Answers for
Appendix A Exercises

Here is the answer to exercise 2 from Chapter 6:

2. Here's one way to do it:

```
@ARGV = reverse @ARGV;
print reverse <>;
```

The first line just takes any filename arguments and reverses them. That way if the user called this script with command line arguments "camel llama alpaca", @ARGV would then contain "alpaca llama camel" instead. The second line reads in all the lines in all the files in @ARGV, flips them end on end, and prints them. If no arguments were passed to the program, then as before, <> works on STDIN instead.

Here is the answer to exercise 2 from Chapter 9:

2. Here's one way to do it:

```
{
  print "Enter a number (999 to quit): ";
  chomp($n = <STDIN>);
  last if $n == 999;
  $sum += $n;
  redo;
}

print "the sum is $sum\n";
```

We're using a naked block with a **redo** and a **last** to get things done this time. Start by printing the prompt and grabbing the number. If it's 999, exit the block with **last** and print out the sum on exit. Otherwise, we add to our running total and use **redo** to execute the block again.

About the Authors

Randal L. Schwartz is an eclectic tradesman and entrepreneur, making his living through software design, technical writing and training, system administration, security consultation, and video production. He is known internationally for his prolific, humorous, and occasionally incorrect spatterings on Usenet—especially his "Just another perl hacker" signoffs in *comp.lang.perl*.

Randal honed his many crafts through seven years of employment at Tektronix, ServioLogic, and Sequent. Since 1985, he has owned and operated Stonehenge Consulting Services in his home town of Portland, Oregon.

Tom Christiansen is a freelance consultant specializing in Perl training and writing. After working for several years for TSR Hobbies (of Dungeons and Dragons fame), he set off for college where he spent a year in Spain and five in the United States dabbling in music, linguistics, programming, and some half-dozen different spoken languages. Tom finally escaped UW-Madison with BAs in Spanish and Computer Science, and an MS in Computer Science.

He then spent five years at Convex as a jack-of-all-trades working on everything from system administration to utility and kernel development, with customer support and training thrown in for good measure. Tom also served two terms on the Board of Directors of the USENIX Association.

With over 15 years' experience in UNIX system administration and programming, Tom presents seminars internationally. Living in the foothills above Boulder, Colorado, surrounded by mule deer, skunks, and the occasional mountain lion and black bear, he takes summers off for hiking, hacking, birding, music making, and gaming.

Colophon

The animal featured on the cover of *Learning Perl* is the llama, a domestic member of the South American camels native to the Andean range. Also included in this llamoid group is the domestic alpaca, and their wild ancestors, the guanaco and the vicuna. All of these animals graze on grasses, which they chew and cud. The wild guanacos can run up to 40 miles per hour and will readily take to water in order to escape danger.

Bones found in ancient human settlements suggest that domestication of the alpaca and llama dates back 4,500 years. In 1531, when Spanish conquistadors overran the Inca Empire in the high Andes they found both animals present in great numbers. These camels are suited for high mountain life; their hemoglobin can take in more oxygen than that of other mammals.

Llamas can weigh up to 300 pounds, and are mainly used as beasts of burden. A packtrain may contain several hundred animals and can travel up to twenty miles per day. Llamas will carry loads up to fifty pounds, but have a tendency to be short tempered and will resort to spitting and biting to demonstrate displeasure. To the people of the Andes, llamas also provide meat, wool for clothing (although the smaller alpaca provides a superior wool), hides for leather, and fat for candles. Their wool can also be braided into rope and rugs, and the dried dung is used for fuel.

Edie Freedman designed this cover and the entire UNIX bestiary that appears on other Nutshell Handbooks. The beasts themselves are adapted from 19th-century engravings from the Dover Pictorial Archive. The cover layout was produced with Quark XPress 3.32 using ITC Garamond from Adobe. Whenever possible, our books use RepKover™, a durable and flexible lay-flat binding. If the page count exceeds RepKover's limit, perfect binding is used.

The inside layout was designed by Nancy Priest and formatted in FrameMaker 5.0 by Mike Sierra using ITC Garamond Light and ITC Garamond Book fonts. Mary Anne Weeks Mayo was the project manager and production editor. Quality control was assured by Jane Ellin, John Files, and Sheryl Avruch. Seth Maislin created the index. Chris Reilley, Linda Mui, and Robert Romano were responsible for the figures. The colophon was written by Michael Kalantarian.

 # More Titles from O'Reilly

Perl

Perl Resource Kit – Win32 Edition

By Dick Hardt, Erik Olson, David Futato &
Brian Jepson
1st Edition August 1998
1,832 pages, Includes 4 books & CD-ROM
ISBN 1-56592-409-6

The *Perl Resource Kit–Win32 Edition* is an
essential tool for Perl programmers who are
expanding their platform expertise to include
Win32, and for Win32 Webmasters and system
administrators who have discovered the power and flexibility of
Perl. The Kit contains some of the latest commercial Win32 Perl
software from Dick Hardt's ActiveState Tool Corp., along with a
collection of Perl modules that run on Win32, and a definitive
documentation set from O'Reilly.

Learning Perl on Win32 Systems

By Randal L. Schwartz,
Erik Olson & Tom Christiansen
1st Edition August 1997
306 pages, ISBN 1-56592-324-3

In this carefully paced course, leading
Perl trainers and a Windows NT practitioner
teach you to program in the language that
promises to emerge as the scripting language
of choice on NT. Based on the "llama" book,
this book features tips for PC users and new NT-specific examples,
along with a foreword by Larry Wall, the creator of Perl, and Dick
Hardt, the creator of Perl for Win32.

Learning Perl/Tk

By Nancy Walsh
1st Edition January 1999
376 pages, ISBN 1-56592-314-6

This tutorial for Perl/Tk, the extension to
Perl for creating graphical user interfaces,
shows how to use Perl/Tk to build graphical,
event-driven applications for both Windows
and UNIX. Rife with illustrations, it teaches
how to implement and configure each
Perl/Tk graphical element.

Mastering Regular Expressions

By Jeffrey E. F. Friedl
1st Edition January 1997
368 pages, ISBN 1-56592-257-3

Regular expressions, a powerful tool for
manipulating text and data, are found in
scripting languages, editors, programming
environments, and specialized tools. In this
book, author Jeffrey Friedl leads you through
the steps of crafting a regular expression that
gets the job done. He examines a variety of tools and uses them in
an extensive array of examples, with a major focus on Perl.

Perl in a Nutshell

By Ellen Siever, Stephen Spainhour &
Nathan Patwardhan
1st Edition December 1998
674 pages, ISBN 1-56592-286-7

The perfect companion for working
programmers, *Perl in a Nutshell* is a
comprehensive reference guide to the
world of Perl. It contains everything you
need to know for all but the most obscure
Perl questions. This wealth of information
is packed into an efficient, extraordinarily usable format.

Perl Cookbook

By Tom Christiansen & Nathan Torkington
1st Edition August 1998
794 pages, ISBN 1-56592-243-3

The *Perl Cookbook* is a comprehensive
collection of problems, solutions, and
practical examples for anyone programming
in Perl. You'll find hundreds of rigorously
reviewed Perl "recipes" for manipulating
strings, numbers, dates, arrays, and hashes;
pattern matching and text substitutions; references, data structures,
objects, and classes; signals and exceptions; and much more.

Perl

Mastering Algorithms with Perl

By Jon Orwant, Jarkko Hietaniemi &
John Macdonald
1st Edition August 1999
704 pages, ISBN 1-56592-398-7

There have been dozens of books on
programming algorithms, but never before
has there been one that uses Perl. Whether
you are an amateur programmer or know a
wide range of algorithms in other languages,
this book will teach you how to carry out traditional programming
tasks in a high-powered, efficient, easy-to-maintain manner with
Perl. Topics range in complexity from sorting and searching to
statistical algorithms, numerical analysis, and encryption.

Programming Perl, 3rd Edition

Larry Wall, Tom Christiansen & Jon Orwant
3rd Edition July 2000
1104 pages, ISBN 0-596-00027-8

Programming Perl is not just a book about
Perl; it is also a unique introduction to the
language and its culture, as one might expect
only from its authors. This third edition has
been expanded to cover Version 5.6 of Perl.
New topics include threading, the compiler,
Unicode, and other features that have been added or improved
since the previous edition.

Advanced Perl Programming

By Sriram Srinivasan
1st Edition August 1997
434 pages, ISBN 1-56592-220-4

This book covers complex techniques for
managing production-ready Perl programs
and explains methods for manipulating
data and objects that may have looked
like magic before. It gives you necessary
background for dealing with networks,
databases, and GUIs, and includes a discussion of internals to
help you program more efficiently and embed Perl within C or
C within Perl.

The Perl CD Bookshelf

By O'Reilly & Associates, Inc.
1st Edition July 1999
Features CD-ROM
ISBN 1-56592-462-2

Perl programmer alert! Six bestselling
O'Reilly Animal Guides are now available
on CD-ROM, easily accessible with your
favorite Web browser: *Perl in a Nutshell;
Programming Perl, 2nd Edition; Perl
Cookbook; Advanced Perl Programming;
Learning Perl;* and *Learning Perl on Win32 Sytems*. As a bonus,
the new hard-copy version of *Perl in a Nutshell* is also included.

Web Programming

VBScript in a Nutshell

By Paul Lomax, Matt Childs, & Ron Petrusha
1st Edition May 2000
512 pages, ISBN 1-56592-720-6

Whether you're using VBScript to create
client-side scripts, ASP applications, WSH
scripts, or programmable Outlook forms,
VBScript in a Nutshell is the only book
you'll need by your side – a complete and
easy-to-use language reference.

mod_perl Pocket Reference

By Andrew Ford
1st Edition November 2000 (est.)
90 pages (est.), ISBN 0-59600-047-2

mod_perl Pocket Reference is a concise,
conveniently formatted reference to all
mod_perl features used in day-to-day
mod_perl programming. This small book
covers functions as well as configuration
directives that help maximize the effectiveness
of the mod_perl Apache module.

Web Programming

CGI Programming with Perl, 2nd Edition

By Shishir Gundavaram
2nd Edition July 2000
470 pages , ISBN 1-56592-419-3

Completely rewritten, this comprehensive
explanation of CGI for those who want to
provide their own Web servers features
Perl 5 techniques and shows how to use two
popular Perl modules, CGI.pm and CGI_lite.
It also covers speed-up techniques, such as
FastCGI and mod_perl, and new material on searching and indexing,
security, generating graphics through ImageMagick, database access
through DBI, Apache configuration, and combining CGI with
JavaScript.

Dynamic HTML: The Definitive Reference

By Danny Goodman
1st Edition July 1998
1088 pages, ISBN 1-56592-494-0

Dynamic HTML: The Definitive Reference is an
indispensable compendium for Web content
developers. It contains complete reference
material for all of the HTML tags, CSS style
attributes, browser document objects, and
JavaScript objects supported by the various
standards and the latest versions of Netscape Navigator and
Microsoft Internet Explorer.

PHP Pocket Reference

By Rasmus Lerdorf
1st Edition January 2000
120 pages, ISBN 1-56592-769-9

The *PHP Pocket Reference* is a handy
quick reference for PHP, an open-source,
HTML-embedded scripting language that
can be used to develop web applications.
This small book acts both as a perfect
tutorial for learning the basics of PHP
syntax and as a reference to the vast
array of functions provided by PHP.

JavaScript: The Definitive Guide, 3rd Edition

By David Flanagan
3rd Edition June 1998
800 pages, ISBN 1-56592-392-8

This third edition of the definitive reference
to JavaScript covers the latest version of the
language, JavaScript 1.2, as supported by
Netscape Navigator 4 and Internet Explorer
4. JavaScript, which is being standardized
under the name ECMAScript, is a scripting
language that can be embedded directly in HTML to give Web
pages programming-language capabilities.

ASP in a Nutshell, 2nd Edition

By A. Keyton Weissinger
2nd Edition July 2000
492 pages, ISBN 1-56592-843-1

ASP in a Nutshell, 2nd Edition, provides
the high-quality reference documentation
that web application developers really need to
create effective Active Server Pages. It focuses
on how features are used in a real application
and highlights little-known or undocumented
features.

Programming ColdFusion

By Rob Brooks-Bilson
1st Edition November 2000 (est.)
500 pages (est.), ISBN 1-56592-698-6

Programming ColdFusion covers everything
you need to know to create effective web
applications with ColdFusion, a powerful
tool for rapid web site development. The
book starts with the basics and quickly moves
to more advanced topics, providing numerous
examples of common web application tasks, so you can learn by
example. Covers ColdFusion 4.5.

Web Programming

Webmaster in a Nutshell, 2nd Edition

By Stephen Spainhour & Robert Eckstein
2nd Edition June 1999
540 pages, ISBN 1-56592-325-1

This indispensable book takes all the essential reference information for the Web and pulls it together into one volume. It covers HTML 4.0, CSS, XML, CGI, SSI, JavaScript 1.2, PHP, HTTP 1.1, and administration for the Apache server.

DocBook: The Definitive Guide

By Norman Walsh & Leonard Muellner
1st Edition October 1999
652 pages, Includes CD-ROM
ISBN 1-56592-580-7

DocBook is a Document Type Definition (DTD) for use with XML (the Extensible Markup Language) and SGML (the Standard Generalized Markup Language). DocBook lets authors in technical groups exchange and reuse technical information. This book contains an introduction to SGML, XML, and the DocBook DTD, plus the complete reference information for DocBook.

Java and XML

By Brett McLaughlin
1st Edition June 2000
498 pages, ISBN 0-596-00016-2

Java revolutionized the programming world by providing a platform-independent programming language. XML takes the revolution a step further with a platform-independent language for interchanging data. *Java and XML* shows how to put the two together, building real-world applications in which both the code and the data are truly portable.

JavaScript Application Cookbook

By Jerry Bradenbaugh
1st Edition September 1999
478 pages, ISBN 1-56592-577-7

JavaScript Application Cookbook literally hands the Webmaster a set of ready-to-go, client-side JavaScript applications with thorough documentation to help them understand and extend the applications. By providing such a set of applications, *JavaScript Application Cookbook* allows Webmasters to immediately add extra functionality to their Web sites.

Practical Internet Groupware

By Jon Udell
1st Edition October 1999
524 pages, ISBN 1-56592-537-8

This revolutionary book tells users, programmers, IS managers, and system administrators how to build Internet groupware applications that organize the casual and chaotic transmission of online information into useful, disciplined, and documented data.

Java in a Nutshell, 3rd Edition

By David Flanagan
3rd Edition November 1999
668 pages, ISBN 1-56592-487-8

The third edition of this bestselling book covers Java 1.2 and 1.3. It contains an advanced introduction to Java and its key APIs and provides quick-reference material on all the classes and interfaces in the following APIs: java.lang, java.io, java.beans, java.math, java.net, java.security, java.text, java.util, and javax.crypto.

O'REILLY®

TO ORDER: **800-998-9938** • **order@oreilly.com** • **http://www.oreilly.com/**

OUR PRODUCTS ARE AVAILABLE AT A BOOKSTORE OR SOFTWARE STORE NEAR YOU.

FOR INFORMATION: **800-998-9938** • **707-829-0515** • **info@oreilly.com**

Web Programming

Enterprise JavaBeans, 2nd Edition

By Richard Monson-Haefel
2nd Edition March 2000
492 pages, ISBN 1-56592-869-5

Enterprise JavaBeans, 2nd Edition
provides a thorough introduction to EJB 1.1
and 1.0 for the enterprise software developer.
It shows you how to develop enterprise Beans
to model your business objects and processes.
The EJB architecture provides a highly flexible
system in which components can easily be reused, and which can
be changed to suit your needs without upsetting other parts of the
system. *Enterprise JavaBeans* teaches you how to take advantage
of the flexibility and simplicity that this powerful new architecture
provides.

Writing Apache Modules with Perl and C

By Lincoln Stein & Doug MacEachern
1st Edition March 1999
746 pages, ISBN 1-56592-567-X

This guide to web programming shows
how to extend the capabilities of the Apache
web server. It explains the design of Apache,
mod_perl, and the Apache API, then
demonstrates how to use them to rewrite
CGI scripts, filter HTML documents on the
server-side, enhance server log functionality, convert file formats
on the fly, and more.

Network Administration

sendmail, 2nd Edition

By Bryan Costales & Eric Allman
2nd Edition January 1997
1050 pages, ISBN 1-56592-222-0

sendmail, 2nd Edition, covers sendmail
Version 8.8 from Berkeley and the standard
versions available on most systems. This
cross-referenced edition offers an expanded
tutorial and solution-oriented examples,
plus topics such as the #error delivery agent,
sendmail's exit values, MIME headers, and how to set up and use
the user database, mailertable, and smrsh.

Network Administration

DNS and BIND, 3rd Edition

By Paul Albitz & Cricket Liu
3rd Edition September 1998
502 pages, ISBN 1-56592-512-2

DNS and BIND discusses one of the Internet's
fundamental building blocks: the distributed
host information database that's responsible
for translating names into addresses, routing
mail to its proper destination, and many other
services. The third edition covers BIND 4.9,
on which most commercial products are currently based, and
BIND 8, which implements many important new features and will
be the basis for the next generation of commercial name servers.

The Networking CD Bookshelf

By O'Reilly & Associates, Inc.
1st Edition March 1999
Features CD-ROM
ISBN 1-56592-523-8

Network administrator alert! Six bestselling
O'Reilly Animal Guides are now available on
CD-ROM, easily accessible with your favorite
Web browser: *TCP/IP Network Administration,
2nd Edition; sendmail, 2nd Edition; sendmail
Desktop Reference; DNS and BIND, 3rd Edition; Practical UNIX &
Internet Security, 2nd Edition;* and *Building Internet Firewalls.* As
a bonus, the new hardcopy version of *DNS and BIND, 3rd Edition*
is also included.

Virtual Private Networks, 2nd Edition

By Charlie Scott, Paul Wolfe & Mike Erwin
2nd Edition December 1998
228 pages, ISBN 1-56592-529-7

This book explains how to plan and build a
Virtual Private Network (VPN), a collection of
technologies that creates secure connections
or "tunnels" over regular Internet lines. It
discusses costs, configuration, and how to
install and use VPN technologies that are
available for Windows NT and UNIX, such as PPTP and L2TP,
Altavista Tunnel, Cisco PIX, and the secure shell (SSH). New
features in the second edition include SSH and an expanded
description of the IPSec standard.

O'REILLY®

TO ORDER: **800-998-9938** • *order@oreilly.com* • *http://www.oreilly.com/*
OUR PRODUCTS ARE AVAILABLE AT A BOOKSTORE OR SOFTWARE STORE NEAR YOU.
FOR INFORMATION: **800-998-9938** • **707-829-0515** • *info@oreilly.com*

Network Administration

Internet Application Protocols: The Definitive Guide

By Eric Hall
1st Edition April 2001 (est.)
700 pages (est.), Includes CD-ROM
ISBN 1-56592-606-4

Internet Application Protocols: The Definitive Guide covers HTTP, SMTP, POP3, IMAP, FTP, DNS, and other key application protocols that do the work of the Internet. Together with *Internet Core Protocols: The Definitive Guide*, this book forms the foundation of a series that provides network administrators with practical reference material to help them troubleshoot their networks. Includes the Surveyor Lite protocol analyzer on CD-ROM.

sendmail Desktop Reference

By Bryan Costales & Eric Allman
1st Edition March 1997
74 pages, ISBN 1-56592-278-6

This quick-reference guide provides a complete overview of the latest version of sendmail (V8.8), from command-line switches to configuration commands, from options declarations to macro definitions, and from m4 features to debugging switches – all packed into a convenient carry-around booklet coauthored by the creator of sendmail. Includes extensive cross-references to *sendmail, 2nd Edition*.

Internet Core Protocols: The Definitive Guide

By Eric Hall
1st Edition February 2000
472 pages, Includes CD-ROM
ISBN 1-56592-572-6

Internet Core Protocols: The Definitive Guide provides the nitty-gritty details of TCP, IP, and UDP. Many network problems can only be debugged by working at the lowest levels – looking at all the bits traveling back and forth on the wire. This guide explains what those bits are and how to interpret them. It's the only book on Internet protocols written with system and network administrators in mind.

TCP/IP Network Administration, 2nd Edition

By Craig Hunt
2nd Edition December 1997
630 pages, ISBN 1-56592-322-7

A complete guide to setting up and running a TCP/IP network for practicing system administrators. Beyond basic setup, this new second edition discusses the Internet routing protocols and provides a tutorial on how to configure important network services. It also includes Linux in addition to BSD and System V TCP/IP implementations.

How to stay in touch with O'Reilly

1. Visit Our Award-Winning Web Site

http://www.oreilly.com/

★ "Top 100 Sites on the Web" —*PC Magazine*
★ "Top 5% Web sites" —*Point Communications*
★ "3-Star site" —*The McKinley Group*

Our web site contains a library of comprehensive product information (including book excerpts and tables of contents), downloadable software, background articles, interviews with technology leaders, links to relevant sites, book cover art, and more. File us in your Bookmarks or Hotlist!

2. Join Our Email Mailing Lists

New Product Releases

To receive automatic email with brief descriptions of all new O'Reilly products as they are released, send email to:
listproc@online.oreilly.com
Put the following information in the first line of your message (*not* in the Subject field):
subscribe oreilly-news

O'Reilly Events

If you'd also like us to send information about trade show events, special promotions, and other O'Reilly events, send email to:
listproc@online.oreilly.com
Put the following information in the first line of your message (*not* in the Subject field):
subscribe oreilly-events

3. Get Examples from Our Books via FTP

There are two ways to access an archive of example files from our books:

Regular FTP

- ftp to:
  ftp.oreilly.com
  (login: anonymous
  password: your email address)
- Point your web browser to:
  ftp://ftp.oreilly.com/

FTPMAIL

- Send an email message to:
  ftpmail@online.oreilly.com
  (Write "help" in the message body)

4. Contact Us via Email

order@oreilly.com
To place a book or software order online. Good for North American and international customers.

subscriptions@oreilly.com
To place an order for any of our newsletters or periodicals.

books@oreilly.com
General questions about any of our books.

software@oreilly.com
For general questions and product information about our software. Check out O'Reilly Software Online at **http://software.oreilly.com/** for software and technical support information. Registered O'Reilly software users send your questions to: **website-support@oreilly.com**

cs@oreilly.com
For answers to problems regarding your order or our products.

booktech@oreilly.com
For book content technical questions or corrections.

proposals@oreilly.com
To submit new book or software proposals to our editors and product managers.

international@oreilly.com
For information about our international distributors or translation queries. For a list of our distributors outside of North America check out:
http://www.oreilly.com/www/order/country.html

5. Work with Us

Check out our website for current employment opportunites:
www.jobs@oreilly.com
Click on "Work with Us"

O'Reilly & Associates, Inc.
101 Morris Street, Sebastopol, CA 95472 USA
TEL   707-829-0515 or 800-998-9938
       (6am to 5pm PST)
FAX   707-829-0104

International Distributors

http://international.oreilly.com/distributors.html

UK, EUROPE, MIDDLE EAST AND AFRICA (EXCEPT FRANCE, GERMANY, AUSTRIA, SWITZERLAND, LUXEMBOURG, AND LIECHTENSTEIN)

INQUIRIES
O'Reilly UK Limited
4 Castle Street
Farnham
Surrey, GU9 7HS
United Kingdom
Telephone: 44-1252-711776
Fax: 44-1252-734211
Email: information@oreilly.co.uk

ORDERS
Wiley Distribution Services Ltd.
1 Oldlands Way
Bognor Regis
West Sussex PO22 9SA
United Kingdom
Telephone: 44-1243-843294
UK Freephone: 0800-243207
Fax: 44-1243-843302 (Europe/EU orders)
or 44-1243-843274 (Middle East/Africa)
Email: cs-books@wiley.co.uk

FRANCE

INQUIRIES & ORDERS
Éditions O'Reilly
18 rue Séguier
75006 Paris, France
Tel: 33-1-40-51-52-30
Fax: 33-1-40-51-52-31
Email: france@oreilly.fr

GERMANY, SWITZERLAND, AUSTRIA, LUXEMBOURG, AND LIECHTENSTEIN

INQUIRIES & ORDERS
O'Reilly Verlag
Balthasarstr. 81
D-50670 Köln, Germany
Telephone: 49-221-973160-91
Fax: 49-221-973160-8
Email: anfragen@oreilly.de (inquiries)
Email: order@oreilly.de (orders)

CANADA (FRENCH LANGUAGE BOOKS)
Les Éditions Flammarion ltée
375, Avenue Laurier Ouest
Montréal (Québec) H2V 2K3
Tel: 00-1-514-277-8807
Fax: 00-1-514-278-2085
Email: info@flammarion.qc.ca

HONG KONG
City Discount Subscription Service, Ltd.
Unit A, 6th Floor, Yan's Tower
27 Wong Chuk Hang Road
Aberdeen, Hong Kong
Tel: 852-2580-3539
Fax: 852-2580-6463
Email: citydis@ppn.com.hk

KOREA
Hanbit Media, Inc.
Chungmu Bldg. 210
Yonnam-dong 568-33
Mapo-gu
Seoul, Korea
Tel: 822-325-0397
Fax: 822-325-9697
Email: hant93@chollian.dacom.co.kr

PHILIPPINES
Global Publishing
G/F Benavides Garden
1186 Benavides Street
Manila, Philippines
Tel: 632-254-8949/632-252-2582
Fax: 632-734-5060/632-252-2733
Email: globalp@pacific.net.ph

TAIWAN
O'Reilly Taiwan
1st Floor, No. 21, Lane 295
Section 1, Fu-Shing South Road
Taipei, 106 Taiwan
Tel: 886-2-27099669
Fax: 886-2-27038802
Email: mori@oreilly.com

INDIA
Shroff Publishers & Distributors Pvt. Ltd.
12, "Roseland", 2nd Floor
180, Waterfield Road, Bandra (West)
Mumbai 400 050
Tel: 91-22-641-1800/643-9910
Fax: 91-22-643-2422
Email: spd@vsnl.com

CHINA
O'Reilly Beijing
SIGMA Building, Suite B809
No. 49 Zhichun Road
Haidian District
Beijing, China PR 100080
Tel: 86-10-8809-7475
Fax: 86-10-8809-7463
Email: beijing@oreilly.com

JAPAN
O'Reilly Japan, Inc.
Yotsuya Y's Building
7 Banch 6, Honshio-cho
Shinjuku-ku
Tokyo 160-0003 Japan
Tel: 81-3-3356-5227
Fax: 81-3-3356-5261
Email: japan@oreilly.com

THAILAND
TransQuest Publishers (Thailand)
535/49 Kasemsuk Yaek 5
Soi Pracharat-Bampen 15
Huay Kwang, Bangkok
Thailand 10310
Tel: 662-6910421 or 6910638
Fax: 662-6902235
Email: puripat@.inet.co.th

ALL OTHER ASIAN COUNTRIES
O'Reilly & Associates, Inc.
101 Morris Street
Sebastopol, CA 95472 USA
Tel: 707-829-0515
Fax: 707-829-0104
Email: order@oreilly.com

AUSTRALIA
Woodslane Pty., Ltd.
7/5 Vuko Place
Warriewood NSW 2102
Australia
Tel: 61-2-9970-5111
Fax: 61-2-9970-5002
Email: info@woodslane.com.au

NEW ZEALAND
Woodslane New Zealand, Ltd.
21 Cooks Street (P.O. Box 575)
Waganui, New Zealand
Tel: 64-6-347-6543
Fax: 64-6-345-4840
Email: info@woodslane.com.au

ARGENTINA
Distribuidora Cuspide
Suipacha 764
1008 Buenos Aires
Argentina
Phone: 5411-4322-8868
Fax: 5411-4322-3456
Email: libros@cuspide.com

O'REILLY®